Working in the Twenty-First Century

ISSUES IN WORK AND HUMAN RESOURCES

Daniel J.B. Mitchell, Series Editor

WORKING IN THE TWENTY-FIRST CENTURY
Policies for Economic Growth Through Training,
Opportunity, and Education
David I. Levine

INCOME INEQUALITY IN AMERICA
An Analysis of Trends
Paul Ryscavage

HARD LABOR
Poor Women and Work in the Post-Welfare Era
Joel F. Handler and Lucie White

Working in the Twenty-First Century

Policies for Economic Growth Through Training, Opportunity, and Education

David I. Levine

M. E. Sharpe
Armonk, New York
London, England

Library of Congress Cataloging-in-Publication Data

Levine, David I., 1960–
Working in the twenty-first century : policies for economic growth
through training, opportunity, and education / David I. Levine.
p. cm. — (Issues in work and human resources)
Includes bibliographical references and index.
ISBN 0–7656–0303–9 (hardcover : alk. paper). —
ISBN 0-7656–0304–7 (pbk. : alk. paper)
1. Full employment policies—United States.   2. Human capital—
Government policy—United States.   3. Ocupational training—
Government policy—United States.   4. Education and state—United States.
5. Employment forecasting—United States.   6. Twenty-first century—Forecasts.
I. Title.   II. Series.
HD5724.L4224 1998
339.5′0973—dc21   98–13865
CIP

Printed in the United States of America

The paper used in this publication meets the minimum requirements of
American National Standard for Information Sciences—
Permanence of Paper for Printed Library Materials,
ANSI Z 39.48-1984.

MV (c)   10   9   8   7   6   5   4   3   2   1
MV (p)   10   9   8   7   6   5   4   3   2   1

To my partner and wife,
Vicki Elliot

TABLE OF CONTENTS

LIST OF BOXES AND FIGURES

Boxes

Figures

SERIES EDITOR'S FOREWORD

The employment relationship, for most people, is the most important economic relationship they will have. It is the major source of income as well as benefits. Public programs, such as Social Security, are tied to the employment relationship. Unlike economic relationships in many other markets, the employment relationship has not been deregulated. Public policies abound in the labor market. Today, there are laws dealing with unions, with the provision of benefit programs, with minimum wages, with safety and health on the job, with retirement, and so on. Many of these laws have been on the books for decades.

But as David Levine points out, the employment relationship is undergoing change. The wage distribution is shifting toward the more skilled and better educated. Employers nowadays complain of skilled-labor shortages; in some cases they turn to Congress and ask for immigration rules to be relaxed so that skilled workers can be obtained from abroad. But despite the shortages in some occupations, real wages have been relatively stagnant since the early 1970s.

Are we condemned to a permanent wide divide between the top and bottom of the wage scale? Can we produce the skills needed for the future, or must we inevitably rely on foreign labor sources to meet those needs? Will our labor regulatory system remain focused on labor markets of the past, dominated by large bureaucratic firms? Or can we adapt to employer demands for more "flexibility" without undermining past gains in working conditions? In short, can we make our economy work better for our employees, their dependents, and—indeed—for society as a whole?

Levine argues that schools and training will be major components in a successful adjustment of the American labor market to the new realities. Other government policies must also change. Efforts must be made to improve labor market opportunities for those who have previously remained outside the economic mainstream.

One area in which the United States stands out as a success, especially when compared with developed countries in Europe, is job creation. European countries have tended to see improvements in real wages but stagnation in job creation and difficulties in the transition to work among the young. One view is that American job growth is in fact due to wage stagnation and European job stagnation is due to its wage trends. What Levine would like to achieve is continued job creation in the United States but with a reduction in social ills. In effect, he would like to see the best of both sides of the Atlantic present in the American workforce of the future.

Too big a challenge? Levine is optimistic that improvements can be made, even if perfection cannot be achieved. Government policy makers must pay more attention to incentives and mis-incentives they create. More consideration must be given to overall policy rather than the one-ill-at-a-time approach that has been traditional. Government interventions must adopt a "customer" sensitivity. And educational policy is one of the most important programs government operates. Clearly, says Levine, major revamps of the incentives of the K–12 system will be needed. And post-high school systems of training and skill acquisition will be essential. Such an approach will allow adjustment to the increased job mobility that is likely to be characteristic of the future workforce.

Just as education needs important reforms, so too does U.S. policy toward job safety, housing, health care, disability, and other social concerns. Throughout his book, Levine offers concrete suggestions for improvement, drawing on available research and approaches that appear promising. Quick fixes, magic bullets, and panaceas are not on offer. But continuous improvement in what we have is proposed. Whether you agree with a particular suggestion or not, Levine's careful development of problem and solution will provoke and inform

Daniel J.B. Mitchell

ACKNOWLEDGMENTS

Many of these ideas were developed while I worked at the Council of Economic Advisers. There I was privileged to work most closely with Maya Federman, who contributed many of the ideas found here. I had excellent colleagues such as Bill Dickens, Tom Kane, Mark Mazur, and Halsey Rogers, and outstanding bosses Laura D'Andrea Tyson, Martin Baily, and Joseph Stiglitz. On disability I worked closely with Susan Daniels, Marie Strahan, and Jane West; on workplace and school regulations with Meghan Kelly, Gaynor McCowan, and Mike Schmidt; on education with Barry White; on reinventing government with Bob Knisely; on public housing with Steve Redburn, Michael Stegman, and Marc Weiss; on work and technology policy with Marie-Louise Caravatti, Frank Emspak, Henry Kelly, and Scott Ralls; on the statistical system with Paul Bugg, Connie Dunham, David Hirschberg, and Katherine Wallman; on urban and youth policy with Sheryl Cashin, Bo Cutter Jr., Paul Dimond, Marcus Stanley, and Judy Wurtzel; and on labor market policy in general with Alan Krueger. I also learned a lot during my six months at the Department of Labor working on workplace issues with Marty Manley, Rob Portman, Jonathan Low, and the staff of the short-lived Office of the American Workplace.

The discussion of the automobile industry draws heavily on many conversations and several coauthored articles with Susan Helper. I have also drawn directly from works coauthored with Brad DeLong, Maya Federman, David Finegold, Thesia Garner, John Greenlees, John Kiely, Duane McGough, Marilyn McNillen, and Kathleen Short. Large sections of chapters 2, 3, and 5 were drawn from chapter 5 of the 1994 *Economic Report of the President*. Although I was the primary author of that chapter, it reflects a collaboration among many at the Council and at several federal agencies.

In short, many of the words here were, in fact, penned by others. I am pleased to share credit for any good ideas with my colleagues. At the same time, many of these colleagues disagreed, sometimes vehemently, with proposals in this volume. Sadly, I retain responsibility for remaining errors. (I leave it to each reader to decide which ideas fall in each category.)

In addition to comments from these coauthors, I received many helpful comments from Carol Chapman, Amanda Datnow, Mark Gilkey, Kara Hartnett, Beth Levine, Daniel Levine, Nancy Levine, Jonathan Leonard,

Eliot Mason, Dan Mitchell, Gary Painter, Siobhan Reilly, David Stern, and George Strauss. Brian Fulfrost helped with the figures. Sarah Bales, Yamile Slebi, and Jimmy Torrez made many suggestions and tracked down a slew of needed facts and references. Students in my 1996 Industrial Relations class read large portions of the book and made many helpful comments. I very much appreciate the assistance of all of these students, friends, and colleagues. I am grateful for the financial support from the Institute of Industrial Relations at U.C. Berkeley and from the Sloan Foundation that helped support this research.

Finally, I must thank Jeremy Elliot Levine. I began the first draft of this book the same month Vicki and I began him. Nine months later I raced to finish a rough draft of the manuscript before his arrival on this planet. I very much appreciate his (barely) holding off arriving until this could be sent to the publisher.

Working in the Twenty-First Century

1

INTRODUCTION

Forty years ago, American schools, businesses, and governments all worked more or less the same way: they were rigidly controlled hierarchies. Most Americans attended boring and rigid schools that prepared them to work at boring and rigid jobs. When Americans needed government services, they got them from rigid government agencies. Schools, businesses, and governments all operated in a machinelike fashion to produce a standard output—whether the "output" was a washing machine from a factory, a semiskilled employee from a school, or a Social Security check from the government.

This production method—essentially an extension of Henry Ford's assembly line—helped raise productivity and standards of living. Schools taught what businesses wanted: punctuality, reliability, and obedience—the virtues of a machine. Businesses put those qualities to work. And government followed suit. Today, however, our major economic challenge is no longer how to produce large quantities of highly standardized goods. Today's trend is away from standard products and toward both high-quality services and customized products. In today's economy, semiskilled and unskilled labor are less valuable. Today's economy needs a different kind of worker—and it isn't getting it. Today's economy also needs a different kind of business and a different kind of government—and it isn't getting enough of those, either.

The result is an economy that has plateaued. Productivity and average living standards are growing much less rapidly than a generation ago. Coupled with low rates of productivity growth, we have high levels of social and economic problems such as child poverty and inequality. Furthermore, businesses aren't very happy with the quality of employees that they get, and employees aren't very happy with the businesses that they work for. And of course nobody's happy with the government.

This volume relates many of our nation's social and economic problems to the combination of these three rigid systems (school, business, and government) and how they reinforce each other. Conversely, this volume shows that these problems are solvable. We can have better schools, better businesses, and better government. To get these desired improvements, we need more flexible businesses that are responsible more to the customer and less to the hierarchy. We must increase accountability to the "customer," whether that customer is receiving a product from a business, an education from a school, or a service from the government.

America at Midcentury

A scant forty years ago, Ford, Chrysler, and General Motors were among the most confident, successful, and admired companies in the world. Their market dominance was based on their manufacturing prowess and their leadership in productivity and quality.

The ideal for a 1950s family was a mother at home and a father at work. Unfortunately, the father's job was often uninteresting: in 1950, 60 percent of jobs were classified as unskilled. The management writings of the time emphasized the efficiency of large hierarchies. In these rigid structures, every worker (and many managers) largely just followed orders and tried to fit in. Moreover, the rigidities of the workplace were repeated in the rigid roles for women, blacks, and other minorities.

On the good side, productivity rose steadily and the fruits of the higher productivity were widely shared. Even regimented jobs such as assembling automobiles provided decent pay. Thus, median family income doubled (after converting into constant 1992 dollars) from $19,000 in 1947 to $39,000 in 1973. Moreover, if the father of this idealized family was a manager or professional, he probably expected that he would have a job for life.

Government at Midcentury

The New Deal and World War II brought government programs a level of legitimacy that was rare in U.S. history. Government policies to make labor markets work better were designed for an idealized version of this economy. For example, employment policy assumed implicitly that health insurance and pensions would be provided by large, stable employers—although such policies remained rare even into the 1950s.

In government, as in the successful businesses of the day, hierarchy was the rule. The New Deal had spawned a set of major social and labor-market programs, such as unemployment insurance, job training, and a small program to give cash grants to widows that evolved into Aid to Families with Dependent Children (AFDC). Most of these programs were run by complex partnerships of federal, state, and local agencies. Typically the federal government gave directions with books of rules and regulations, state governments transmitted those directions and added on further rules, and local offices administered the hundreds of programs.

America at Century's End

The fathers who worked during the 1950s have largely now retired. Their sons and grandsons, as well as their daughters and granddaughters, are working in an economy very different from the economy described above.

Ford and Chrysler have each almost gone out of business (before successful rebirths). The defeated nations that America aided in the 1950s now rival the United States in terms of living standards and technology. Within the United States, productivity growth has slowed to a trickle.

Thus, the typical family's income has barely budged since the early 1970s. (If median family income had continued to grow at the 1949–73 rate, it would have almost doubled again, growing to more than $70,000.)

Moreover, the productivity growth that remains is no longer evenly shared (Figure 1.1). Although all portions of the income distribution benefited from growth in the generation after World War II, even the much lower benefits of growth have not been enjoyed by the less advantaged in the last quarter century.

While even in the 1950s most employees had insecure jobs, by the 1990s perceptions of insecurity now pervade all levels of the organization. Even managers working for large employers often fear for their jobs.

Families have changed dramatically as well. Most mothers now work for pay, as well as in the home. In addition, most children spend time living with only one parent, almost always a mother. Unfortunately, almost half of female-headed families are poor. While 14 percent of children lived in poverty in 1970, 22 percent were in poverty by 1996.

The declining labor market prospects for many low-skilled workers are matched by increasing costs of failed social policy. For example, the nation can expect to pay roughly $70,000 for prison costs for the average male high school dropout. (This calculation discounts future costs over the next thirty years into current dollars. It is the average for all dropouts; the figure for those who actually go to prison is much higher.)

In contrast to the United States at midcentury, by the year 2000 only 12 percent of new jobs are expected to require low or no skills (Hoye and Tegger 1996). The new economy has increased opportunity for those who excel at working as teams and solving problems. These new skills have become essential even on the automobile assembly line. They are even more crucial in the growing number of jobs dealing with information, computers, and customer service.

In spite of the slowdown in growth, new technologies and new ways of organizing work hold the potential for more interesting jobs and more productive workplaces. Most large organizations are redesigning themselves to

Figure 1.1 **Family Income, Average Annual Change**

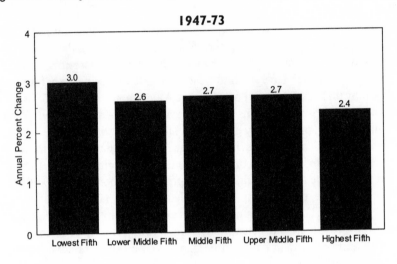

1947-73

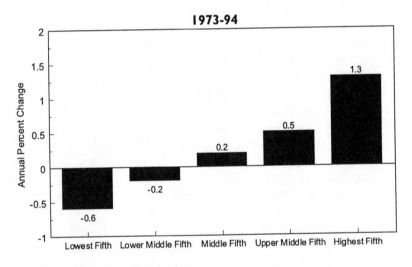

1973-94

Source: Mishel, Bernstein, and Schmitt 1997, 57.

be more flexible and responsive to their customers. A modest number of workplaces have reorganized so that front-line workers have more skills, more autonomy, and more rewards for solving their customers' problems. These innovative workplaces can produce better outcomes for both businesses and employees.

A Government for the New Century

Unlike the post–World War II era, the government is now held in low esteem by much of society. The small program to give cash grants to widows has grown into a welfare state. The great programs of the New Deal are now commonly thought of as morally bankrupt (welfare) or as soon-to-be literally bankrupt (Social Security).

Too many programs provide citizens (as employees, welfare recipients, managers, etc.) with poor incentives. Too many programs are based on rigid command-and-control rules. These rules, in turn, too often provide government agencies and service providers with poor incentives. Too often, multiple agencies with conflicting rules and uncoordinated approaches address a common problem. The resulting decisions often focus on the short run or on solving a piece of a problem, not on creating value for the nation's citizenry. It is always important to spend money cost-effectively, but the urgency rises as government spending declines in purchasing power. It is equally crucial for programs to improve continuously. Unfortunately, our government programs are often not as cost effective as they could be.

Overview of the Book

The bad news is that American productivity and living standards are no longer increasing at the rate of a generation ago. Moreover, because of rising inequality, living standards are actually declining for large segments of the population (chapter 2).

The good news is that flexible, customer-focused workplaces can improve productivity and the quality of worklife (chapter 3). Just as rigidities almost put Ford and Chrysler out of business, important lessons can be learned from their revival. Unfortunately, both government and markets work imperfectly—and a number of these imperfections reduce the adoption of flexible and customer-focused workplaces (chapter 4). We appear to be trapped in an inefficient but fairly stable situation where most employers choose rigid workplaces, in part because of a shortage of skilled employees. Government programs, in turn, are also typically rigid and hierarchical (in spite of the important efforts to begin moving to more flexible models).

The argument of this book can be summed up by looking at the interaction of the structure of workplaces, the skills of the workforce, and the design of government programs (Figure 1.2). Each of these is both a cause and an effect of the other two.

The increasingly demanding standards of customers are inducing many enterprises to move to high-skill and flexible workplaces. At the same time,

Figure 1.2 **Connections Between New Workplaces, New Skills, and New Government Policies**

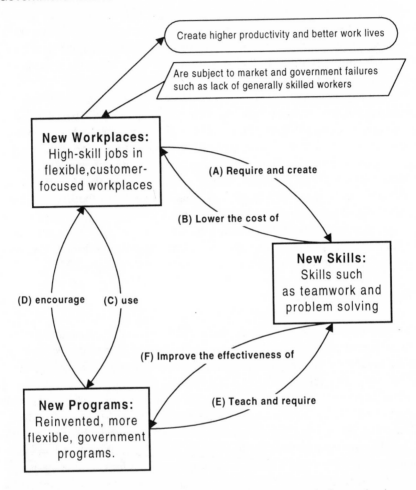

these high-skill workplaces remain the minority. This relative rarity in part reflects market imperfections that lead to relatively few workers who have the needed skills (chapter 4). The ensuing shortage of workers skilled in problem solving and teamwork slows the spread of high-skill workplaces (path A in Figure 1.2).

The solution for this problem is found in schools. For generations, a key goal of many schools has been to teach students to show up on time and follow rules. These were often key skills of the nation's industrial economy at midcentury.

In the new economy, an increasing fraction of workers must know how to work together to solve problems. Because work, technology, and organizations change so rapidly, workers also need the skills of continuous learning.

We must undertake an ambitious agenda of lifelong learning to help American workers respond to the challenges of, and grasp the opportunities afforded by, the new economic realities. Schools, training programs, and skills certifications for students and employees must go beyond the basics to include teamwork, problem solving, and other skills of the new economy (path E in the figure; see chapters 5, 6). Increasing the proportion of the workforce trained in these skills is important because having a workforce with skills such as teamwork and problem solving lowers the cost of creating high-skill jobs in flexible, customer-focused workplaces (path B in the figure; see chapter 3). More generally, government regulations and programs must encourage, not impede, workplaces that create high-skill, high-wage jobs. Government policies for the new economy must certify and reward these high-skilled workplaces while removing legal and other barriers (path D in the figure; see chapters 7, 8).

The public sector must change as rapidly as the private sector. We must take the management lessons of today's best organizations and apply the relevant ones to improve government policies. Although many government programs are not as effective as they should be, reinvented programs can do much better (path C in the figure; see chapter 4). To do this, reinvented government programs should use skills such as teamwork and problem solving (path F in the figure; see chapters 4, 7) to implement five key lessons.

First, reinvented programs must provide good incentives for citizens in their many roles: taxpayers, workers, employers, welfare recipients, and so forth. For example, nobody should ever be made worse off by working, even if they currently receive welfare or a disability stipend.

Second, incentives do not matter just for welfare recipients. The federal government must also provide good incentives for those who provide most government services: states, local governments, suppliers, and direct service providers such as nonprofit organizations. Often the federal government can provide incentives to service providers by giving citizens more discretion concerning where they will receive government-funded services. In other instances, states or localities should have increased autonomy. In all cases, increased autonomy should be accompanied by accountability for results.

Third, the programs should focus on satisfying citizens' needs, even if the government has to reorganize. From the customer's point of view, the organization of the government, statutes, funding streams, and congressional committees should not interfere with good service. This simple idea should hold whether the customer is a welfare mother, a small business owner, or an employee looking for safety information. Advanced information technologies such as the Internet often are key elements of customer-focused solutions.

Fourth, each program must be designed to guarantee continuous improvement. Programs must constantly gather data about their effectiveness and use these data to improve their operations.

Finally, we must not be afraid to invest for long-term payoffs. This is especially true in social policy, where so many investments affect our children.

This analysis builds on past work on reinventing government (Gingrich 1995; Gore 1993, 1995; Osborne and Gaebler 1992; Wilson, n.d.), and goes beyond it in several ways. First, I bring a more nuanced view to theories of market and nonmarket incentives. While many schemes sound good, all schemes have incentives for undesirable behavior. Given that all schemes have flaws, I examine the existing evidence on what works (and what does not) when evaluating alternatives. Second, I draw on the experience of leading private-sector firms that have addressed similar problems, often in ways that are quite different from the solutions prescribed by past government reformers. Often these solutions involve incentives for partners to implement quality improvement programs. Finally, because no perfect solution exists, I emphasize that systems must be designed to guarantee learning and improvement.

A Life-Cycle Approach

This book discusses how labor market and social policies must change to adapt to the realities of the new economy. These policies run throughout a citizen's life cycle. The nation cannot afford cradle-to-grave income supports (and many would not endorse the lower work effort that would follow). At the same time, the nation cannot afford to ignore a life cycle of investments that can increase equity, improve incentives and opportunity, and create high returns.

The analysis begins with policies to help children and improve schools, then moves on to programs to finance college and to help students move from school to work. The middle portion of the book discusses policies to improve workplaces, with an emphasis on improving the regulation of workplaces. Because the vast majority of jobs do not last a lifetime, the following section discusses policies to help people move between jobs.

At each step, government programs must not become traps, perhaps by guaranteeing a below-poverty-level income. The counterpart to programs that provide good incentives for citizens is requiring citizens to take responsibility. That is, effective programs typically provide adequate levels of opportunity but do not guarantee a certain level of success.

Updating and Including

Finally, three large, overlapping groups are usually not fully participating in the "new economy"—people between jobs (that is, unemployed), the ghetto poor, and disabled people receiving government income assistance. Although often thought of as separate populations, membership in these groups is often quite dynamic. Virtually every family in the United States has members that spend at least part of their lives in one or more of these groups.

The new economy presents new challenges to these groups, as well as new opportunities. Our policies for the unemployed, ghetto youth, and the disabled must adapt to the new realities while preparing all citizens to succeed in the new economy.

The Unemployed (or Those Who Soon May Be)

Many of our national policies, ranging from pensions to health insurance, evolved for a world in which people held a single job most of their working life. At the same time, most employees hold many jobs over their lifetimes. Thus, our programs must help employees move between employers without loss of living standards, rewards for skills, pensions, or (most important) health insurance.

Residents in Our Worst Neighborhoods

In some American neighborhoods, fewer than half the households have an employed adult, fewer than half the youth graduate from high school, and teen pregnancy and crime are common. We must reinvent our urban and rural policies to make it easier to leave these neighborhoods, both by reinventing public housing and by creating an integrated plan to improve the schools and youth policies of these neighborhoods.

The Disabled

In the old economy, everyone in a wheelchair was assumed to be unable to work. Those declared as disabled were eligible for a pension (often less than the poverty line), but only if they did not work. In an era when computers filled large rooms and most work was manual, such an assumption made some sense.

Now, a computer more powerful than any available in the 1950s fits in one hand, and most employees use a computer at work. Thus, the assumption that those in wheelchairs cannot work is wrong more often than not. Our programs must embrace new technology and give citizens the skills they need to use it—not trap them in programs that impede such learning.

Conclusion

Books have been written on each topic discussed in this volume, such as education, regulation, or disability. There are two advantages to covering these topics in an integrated framework.

First, many of the challenges are common to different spheres of policy. Rising income inequality, changes in work organization, and increased use of computers create challenges and opportunities for all aspects of social and labor market policy. At the same time, a similar set of problems and rigidities affects most government programs.

Second, and as a result of the first point, a similar set of lessons reappears in almost every chapter of this book. Not coincidentally, these lessons are often similar to (although not identical to) those learned at the nation's best-run businesses.

After a generation of well-meaning government programs and of social science research on social problems, it is clear that government has no magic bullet to solve all our problems. Government programs (even ones as pervasive as public schools) will never be more important than families, cultural and religious institutions, or perhaps even television. Ideally, all these institutions should align in teaching the virtues of hard work, teamwork, and learning as activities both joyful and useful. On the one hand, it is unrealistic to expect schools and other government programs to teach these virtues unassisted. On the other hand, it is crucial that all government programs align to support these virtues: to make work pay, to teach and support teamwork, and to make learning both engaging and fruitful.

It goes without saying that we cannot afford ineffective government programs. At the same time, we cannot afford to allow the government to ignore the problems of slow growth, poverty, or unemployment. The good news is that wise investments can address these problems, raise Americans' living standards, and create a nation where every child has a much greater opportunity to succeed.

2

STAGNATION FOR MOST, DECLINE FOR MANY

> Productivity growth has slowed to a crawl since 1973. Although difficult to measure, income growth has slowed for most and has been reversed for many Americans. Inequality is also difficult to measure, but all measures of inequality show it has risen as growth has slowed.

In the last generation, the United States has created more jobs than western Europe and Japan combined. At the same time, productivity growth has been much lower in the United States, and wage growth—especially for the bottom half of wage earners—has been far worse. This chapter outlines the evidence on wages and incomes, while the rest of the book describes how to avoid the trade-off many have assumed exists between equality and growth.

Hearing liberals and conservatives chatter, some observers might be confused about how well the U.S. economy has done over the past twenty-five years. In fact, the incomes of Americans show two unmistakable trends in the last generation.

First, all measures of income show much slower growth since 1973 than during the previous twenty-five years. For example, the median real hourly wage declined by 0.3 percent per year between 1973 and 1995, compared to its growth of roughly 2.5 percent a year during the previous quarter century. This turnaround was more dramatic than the slowdown in worker productivity growth, from 2.5 percent per year to only 1 percent.

Second, all measures of income and living standards show growing inequality since 1973, in contrast to the stable or slight equalization of growth during the preceding generation. For example, the male at the tenth percentile of the earnings distribution (that is, earning more than 10 percent of the male work force) earned 13 percent less per hour in 1995 ($5.06) than in 1973 ($5.76), while the earnings of the male at the ninetieth percentile rose 6 percent, from $21.10 to $22.35 (Mishel et al. 1997, 141. All figures are in 1995 dollars.). Women still earn less than men on average, but the gap closed somewhat over this period (largely as average male earnings declined). At the same time, inequality also increased among women.

The combination of slow growth and rising inequality led the bottom part of the income distribution to become worse off. Because so many ways exist to measure incomes, different measures show slightly different pictures: Did real income decline for 30 percent of the population, or for 60 percent? Has the upper few percent of the income distribution enjoyed half the total growth, or even more? In spite of these disagreements, the two basic facts of slower growth and widening inequality are not in dispute.

Different Versions of the Same Story

Some measures of income can make the story a little cheerier than that indicated by the declining real median wage. Mean wages (the average of all wages earned) have risen slightly since 1973 as high-end wages have grown faster while those in the bottom have dropped. In addition, because the cost of health insurance has risen faster than the rate of inflation, average total compensation (wages plus the cost of benefits) has increased slightly faster than wages. In addition, inequality of consumption has increased, but not as rapidly as has inequality of income (Cutler and Katz 1992).

Moreover, it is very difficult to measure the value of totally new goods such as personal computers or the change in average prices when people buy more goods at discount outlets such as warehouse stores. Thus, several different measures of inflation show slightly lower inflation and slightly faster real wage growth than is indicated by the best official version of the Consumer Price Index (that is, version CPI-U-X1).

Regardless of the various measures one can choose, the two basic facts remain: growth of mean wages, compensation, family income and consumption have all slowed since 1973. For example, the slowdown in productivity growth and in wage growth are at least four times larger than any plausible mismeasurement of inflation. In addition, all of these measures show widening inequality.

Other measures of living standards give a slightly drearier story than median wage decline coupled with growing wage inequality. Inequality after taxes and transfers grew slightly more rapidly than before taxes. Although it is difficult to make comparisons directly, it appears that inequality of wealth also increased, but less rapidly than did income inequality. In 1983 the top fifth owned 81.3 percent of wealth, while in 1992 that fraction had risen to 83.8 percent (Mishel et al. 1997, table 5.5, citing Wolff 1996). If we are concerned about the next generation, one result of the growth in inequality is particularly troublesome: child poverty rates have increased from 14 percent in 1980 to 22 percent in 1995. (On the cheery side, elderly poverty rates have declined markedly since the late 1960s.)

To muddy the waters further, multiple measures of inequality exist. Fortunately for those trying to sum up the state of the economy (although not so fortunately for those at the low end of the income distribution), all of these different measures show increases in inequality. Inequality has grown between groups with the same number of years of education, and within groups of same years of education. Inequality has grown between those at the top of the ladder versus those at the bottom, between blue-collar and managerial occupations, between those with a college education and those with less (Figure 2.1). In figures not shown, inequality has grown between those with more and those with less labor market experience, and within groups with similar levels of experience. More arcane measures of inequality such as the Gini coefficient or the standard deviation of the logarithm of wages also reflect growing inequality.

Furthermore, the person at the bottom of the income distribution in one year is not the same individual as the person at the bottom a generation later. This can matter because incomes fluctuate more now than they used to. Increased fluctuations, by themselves, will increase inequality measured on an annual basis. Nevertheless, if the fluctuations tend to average out, inequality measured over several years' time might not have risen. In fact, inequality appears to have increased as rapidly when measured over several years as when measured on an annual basis (Gottschalk and Moffitt 1994).

The Costs and Benefits of a Dynamic Economy

The United States has a dynamic economy. This dynamism is reflected, for example, in the 37 million additional jobs the U.S. economy created between 1973 and 1995 (U.S. Council of Economic Advisers 1995).

On the downside, American dynamism includes high rates of job loss, often followed by declining earnings and living standards. Each year more than 2 million U.S. workers permanently lose their jobs through no fault of their own, when plants close or there are mass layoffs. Although most dislocated workers find new jobs within fifteen weeks of their job loss, 15 percent of all workers displaced between 1987 and 1991 remained unemployed for more than six months. Older workers and those with less education were the least likely to find a new job after displacement (U.S. Council of Economic Advisers 1995). Of those involuntarily displaced workers fortunate enough to find new employment, 47 percent suffered a decrease in their wages. Moreover, these lower wages were persistent; six or more years after displacement, earnings remain 10 percent below what the worker would have been expected to earn (U.S. Council of Economic Advisers 1996b).

In recent years, Americans have reported declining perceptions of job security. In one poll, the proportion of Americans who "frequently worry about being laid off" has risen from 22 percent in 1988 to 46 percent in 1995 (Schellhardt 1996). The same International Survey Research

16

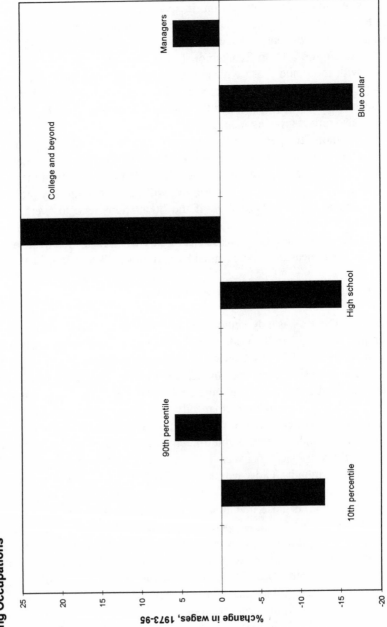

Figure 2.1 Inequality Has Grown Among Men—Between the Top and the Bottom, Between Education Groups, and Among Occupations

Corporation poll reported that between 1988 and 1995, the proportion who felt sure their job was secure if they performed well declined from 73 to 50 percent. Some of this increase may reflect the emphasis in the popular press on the declining importance of long-term employment in the United States, particularly at large employers such as AT&T and IBM, which were once famous for their lifetime jobs.

Interestingly, the academic research on this topic has presented a more mixed picture. Specifically, the average tenure of U.S. workers has not declined markedly in the past fifteen years (Diebold et al. 1997).

This fact masks several important trends that indicate the press accounts are not completely misleading. Most importantly, average tenure has declined for men. This decline has been most rapid for men who did not complete high school. Moreover, consistent with the press accounts of the downsizing of middle managers, rates of job loss of middle-aged, more educated men have also increased. Job loss remains more common for blue-collar workers, but rates of job loss have increased most rapidly for the formerly more protected categories.

The average job tenure (that is, at a single employer) in the economy is almost stable because average tenure has increased for women at the same time it has decreased for men. To the extent that women's higher average tenure reflects their increased commitment to careers (as opposed to full-time work in the home), this increase in tenure may still mask a shortfall of the supply of long-term jobs relative to the demand.

In any case, any *change* in rates of turnover or displacement are of only modest importance. Most jobs in the United States do not last very long, and it is important to create institutions to increase tenure when it is efficient (for example, due to firm-specific skills), and to facilitate what will always be high rates of movement between employers.

In addition, earnings are highly variable. While two thirds of families with heads of prime working age had higher incomes at the end of the 1980s than at the beginning, a third experienced declines. Moreover, this measure of the variability of earnings has risen. During the 1970s only 21 percent experienced a fall in incomes (Rose 1994, 20).

A recent study by the Census Bureau provides more evidence on the importance of fluctuating incomes. The study found that within a thirty-two-month spell more than 16 percent of all workers employed full-time experienced a spell of poverty (Shea 1995). Furthermore, during the most recent recession (1990–91), 31 percent of food stamp recipients previously had an hourly wage of at least $7.

To the extent that people have difficulty maintaining their consumption when they suffer temporary reductions in income, an increase in the variability of transitory income can reduce the nation's average well being. There is substantial evidence that short-term changes in income lead to changes in consumption for most American households (Campbell and Mankiw 1990). An implication of the variability of consumption is that social insurance that redistributes income from people who are having a good year to those having a bad year can increase the well-being of American families when measured over their lifetime.

Inequality is not always a problem, particularly if it provides incentives that increase productivity and average living standards. Unfortunately, there is no evidence that the widening inequality in the United States has increased incentives substantially. Productivity growth between 1948 and 1973 was far more rapid than growth since 1973, while inequality was declining in the first period and rising in the second.

The dynamics of families is also important. The typical child born today will spend some portion of his or her childhood living with only one parent. Unfortunately, poverty rates for children in single-parent households are close to 50 percent. Almost half of all spells on welfare (45 percent) begin as a result of divorce or separation (Bane and Ellwood 1994).

Even intact families are at risk, particularly if only one parent works. In 1992, one in seven men did not earn enough to support a family of four above the poverty line in 1992. This ratio has almost doubled since 1979. Recessions worsen the risk of poverty; each percentage point increase in unemployment raises the poverty rate about 0.7 points, or almost 2 million people (Blank and Blinder 1986).

The result is an economy in which ordinary working Americans find themselves at risk of job loss, of lower earnings, and of poverty. For example, over a third of children spend at least a year in poverty before they turn eighteen (Mishel et al. 1997).

Poverty

From 1960 to 1973, the nation's overall poverty rate fell from 22 percent to 11 percent; it then rose to 15 percent by 1995. Poverty rates for children have been even higher: 27 percent in 1960, 14 percent in 1973, and 22 percent in 1995 (Figure 2.2). The rise in poverty remains even after taxes and transfers are accounted for; poverty rates by this measure rose from 9 percent in 1979 to 12 percent in 1993 (comparable figures are not available prior to 1979).

Measuring Poverty

In the United States, a family is defined as poor if it has a cash income below the official poverty line for a given family size. The poverty line in

Figure 2.2 Poverty Rates for All Americans, 1966–1996

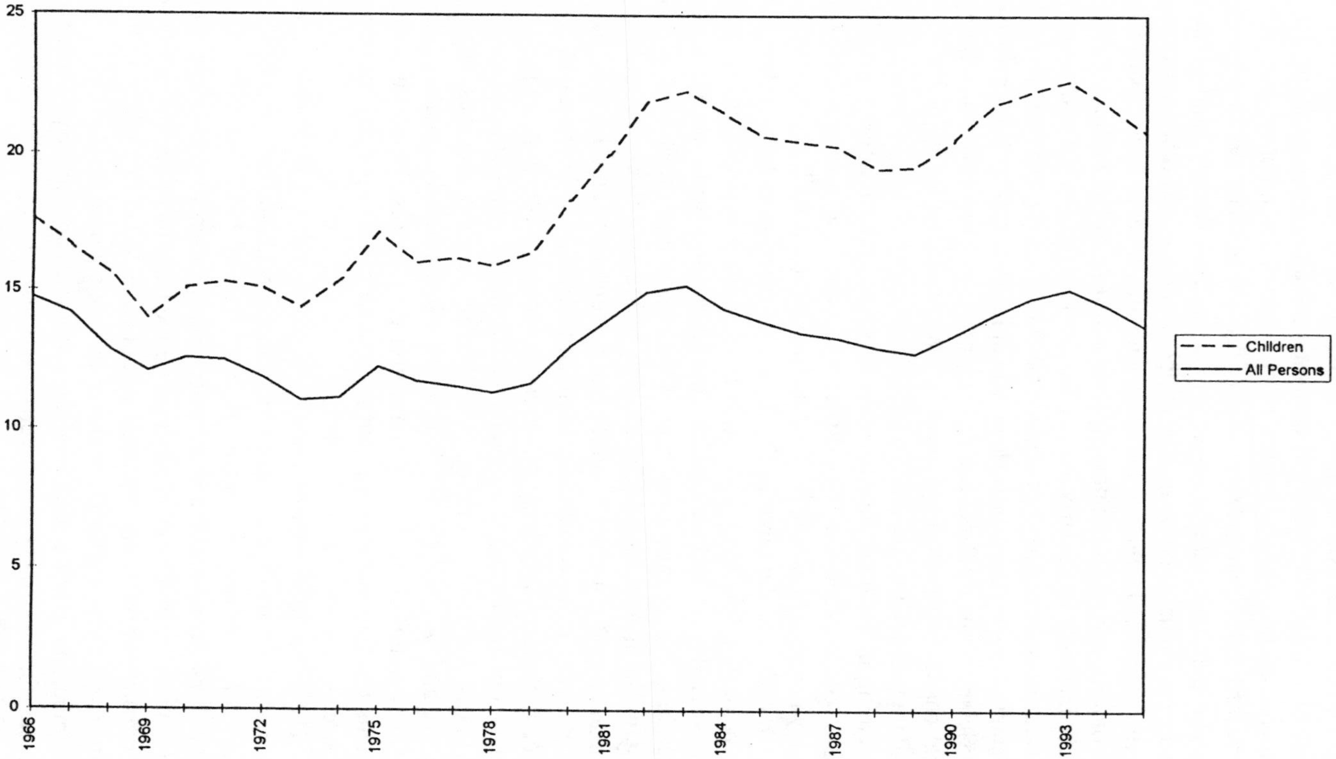

the United States was set in the early 1960s by taking an estimate of the cost of a minimum adequate diet multiplied by three to allow for other expenses. The poverty line has been adjusted for inflation, but otherwise remains little unchanged since then (Citro and Michael 1995).

The measured rate of poverty may be misleadingly high because the focus on annual income ignores homeownership and other assets that can permit reasonable living standards even when income is low (particularly if income is low only temporarily). In addition, some families underreport their income, particularly on tax forms. Finally, the official poverty rate based on income does not include taxes or in-kind transfers such as food stamps or government-provided medical insurance. (The National Academy of Science Poverty Panel has recently released a report recommending several changes to the official poverty measure including adjusting for taxes and transfers [Citro and Michael 1995].)

Going in the other direction, the measured rate of poverty may be misleadingly low because it is difficult to count the homeless and because many people who would be poor are in institutions such as jails and prisons.

In addition, the poverty line is not adjusted over time. When looking at poverty levels over long periods of time, it is important to note that the socially defined standard of living required to be a citizen of good standing can change over time. (This argument dates back at least to Adam Smith.) In many schools sixty years ago, there was only modest social stigma if a child's family had no telephone and the child had head lice. Now, in most schools such children would be outcasts. Thus, a recent National Academy of Sciences report on revising the poverty line advocates increasing the poverty cutoff in line with consumer spending patterns for food, clothing, and housing for the previous three years (Citro and Michael 1995). Thus, comparisons based on material deprivations are important, but by definition they ignore important social elements that can make people with the same calories per day meaningfully poorer in one era than in another.

The increase in poverty rates in recent decades is somewhat surprising because the growth in average family incomes should have reduced poverty rates by over two percentage points between 1973 and 1991. Unfortunately, as documented above, wages have fallen for low-wage workers. This increase in inequality has undone the benefits of economic growth for low-wage workers, and by itself would have added two points to the poverty rates. Even worse, the increase in single-parent households is roughly as important as the rise in inequality in increasing poverty. Thus, the two forces together have led poverty rates to rise, not fall (Danzinger and Gottschalk 1995, 93–111).

How Poor Are the Poor?

The difficulties with measuring poverty have led some analysts to conclude that few of those with incomes below the poverty line are meaningfully "poor" in the sense of suffering much deprivation. For example, Robert Rector (1992) analyzes the 1989 American Housing Survey and concludes that most people officially identified as poor are "well housed." He notes that nearly 40 percent of all households with incomes below the poverty line own their own home, and the median value of homes owned by the poor is 58 percent of the median value of all homes owned in America. In addition, he finds that only 8 percent of poor households are overcrowded (defined as more than one person per room), and 53 percent of poor households have air-conditioning.

Although the paper is subtitled "Lessons for Welfare Reform," in most cases Rector's tabulations do not focus on single-parent families, the group most affected by welfare reform. One exception is illuminating: For home-ownership, he emphasizes that 40 percent of all poor households own their own home. At the same time, he calculates that only 18 percent of poor, single-parent families own their own home. Only this population was typically eligible for Aid to Families with Dependent Children, the largest cash welfare program. The elderly and two-parent households rarely receive AFDC. Thus, focusing on all poor households, instead of on those potentially eligible for welfare, is misleading.

To understand better the living standards of the poor and nonpoor, I worked with a group of experts from the federal statistical agencies to analyze a broad array of national surveys (Federman et al. 1996). We promoted comparability across surveys as much as possible. In all but a few of the measures we could identify, individuals in poor households were significantly worse off than those in nonpoor families.

We found that 71 percent of the expenditures of families that spent less than the poverty line is for food, shelter, utilities, and apparel, compared to 46 percent for families of the nonpoor. For those in poor, single-parent families, the share spent on these necessities is 80 percent. For nonmaterial aspects of life, the living standards of the poor diverge even more than for consumption. Those living in poor households are twice as likely to be victims of violent crimes (robbery, assault, and rape) as are the nonpoor. Those in poor, single-parent families are more than three times as likely to be victimized. Infant mortality rates also differ sharply: 13.5 out of every 1,000 infants born to poor mothers die within their first year, compared to 8.3 per 1,000 among the nonpoor.

Twenty-seven percent of the poor live in families that report two or more of the following: eviction in the past year, crowding (more than one person per room), having moderate or severe housing upkeep problems, having gas or electricity turned off in the past year, having the phone disconnected in the past year, not having enough food in the past four months, living without a refrigerator, living without a stove, and living without a telephone. Only 3 percent of the nonpoor report two or more of these events. The mean number of these events per poor family is just over one. In short, even with its problems, the current poverty measure appears to identify primarily families suffering deprivations. Presumably a more accurate poverty line would show a higher proportion of the poor with serious deprivations, but there is no reason to believe it would identify substantially fewer poor families.

The Declining Fortunes of Black Americans

Black workers have been particularly harmed by recent earnings trends. After a decade of progress following the Civil Rights Act of 1964, trends in the relative earnings of blacks and whites reversed. In the early 1960s, the wage gap between a black man and a white man of similar age and education averaged over 20 percent. This gap closed to less than 10 percent in the mid-1970s, but much of this gain has eroded (Bound and Freeman 1992). (Hispanics have suffered similar negative trends, but the lack of data on their earnings over a sufficiently long period makes comparisons difficult.) In addition, the proportion of black men over twenty years old who are employed has declined, from about 6 percentage points less than the rate for whites to 10 percentage points, over the past twenty years. The drop in employment is due to a decline in black labor force participation as well as increases in black unemployment.

In contrast to the decline in relative earnings, years of school completed and test scores among blacks have risen relative to whites. The difference in high school graduation rates between blacks and whites has narrowed sharply. From 1973 to 1992, dropout rates for blacks fell from 12.3 percentage points more than for whites to only 4.1 percentage points more. Black test scores (as measured by the National Assessment for Educational Progress) increased rapidly from 1978 to 1988, although they have fallen slightly since then; meanwhile, white test scores rose only slightly.

The bad news on black employment and the relatively good news on black test scores are both much worse in a subset of America's very poor inner-city neighborhoods. In many inner-city districts the dropout rate remains above 40 percent, and Hispanic dropout rates remain very high (McNeil 1996, 4). In some of these ghettos, as few as 40 percent of black men are employed—that is half the male employment rate for the nation as a whole.

An increasing portion of poor Americans, especially those of color, live in neighborhoods with very high concentrations of poverty (Jargowsky 1994). As poverty rates in America's ghettos have increased, fewer ghetto youths live with employed parents, and all ghetto youths have fewer employed neighbors. The lack of job market connections, in turn, appears to be an important factor in high nonemployment rates of ghetto youth (O'Regan and Quigley 1996).

Links to the job market provide jobholders with several related benefits. In neighborhoods with high employment rates, youths are more likely to hear about available job openings. Young people in such neighborhoods also learn more about the requirements of each job, so they are more likely to select a job that fits them well. Youths also learn the basic skills of getting and holding a job, such as how to dress for an interview and the importance of showing up on time.

Employers often prefer applicants who receive referrals because the referring person can provide information about the applicant and often screens applicants. Those making referrals have particularly strong incentives to identify good workers and to promote good performance on the job if they would like to make additional referrals in the future. (Adriana Kugler [1996] reviews these theories and the evidence concerning them.) The result of living in neighborhoods with low employment rates is that ghetto youth often lack all these benefits.

At the same time that inner cities have seen job opportunities declining and many schools remaining inadequate, a majority of young black male high school dropouts have turned to illegal activities for income. (Although this fact is dramatic, it is important to remember that the vast majority of black youth graduate from high school, as noted above.) Surveys indicate that young black men are more likely now than a decade ago to perceive greater rewards from crime than from regular employment. Young persons' participation in crime has adverse effects on their likelihood of future employment, especially if their activities lead to incarceration. These problems feed on each other: a child's chances of attending a low-quality school, becoming a teen parent, dropping out of school, living with only one parent, and having parents who do not work for pay are all associated with living in a poor neighborhood (Crane 1991).

Racial and ethnic discrimination remains a significant barrier for minorities in the job market. Direct measures of discrimination in employment are available from experiments in which similarly qualified white and black candidates, or white and Hispanic candidates, applied for the same job. In a series of experiments in Chicago, Washington, D.C., and Denver, whites received roughly three job offers for every two received by a matched black or Hispanic (Fix and Struyk 1993). In anonymous interviews, many employers also freely admit to preferring white applicants to black applicants (Kirschenman and Neckerman 1991; Moss and Tilly 1995).

Government antidiscrimination efforts became less aggressive in the 1980s, and this may account for some of the persistence of discrimination. An analysis of data collected by the Equal Employment Opportunity Commission (EEOC) and the Office of Federal Contract Compliance Programs (OFCCP) and its precursors shows that enforcement of affirmative action rules between 1974 and 1980 improved the job opportunities of black men with federal contractors. By the latter part of that period, affirmative action also helped both black and white women. In the 1980–84 period the enforcement of affirmative action was not as spirited as previously, and coverage by the federal government affirmative action policies was no longer associated with gains in black employment (Leonard 1990).

Growth of the Underclass?

Former Secretary of Education William Bennett (1995, 161) has argued that thirty years of our welfare system has produced "an underclass which is much larger, more violent, more poorly educated" than a generation ago. In fact, these claims are overstated. Although, as noted earlier, poverty and out-of-wedlock fertility are rising, many measures of the "underclass" show declining or stable size (Jencks and Peterson 1991). For example, many descriptions of the underclass focus on concentrations of the poor in largely minority ghettos. The good news is that ghettos in America are not growing rapidly. A higher proportion of poor people in 1980 lived in neighborhoods that were more than 40 percent poor than in 1970s, for example, but this fact appears to be due solely to the growing fraction of the population that is poor—not to any increase in concentration of the poor.

In addition, black high school dropouts are a large element of most definitions of the underclass. As noted earlier, blacks' high school graduation rates and test scores are up relative to those of whites, not down. Moreover, crime rates have been roughly stable since 1973, as reported on victimization surveys (although crime rates did rise in the 1960s, and serious crimes may have become slightly more concentrated in poor urban areas).

Conclusion

Compared to its trading partners, the United States has excelled in job creation. At the same time, the industrialized nations of western Europe and

East Asia have coupled better productivity growth with higher wage growth, especially for low-skill workers. In the United States we have seen widening inequality of wages, incomes, and living standards. The gaps have grown overall, as well as between those of different education, experience, or race. (The gender wage gap is the primary exception, although this has narrowed as men's wages have fallen, more than as women's wages have risen.) The nation's rates of poverty, especially for children, remain at unconscionable levels. The United States is alone among the industrialized nations in experiencing high and rapidly rising child poverty.

Some observers have hypothesized that an inevitable trade-off occurs between job growth and earnings inequality. The rest of this volume outlines policies that improve skills and promote new, high-productivity enterprises that can avoid this tradeoff. Before describing these solutions, we must understand the sources of the slower productivity growth and growing inequality that plague the nation.

3

GETTING INTO THIS MESS

> Liberals often (correctly) point out the failings of the free market, such as under-investment in human capital, managers who are not sufficiently rewarded for investments in their company's long-term capabilities, and high levels of inequality. Conservatives often (correctly) point out the failings of the government, such as its poor incentives for citizens, poor incentives for government agencies and partners, multiple programs and agencies that do not coordinate, rigid command-and-control rules, and inadequate willingness to invest for the long term.

Liberals tend to emphasize the many imperfections of the market, particularly the market for labor. Conservatives often reply by mentioning the many imperfections of government-proposed solutions. Unfortunately, the two sides often speak past each other, when in fact both are often correct.

This and the following chapter provide a framework for thinking about what works and what does not work in terms of creating effective government programs. This chapter outlines several important market failures that affect the labor market. It then outlines how several changes in the economy have amplified these market failures, worsening outcomes for many Americans. It then takes a detour through the private sector to examine the experience of rigid command-and-control hierarchy in the U.S. auto industry. It then shows how similar rigidities are pervasive in the U.S. government. These government failures have led to a number of unimpressive programs and to systematic failures in solving many important problems. The next chapter indicates how many of the principles of reinvention present in the U.S. auto industry can help solve the similar problems of government.

Market Failures

The fall of the Iron Curtain has reassured many Americans that the free market system works better than what was (until recently) its main alternative—state-directed central planning under a dictatorship. Markets give incentives for companies to respond to the desires of the purchasing public. Markets also determine prices that transmit information about where shortages are forming. Finally, the price system provides incentives for companies to be both innovative and efficient.

Alongside their many advantages, markets often have a number of failures that can inhibit efficient investment in skills and efficient schools and workplaces. This section describes a number of these market failures.

The Theory of Human Capital

When training is useful primarily at a single employer, neither the employees nor the employer will be willing to invest the efficient amount in training. In this situation, both are afraid the other will capture all the returns to the sunk investment (Becker 1975; Malcomson 1997).

In other instances, training is useful at many enterprises. In some cases, employees will pay for this training, perhaps with a low starting wage. For example, both medical residents and construction apprentices appear to receive low wages in part because of the valuable skills they acquire. Unfortunately, many employees are unable to pay for training because they have no financial assets. In addition, workers may be unwilling to pay for training implicitly with lower wages because they fear employers will not provide promised training of high quality, or fear the training will not lead to higher future wages. Thus, generally useful training can also be underprovided by the free market (Levine 1995, ch. 5).

Youth Labor Markets

For the majority of young Americans, the transition from high school to the workplace does not involve a degree from a four-year college. Although most high school graduates enter two- or four-year colleges, only one in four young Americans will graduate from college with a bachelor's degree. The typical new entrant will hold nine new jobs in his or her first ten years in the labor market (Stern et al. 1995).

Many of these new jobs last only a few months, three out of five end in less than two years (Bishop 1993, 339). Much of this churning is ultimately valuable, as young workers learn what they want from a job, and employers and employees find good matches. At the same time, the amount of churning in the United States appears inefficiently high. For example, it is higher than that of any other industrialized nation (Bishop 1993, 339). It is also accompanied by unemployment rates for eighteen- and nineteen-year-olds that are triple those of adults (Stern et al. 1995, 5).

At the same time, youth unemployment rates in the United States are low relative to those in Europe. Moreover, the high level of employment regulation in Europe may contribute both to low rates of job mobility and to high unemployment gaps (Siebert [1997]; but see Nickel [1997] for an opposing view.) The relatively high wages and low youth unemployment rates in West Germany before reunification indicate that better labor market outcomes for youth may be possible in the United States as well (see box 5.4).

Moreover, although roughly half of new hires have job-relevant experience, only 7 percent demonstrate a skill certification to the new employer. (Typical skill certifications include passing a medical board for a doctor or becoming a journeyman after a construction apprenticeship.) Unsurprisingly, employers report they are then pleasantly surprised by the skills of these experienced workers (Bishop 1993, 343). It is likely that if employees could more convincingly signal their past experience and skills, they would find more productive and higher-paid matches more rapidly.

Finance Problems

Investments in employees' skills and in the company's reputation as a trustworthy employer and business partner frequently take years to pay off. Managers are able to inform investors about their investments through many avenues. Yet investors will almost always have better information on, and thus likely pay more attention to, investments that are reported in publicly available financial statements and that are comparable across time and between companies. Informing investors about investments in human resources is more difficult because no common language exists to describe them in a way that allows outsiders to assess their value. Current accounting rules do not measure the investment that managers make in building a high-quality workforce and in producing high-quality goods. Instead, such spending shows up only as lower cash flow and earnings in the short run (Levine 1995, ch. 3; Porter 1992).

Partly because of these communication problems, corporate managers in a recent survey rated employee satisfaction, turnover, and training expenditures the three least important of nineteen measures of financial and nonfinancial performance to report to outside investors. These measures not only lagged behind earnings (ranked first) and capital expenditures (fourteenth), but even lost out to corporate ethics statements (sixteenth) (Eccles and Mavrinac 1994). Importantly, capital markets with richer information flows (as hold in much of Japan and Germany, for example) have smaller problems monitoring such investments (Porter 1992).

Because human resource investments are so hard to measure and monitor, they may be especially sensitive to cutbacks during downturns in a corporation's cash flow. These information problems, plus the general difficulty that investors have in knowing whether managers are investing for the long run, can lead to fewer high-skill, high-involvement workplaces than would be efficient.

Other Market Failures

A host of other market and government imperfections can impede high-skill workplaces. (Levine [1995, chs. 5, 6] provides more detailed explanations and empirical evidence on these points.) For example, each high-quality producer and each employer that keeps its promises helps improve the reputation for its industry and region. Unfortunately, they do not receive payments for these positive "reputational externalities" that help other companies. In addition, high-involvement workplaces tend to offer lower wage differentials to promote cohesiveness between front-line employees and managers. Other employers using different incentive schemes can offer inefficiently wide wage differentials that penalize employers that maintain enhancing cohesiveness-enhancing wage policies. In yet another example, when unemployment is high, employers may find it less expensive to rely on the threat of unemployment to motivate employees and forego a strategy based on interesting work and skilled workers. When the threat of unemployment is used to discipline workers, the economy generates an inefficiently high level of unemployment. (This result is proven formally in what economists refer to as efficiency wage models [Shapiro and Stiglitz 1984].)

The long-term commitment of high-performance organizations to their workforces can have favorable macroeconomic effects. Under reasonable assumptions, each firm that avoids layoffs helps stabilize demand for other firms' products, which the original firm's workers, by keeping their jobs, are able to continue purchasing. High-performance organizations usually try to build trust and protect their investments in workers by minimizing layoffs. Thus, when an economy has many high-performance workplaces it may well find that its recessions become less severe.

The present system of unemployment insurance sometimes *encourages* layoffs. Employers in most states pay unemployment insurance premiums that are not closely related to their record of past layoffs. As a result, companies that avoid layoffs implicitly subsidize those that frequently lay off workers (Marks [1984] and Topel [1984] provide empirical evidence on this point).

Another set of problems centers on deficiencies in the incentive system facing American managers. Many American managers have spent years in workplaces designed for top-down control, not for encouraging initiative from low-level workers. In addition, new work practices diffuse slowly partly for the same reason management initiatives often diffuse slowly—

learning takes time. A number of innovations ranging from hybrid corn varieties to the divisional corporate structure have taken a generation or longer to spread to half the companies that would eventually adopt them, and employee involvement appears to be no exception.

A legal difficulty augments these problems. Some high-performance work practices have been subject to challenge under U.S. labor law, which has developed within a decades-long adversarial system of worker-management relations. Some forms of substantive employee involvement have been found to be in violation of the National Labor Relations Act because they are deemed the equivalent of "company-dominated unions" or blur the legal line between workers and managers.

In addition, no single school, state, or employer captures all the benefits concerning improvements in teaching technology. In economists' lingo, information is a public good, worth more to society than to the ones who create it. Because of this public good-problem, the federal government has a role in promoting and subsidizing research into how people learn, what programs work, and so forth.

Externalities of Redistribution

A similar public-good problem arises concerning redistribution. The majority of Americans might be willing to pay $500 to eliminate childhood hunger and deprivation if everyone else contributed a like amount, but each person might also rationally realize their own contribution would have a negligible effect on overall childhood poverty. Thus, antipoverty programs can be a form of public good as well.

Finally, social insurance is also a public good in some cases. People may want to buy insurance against events that are hard to predict: a long life that requires a big retirement savings, a divorce that reduces children's standard of living, or a disability that cuts short one's work life. Such insurance can maximize the expected happiness of a family, even if it somewhat lowers incentives to work and save. Unfortunately, private insurance companies may be unwilling to offer such insurance for fear that those most likely to live a long time, get divorced, or suffer disability will apply. (Economists call this "adverse selection.") When most people want insurance, but insurance companies cannot profitably enter the market, government-imposed provision or requirement to purchase private insurance can be efficient.

Equity and Equality of Opportunity

At their best, markets distribute income efficiently in the narrow sense that no policy can help every single person. Unfortunately, even when no market imperfections exist, markets do not guarantee that the resulting income distribution is fair. For example, giving 100 percent of a pie to Adam and none to Betty can be efficient, even when it is not fair. Increasing fairness, however, has problems of its own. First, people rarely agree on what is fair distribution of income. Even when they do, tradeoffs usually exist: most programs to equalize incomes also reduce incentives to work and save.

The ethical value of equality of opportunity implies that inequalities that are not a person's own fault are more serious than those created by a person's past choices. In a rare exception to economists' grumpy insistence on tradeoffs, reducing these inequalities usually also has fewer bad effects on incentives than does reducing inequality of outcomes. In fact, equalizing opportunity can often increase efficiency and economic growth. A key goal for social policy is to identify interventions that increase opportunity for the disadvantaged. In many cases, as noted below, these interventions will involve investing in children and youth.

Changes in the Economy

Government policy was designed for a more stable world. The stability was often lacking even in the "old model's" heyday, leading to problems such as large numbers of families with no health insurance even in the 1950s and 1960s. The lack of fit between policies and the reality they are designed for has worsened in the more dynamic economy of the 1990s. In addition, many of the changes in the economy worsened the effects of these market failures, making both the inefficiency and the inequity of the market more of a problem.

Although a complete explanation of the declining economic fortunes of so many American workers and families is lacking, most economists believe that a shift in the demand for labor in favor of more highly skilled, more highly educated workers has played a key role. Such a shift is the only explanation consistent with the fact that even though the percentage of the labor force with a college degree increased from 16.4 percent in 1973 to 27 percent in 1993, the same period saw a pronounced increase in the relative wages of college graduates.

In part, the shift in demand in favor of more educated workers reflects a shift in employment away from those goods-producing sectors that have disproportionately provided high-wage opportunities for blue-collar men and toward medical, business, and other services that disproportionately employ college graduates and women. In addition, employment has grown in such low-wage sectors as retail trade, which disproportionately provide employment opportunities to those with only a high school education. These interindustry shifts appear to explain some of the decline in the wages of high school graduates over the past twenty years.

The economy now faces higher levels of global competition, putting downward pressure on many workers' wages. While less than 9 percent of the U.S. economy was traded in 1959, 24 percent was traded in 1995. (The share traded is defined as [exports + imports] / GDP.) At the same time, a number of studies have found that the easily measured effects of trade on the wage distribution were modest, explaining perhaps 20 percent of the rise in inequality.

These effects of trade on inequality may be larger if the internationalization of the U.S. economy also affects wages indirectly—for example, if the threat of increased import competition or the relocation of a factory to another country undermines workers' bargaining power. It is not known how important such effects have been. Nevertheless, even the largest estimates of the effects of trade imply that the majority of the demand shift originated domestically. Trade may also become a more important factor in the future, as international commerce continues to expand.

For much of this century, government has regulated large portions of the economy to keep prices stable. Often at the expense of consumers, these rules usually increased the ability of employers to pay high wages and good benefits. In the past two decades, deregulation has hit enormous sectors of the economy, including transportation (railroads, intercity buses, interstate trucking, and airlines), finance (savings and loans, banks, and brokerages), and utilities (local and national phone service, power generation, and cable television). Roughly one in eleven workers is employed in these industries, which no longer enjoy government-sanctioned protection from market forces (Fortin and Lemieux 1997).

Immigration has increased the relative supply of less skilled labor in the United States and has contributed to the increasing inequality of income, but the effect has been small. One study found that immigration explained less than 1 percent of the change in the college–high school wage differential between 1980 and 1988. Although immigration flows were considerably larger in the late 1980s than in the early 1980s, this study makes it seem unlikely that the recent contribution of immigration could be more than a few percentage points of the total change.

Within-industry shifts in labor demand away from less-educated workers are the most important factor behind their eroding wages, not the shift out of manufacturing. On the basis of current research—much of which remains anecdotal or indirect in nature—most economists believe that such shifts in turn are primarily the result of economy-wide technological and organizational changes in how work is performed. The computerization of work appears important. Recent empirical evidence indicates that workers who use computers are paid on average 15 percent higher wages than those who do not (Krueger 1993, but see Di Nardo and Pischke 1996). And the use of computers in the workplace has increased significantly in recent years: between 1984 and 1993, the share of the labor force using computers on the job increased from 25 percent to 47 percent (Krueger 1993). By the time this book is in print, the majority of the U.S. workforce will use computers at work. Within a few years, most Americans will have access not only to a personal computer but also to the Internet at home, work, or (at a minimum) a local school or library.

In addition to shifts in labor demand, two institutional factors appear to have contributed to the increase in earnings inequality over the past twenty years. One of these is the decline in the proportion of workers belonging to unions. Unions tend to raise wages for workers who would otherwise be in the bottom half of the wage distribution. The share of the labor force belonging to unions fell from 26 percent in 1973 to 15 percent (and only 11 percent of the private-sector labor force) by 1996. The precipitous decline in unionization explains a modest but significant portion of the increase in wage inequality during the past fifteen years, especially among men.

The decline in the real value of the minimum wage has further contributed to greater wage dispersion. The minimum wage rose from $4.25 in 1995 to $5.15 in 1997. At the same time, it did not been keep up with inflation during most all of the 1980s. Thus, even with the low inflation of the 1990s, the minimum wage will return to about 27 percent below its 1979 peak by the year 2000 (Mishel et al. 1997, 205). Because women are almost twice as likely as men to work at minimum-wage jobs, the erosion of its value has had its largest effect at the lower end of the female wage distribution. Recent empirical research finds that modest increases in the minimum wage from historically low levels in the late 1980s were associated with reductions in both wage and income inequality without significant adverse effects on employment.

Of workers affected by the 1996–97 increases in the federal minimum wage, the average minimum-wage worker contributed about half of his or her family's total earnings. Contrary to some press reports emphasizing the youth of minimum-wage recipients, 74 percent were aged 20 and over (Mishel et al. 1997, 207). Because of the changes in the wage structure discussed earlier, the characteristics of workers receiving the minimum wage are now somewhat different from those of workers in the past. In an analysis of the 1990 minimum-wage increase, about 20 percent of minimum-wage earners were poor, and another 13 percent were near poor (earning between 100 and 150 percent of the poverty line). Moreover, 36 percent were the only wage earner in the family.

In short, the economy is quite different from what it was a generation ago. In many cases, government policies were far too rigid even then. Now, with the massive changes and the increased challenges of the new economy, an increasing portion of the policies no longer succeed in achieving their goals. The need for effective policies has not diminished; thus, it is increasingly important to reinvent government policies to fit and to take advantage of the new economy.

Government Failures: Command and Control

In 1992 the American people elected William J. Clinton president, in large part because of his promise to "reinvent government." Evidently dissatisfied with the pace of reinvention, two years later they elected an antigovernment Republican majority to Congress. In one recent poll, just 15 percent of those surveyed have a great deal of confidence in the federal government, down from the 45 percent reported in 1975—two years after Watergate (*Washington Times*, April 19, 1995, sec. A, p. 7).

To understand the current disrespect for government we must understand how the federal government operates. And to understand how the federal government operates, it is useful to study the successes, near demise, and recovery of one of the paragons of American capitalism in this century: Ford Motor Company.

Both the private-sector bureaucracies of the auto companies and the public-sector bureaucracy of the federal government were designed to meet similar objectives. After midcentury successes, both sets of hierarchies ran into severe problems, for similar reasons. Finally, both sets of bureaucracies have a related set of potentially more fruitful alternative means of organizing themselves. These alternatives are based on judicious use of markets instead of hierarchies, relying more on trust (and verification) than on command-and-control regulation, and redesigning the internal operation of the organization to permit all employees to improve service and productivity.

Of course, not all management principles that are appropriate for the private sector apply to government. For example, government agencies have no simple profit-and-loss bottom line but must be accountable to taxpayers, Congress, executive branch decision makers, as well as the citizens they serve or monitor. In spite of the differences, many of the problems of large private sector's organizations also show up in the public sector, and many of the private-sector's best practices apply as well.

The Auto Industry Example

The problems and responses of the U.S. auto industry can help us understand the problems and opportunities for improving government. This example is not meant to indict private-sector management; in fact, the response of Ford to its problems (described in the next chapter) has much to teach the public sector. This example is intended to illustrate the dilemma common to all large organizations whose top management does not trust employees and suppliers. In both public and private sectors, this distrust leads to detailed rules that limit the organization's ability to adapt.

Command-and-Control Regulations

Ford was for many years one of the largest nongovernmental hierarchies in the world. By the 1950s and 1960s, its relations with employees and suppliers reflected the height of command-and-control regulations. Assembly-line workers were told precisely how to do a job and were given no discretion in how to carry out their task. Suppliers were given detailed instructions to the fraction of an inch about how to produce each part. Because managers trusted neither workers nor suppliers, they gave them extraordinarily detailed instructions about what to do. Unfortunately, these instructions were often outdated and never took into account all the information the workers or suppliers who actually performed the task had.

Lack of Coordination and Integration

One problem came to be known as the "stovepipe" focus of each part of the organization—they solved their own problems, with little attention to those of others. The design department designed the new model, then "threw the drawings over the wall" to the engineering department, which converted the new design to engineering specifications. The engineering department in turn passed these specifications to the manufacturing staff at division headquarters, who designed the basic equipment and line configuration. The staff finally passed this process specification to the plant engineers, who installed equipment on the factory floor and organized the specific assembly tasks. Little coordination occurred to help the assembly-line worker who had to put the vehicle together do his or her job.

Similar problems occurred between divisions. At General Motors, auto bodies were designed by a different division than the rest of the car. In one incident, the division producing the car bodies resolved a design dispute by saying, "If you want this car to have some doors, you'll do it our way" (quoted in Helper 1991b, 804).

Poor Incentives for People

The front-line workers had neither the training, motivation nor mechanisms to improve how the work was done. The mentality of management was summed up by an automobile industry executive: "The average man won't really do a day's work unless he is caught and cannot get out of it." The result was a system where workers' incentives were to hide new ideas, not to come up with ways to improve cars or production.

Instead of relying on ideas from the bottom, Ford created an "enormous bleeding organization, governed by a huge centralized bureaucracy" (Shook 1990). At each level, managers and (especially) front-line workers were told to perform narrowly circumscribed tasks, with little ability or incentive to improve how work was organized. The goal was to create a stable and successful system at performing repetitive tasks in a predictable fashion. The mindset and organizational design were quite different from the Japanese approach of creating opportunities for continuous experimentation, learning, and improvement.

Poor Incentives for Partners

Relations with suppliers and dealers—Ford's crucial business partners—were equally low on trust and communication (Shook 1990). Supplier relations are key because most of the value added of an automobile has always been produced by suppliers, not the auto companies themselves. The large auto companies designed parts precisely and then had multiple suppliers bid on the job of making each part. Again, in most cases, Ford had no mechanism to work with suppliers to improve the parts or technology.

Command-and-control rules solve a number of problems in a low-trust environment. Ford gave detailed plans to suppliers to ensure suppliers would bid competitively. The goals were lower average costs and no fear that suppliers could "hold up" Ford for a higher price. Basing buying decisions on price also lowered the influence of corruption and bribery, a perennial problem in the arena of supplier relations (Shook 1990).

In-house divisions made almost half the parts of a Ford car. The lack of competition these divisions faced when selling to Ford lowered their incentive to produce world-class-quality parts and lowered Ford's ability to produce world-class-quality cars. (GM had more and Chrysler had fewer mandatory purchases from in-house suppliers.) The captured market also reduced workers' incentive for higher productivity because, with no new markets to capture, higher productivity could only lower employment.

The costs of Ford's command-and-control regulations are equally clear. Ford had no means to learn from its suppliers. At the same time, suppliers' incentives were to hide new knowledge so that they could make more money, not to share ideas to maximize value for customers. Suppliers, in turn, were cut off from information on the "big picture"—they just followed their detailed instructions. Innovation, quality, efficiency, and responsiveness to the customer were all reduced.

A Short-Term Focus

An organization will be more successful in the long run if it invests in its workers' skills, in its capabilities to adapt and change, and in its reputation with customers. At Ford, in contrast, managers were rewarded for moving cars to customers. Most managers moved to a new job within two or three years of arriving at a new assignment. Thus, it made little sense to forego short-run productivity for assets that are valuable only in the long-run.

Failure to Update as the Nation Changes

In the mid-1970s the price of gasoline skyrocketed, and the share of small cars doubled from 15 to 30 percent of the market (Shook 1990). Ford found itself unable to compete in the small-car segment.

Part of the problem was a lack of flexibility, with no company-wide effort to adapt to the new realities. Ford's emphasis on centralization did not permit different regions to feedback to headquarters the problems they faced—leading Ford to become almost irrelevant in some of the more innovative auto markets such as California.

Inefficiencies of the Old Regime

The results for the U.S. auto industry are well known. From 1978 to 1982, Ford's sales fell by half. From 1980 to 1982, Ford lost $3.3 billion, roughly 40 percent of the company's net worth (Shook 1990).

Part of the problem was a reputation for low quality, both in how each car worked and in how each was designed. These problems were tragically highlighted by stories of exploding Pintos, but quality problems pervaded Ford's reputation. More generally, Ford products were of low quality, earning a reputation that FORD stood for "Fix Or Repair Daily" (Shook 1990).

In short, the U.S. automakers implemented low-skill, low-autonomy workplaces replete with command-and-control regulations. To some extent, the lack of reliance on high-skill workers and workplaces was to be expected, given the many market failures described earlier. At the same time, the crises of the early 1980s led the auto companies to realize that they could no longer afford their rigid, command-and-control organization. Instead, they needed to reinvent themselves as more flexible, customer-focused organizations.

Familiar Problems in the Public Sector

Just as the large auto companies were for many decades (and remain to some extent), government is hobbled by a culture of command and control. Within the government bureaucracies, millions of hard-working civil servants are often stopped from serving the public competently. When the federal government interacts with states, cities, and local service providers, detailed regulations concerning how each agency can spend hundreds of funding streams impede the agency from focusing on its goals. Parts of the federal government, other levels of government, companies and their employees are too often told how to achieve a goal, instead of being given the standard and permitted to find their own best means to meet it. Finally, citizens are often frustrated by the reams of red tape that stand between them and a pleasant interaction with a government office, whether applying for a license at the Department of Motor Vehicles or selling advanced computer software to the Department of Defense.

These regulations arose to reduce corruption and to ensure fair treatment of all citizens. These goals are crucial. For better or worse, the current system of detailed regulations often leads to sufficient inefficiencies that more flexible replacements can better achieve these outcomes along with improving productivity and service.

Lack of Coordination and Integration

The piece-by-piece stovepipe focus reappears with a vengeance in the public sector. Each agency has its own enabling legislation, its own line in the federal budget, its own cabinet-rank officer or agency head, and its own set of committees in each house of Congress. Although most employees at each agency try to do a good job, they are often hindered by their own rules or those of related agencies, often including those agencies working toward the same goal. Each time Congress addresses a problem, it tends to create a distinct program or categorical grant. Each of these, in turn, typically has its own rules, creating a proliferation of regulations. Multiple programs addressing a common group of citizens often have divergent definitions and regulations. When grants define a population to be served or a problem to address, they may not fit the holistic approach many service providers would prefer. As an increasing proportion of grants have required follow-up performance information, agencies have had to collect a bewildering array of performance measures.

For example, when people lose their jobs, they often must visit different offices for signing up for unemployment insurance, job training, and information on job openings. Classes that receive funding for disadvantaged workers through many federal programs have limits on mixing students funded through other programs.

For those workers who have jobs (and their managers), the resulting workplace regulations often have different rules on how to monitor different hazards, keep records, and the frequency of required medical checkups. In addition, a law-abiding business could be scheduled, merely by coincidence, for multiple random audits the same week, one for safety, one for enforcing overtime rules. Sometimes rules even conflict, leaving the manager with a dilemma. Even basic definitions such as *employee, wages,* and *employer* differ across agencies and between states.

Welfare recipients must deal with separate agencies for assistance for income, housing, nutrition (food stamps), medical care, child care, training, and a few other categories. Although at the local level these are often administered from only a few offices, within each office the myriad of rules concerning each program make life a complicated disaster. For example, some assistance is based on the income of the individual, some for the family, some for the household (including unmarried adults staying there), some for everyone sharing a kitchen (which could even include other households).

Importantly, most programs phase out their benefits as incomes rise. Unfortunately, with all of these phase-out ranges overlapping, it is possible for a poor family to lose far more than a dollar's worth of assistance when its income goes up by a dollar.

Programs to help poor neighborhoods or regions are funded by the federal departments of Agriculture, Commerce, Defense, Education, Health and Human Services, Housing and Urban Development, Justice, Labor, and several independent agencies such as the Environmental Protection Agency. In Oakland, California, nine bodies exist to try to coordinate youth employment policy (Rubin and Kaplan 1995).

Within the disability system, a person will often be assessed for disability separately by medical doctors for medical care, by a school, by workers' compensation, by a private disability insurance company, by several layers of gatekeepers for public disability insurance, by vocational rehabilitation service providers, and several others. Because most people with disabilities (especially before receiving assistance) have difficulty getting to appointments and filling out detailed forms, the nonsystem is often disastrous for them.

Command-and-Control Regulations

At each level of the government hierarchy, those on top give detailed directions to those below. These command-and-control rules and regulations are given partly to ensure that subordinates focus on the goals and methods the top deems most socially (or politically) useful. These regulations are also intended to ensure that no scandals occur on the boss's watch. Finally, detailed regulations grow in part due to a lack of understanding of the value of flexibility in satisfying citizens' needs. The pattern is played out at each level. First, Congress often writes rigid and detailed laws so that agencies behave as Congress intends. Agencies then write regulations that have been approved by literally hundreds of lawyers but are not intended to be comprehensible to a manager, citizen, or mayor. The government executives implementing these laws and regulations then create detailed rules governing their employees, not to satisfy citizens, but to avoid scandals and satisfy powerful interest groups.

Federal regulations can be incredibly difficult to modify. For example, one agency used an eighteen-foot chart with 373 boxes to describe its process of passing a regulation (U.S. Office of the Vice President 1993). The complicated and lengthy process implies that revisions are rare, even when new evidence or circumstances motivate both regulators and the regulated to agree on desired changes.

When regulating workplaces, too often regulators describe a particular technology to achieve a goal, instead of announcing a goal and permitting employees and employers choices about how to achieve that goal in the most cost-effective fashion.

In the county welfare office, the poor welfare official must try to determine eligibility for a dozen or so possible programs, each with distinct rules on matters such as the maximum value of the applicant's car. In the disability system, the rules governing who is disabled "enough" to be eligible for a pension fill a bookshelf more than twenty feet long. Then the judge who hears appeals obeys a *different* set of rules(!).

Unfortunately, the detailed nature of regulations evolves because they solve problems. Some managers at regulated companies do not like discretion because they fear inspectors will punish them if the line is blurry. For example, if regulators say, "Post a notice," some companies want to know how big the sign must be. Regulatory agency employees often prefer detailed rules so that they will not be accused of misconduct. A government oversight body—inspector general or Congress's watchdog agency, the General Accounting Office (GAO), a court, a political appointee, or (worst of all) the press can pounce on discretionary acts with which they disagree. Detailed rules protect subordinates from attack in the short run, even as the mass of often outdated and inflexible rules increases attacks on government in the long run.

In spite of (or sometimes because of) the detailed nature, regulations always have unintended consequences. Regulators create rules about once a decade, while those regulated respond to those incentives every day. It is the nature of regulations that those regulated try to figure out tricks, and these tricks are often socially costly ways to evade regulations. At best, regulators get just what they ask for, not their true goals.

Often a single case with a bad effect (as determined by the courts or regulators or public opinion) leads to a new blanket regulation. Congress and the press descend on these cases to attack the entire program. The public reacts vigorously to horror stories of a Welfare Queen and her Cadillac but appears less concerned if $1 million in regulatory burden and enforcement stops only $100,000 in fraud. One highly publicized Welfare Queen or $200 hammer costs an agency (and its employees) far more political capital than imposing a large regulatory burden. Sometimes the new regulation is perverse, as when welfare rules (until recently) prohibited applicants from owning almost any car worth enough that it could actually be useful for commuting.

Poor Incentives for People

Just as the auto industry's workplace had poor incentives for workers, many government employees are hamstrung by the same volumes of rules and regulations that frustrates citizens.

In many parts of the government, incentives are based on processing speed and accuracy of obeying all the rules—not for results. Thus, employees of the system of unemployment insurance, employment search assistance, and job retraining do not receive positive feedback for finding people jobs as often as they do for just filling out the forms quickly and accurately.

The regulatory system often rewards the number of inspections, but not actual safety, or the number of employers who are training supervisors to avoid sexual harassment. Employers, conversely, sometimes face incentives to obey the letter of the law, not the objectives of the regulations.

Within the welfare system, it is remarkable that as many women work as we observe. Because of the loss of cash benefits, food stamps, housing benefits (for some), health insurance (after a waiting period), and other benefits, it is often not a rational act to work. (In spite of this finding, welfare has only a modest effect on reducing recipients' labor supply. Current research indicates that completely *eliminating* cash welfare would only increase recipients' labor supply from nine hours now to fourteen hours a week—still far too little to support a family.)

In addition, the current system permits noncustodial parents (usually fathers) to avoid paying full child support in half or more of single-parent families

(Shell 1996). Children can only benefit from the support of two parents, instead of only one. Furthermore, although the overall effects appear small, the welfare system must reduce the "marriage tax" implicit in many programs.

Within the disability system, the Social Security Administration defines "working disabled" as a contradiction in terms. People who work are at risk of losing their cash stipend, health insurance, and a host of other benefits such as training, personal assistants, and housing assistance. Because disabled people are unlikely ever to find a job with health insurance that will cover their preexisting disability, the loss of health insurance alone implies that work can virtually never be a rational decision. Coupled with other disincentives, the reduction in living standards when taking a full-time minimum-wage job is phenomenal.

Poor Incentives for Partners

The federal government historically has relied on three organizational relationships to accomplish its goals: command-and-control regulations to employers, state and local governments, and direct service providers; procurement via arm's-length agreements with suppliers; and direct provision by government employees. Each has suffered from excess direction from the top and not enough flexibility, accountability, or continuous improvement.

In all three sets of relationships, the federal government has acted as if it knew precisely how to accomplish its goals, even though teachers often have ideas how to teach a disabled child, managers and workers have valuable ideas concerning how to improve safety, suppliers have ideas about how to build a computer system, and government employees have ideas about how better to serve their customers (also known as citizens). Just as Ford's detailed division of labor and centralized control cut off learning from its suppliers and employees, the heavy hand of government's centralized rules and regulations stifle innovation by each of these groups.

For example, multiple categorical grants to states—each with its own regulations and accounting for funds—encourage the states to spend a significant sum checking that each dollar goes to its intended purpose. States and cities often maintain multiple programs even if it is more efficient to merge multiple funding streams all directed at a common group (e.g., disadvantaged youth or the recently disabled).

Funding streams rarely reward success. In many cases, funding increases when problems worsen. This system insures states against bad luck but provides poor incentives. Governors should be rewarded for fixing, not worsening, problems.

Government employees are often hamstrung by detailed rules, regulations, and laws that prevent them from focusing regulatory attention on the "bad actors" while assisting the majority of employers in complying with the law. Employers, at the same time, face incentives to obey the letter of the law, even if they know how to achieve more safety (or whatever else the goal of the regulation is) at lower cost.

Failure to Update Programs as the Nation Changes

Many of our schools are little changed from seventy-five years ago. Our welfare system was set up for widows, not for divorced and never-married mothers. Our disability system was established to help people whose bodies gave out a few years before Social Security retirement age. Our pension and health-care systems were established as if workers stayed at a single employer for most of their careers. Our regulatory system has no means to adapt to the very different situations of millions of workplaces.

In each of these cases, well-meaning policies have not kept up with changes in workplaces, technology, and families. As society and the economy change, each social policy must adapt or (sometimes) be rebuilt from scratch. All too often, instead we see ever-increasing rules and regulations, each responding to a perceived problem in the existing rules. Although the problems were often real, the new rulings add up to morass of paperwork that sometimes nobody can follow. Adapting the masses of regulations to new circumstances is even more difficult.

Inefficiencies of the Old Regime

Just as the large auto companies' rigid top-down system led to declining popularity, the government rigidities have led to many of its problems, detailed in the chapters to follow. These range from safety regulations that do not improve safety to aid to the disabled that dooms recipients to a lifetime of poverty.

The result is a system in which common sense is given little reign. Rules often burden government employees from doing what they know is the right thing. Local service providers spend millions of hours complying with contradictory federal rules, while not serving the clients they want to help. Citizens lose confidence in their government. Just as the U.S. automobile industry had to suffer a severe crisis in the early 1980s to spark changes in organization, governments at all levels in the United States may need a similar crisis to spark fundamental change. The parallels with the auto industry are somewhat discouraging because large-scale job loss and customer dissatisfaction were needed to spark needed changes. The parallels with the auto industry are also somewhat encouraging because that industry has recovered to world-class levels in productivity and quality—now we need federal, state and local governments in the United States to reinvent their relationship with each other and with citizens and companies to create similar improvements.

Conclusion

The slowing growth of productivity and earnings has led many to suspect that markets may not work as well as one might hope. Unfortunately, economic research supports this hypothesis—labor markets are subject to a number of market failures. These failures lead to less investment in skills by children and adults than would be economically efficient. Related failures lead companies to underinvest in their workers, and to create relatively few of the high-skill workplaces that lead to high performance.

At the same time, rigid systems of command-and-control regulations imply that government programs often do not work as well as one might hope. Over and over again, we find programs that lack coordination, detailed and rigid regulations, poor incentives for individuals and for business partners, and programs becoming out of date.

No simple remedy can solve the problems of government. At the same time, as the next chapter describes, some basic lessons of management have helped leading private-sector employers escape their related dilemma. Fortunately, many of these management lessons apply as well to the public sector. Careful application of the relevant lessons can help alleviate the imperfections of government and make it a more useful instrument in alleviating the problems of markets.

4

GETTING OUT OF THIS MESS:
INVEST AND REINVENT

This chapter explains principles to improve incentives for citizens in their many roles as well as for partners such as states and local governments. Improved incentives often involve giving citizens more choice concerning who will deliver services. Programs must focus on satisfying citizens' needs, even if the government has to reorganize. Each program must be designed to guarantee continuous improvement. Finally, we must not be afraid to invest in the future, especially in our children.

The previous chapters have described both external and internal challenges for government. The external challenges include an environment that has become more challenging, with rapid innovation, deregulated markets, and more foreign trade. The most difficult aspects of this new environment are slower productivity growth and rising inequality.

The internal challenges of government involve poor incentives for citizens, poor incentives for government agencies, narrowly focused agencies with uncoordinated agendas, rigid command-and-control rules, and an unwillingness to invest in the long term.

These problems were familiar to the U.S. auto industry. Fortunately, many parts of that industry have moved away from rigid command-and-control systems to more flexible and customer-responsive organization. In leading workplaces of the private (and public) sector, high-skilled workers and reorganized work that can be highly effective. In these workplaces, all employees have the skills, incentives, and authority and responsibility to solve problems for their customers. Although numerous barriers exist to these high-skill workplaces, current evidence (surveyed below) suggests they can increase profits and stock market value, as well as productivity and quality.

In addition, many of the principles that have led the U.S. auto industry back from the brink of massive bankruptcy also apply to the even larger hierarchies of government. The chapter closes with a discussion of the subset of principles of the reinvented workplaces of the private sector that can drive change in the public sector. Using these principles we can create government programs that

- Improve incentives and accountability for individuals
- Provide incentives, flexibility, and accountability for organizations such as service providers and employers

- Guarantee continuous improvement
- Focus on citizens' needs
- Invest in the long term

Such programs will often bring the power of the market to bear in helping government solve market failures and empower people to solve their own problems with help from the government, but not with detailed rules from the government.

The rest of the book then uses these principles to examine key questions of U.S. public policy, largely with the goal of increasing the number of high-skilled jobs. Our policies can address the supply of skilled workers by preparing all Americans to work in teams and solve problems on the job. This new set of skills should be taught by schools, training programs, and other means of disseminating information. Our policies can also address the demand for these skills by promoting high-skill workplaces in our regulatory, unemployment insurance, and other policies.

The Private Sector's Solutions

In the early 1980s, the crisis that threatened its very existence convinced Ford's top managers that their command-and-control technique of dealing with suppliers and employees was no longer tenable. The system had low flexibility, low learning, and high mistrust. Ford knew it could not compete with a workforce and supplier base that was not given the ability and incentives constantly to contribute ideas. High-communication relations with suppliers and high-involvement work systems for employees became the order of the day.

Get Incentives Right for People

The example of employee involvement in Japan convinced many at Ford that workers had valuable ideas to contribute. Many initially suspected employee involvement of being a Japanese-specific phenomenon. Then Toyota was able to take over one of GM's most troubled plants and turn it into a world-class performer. Toyota accomplished this in spite of the return of the same GM workforce, and the same United Auto Workers (UAW) union and leadership. (For more on the NUMMI joint venture, see Levine 1995, ch. 2, and Adler et al. 1997.)

Ford's reinvention began literally where Henry Ford's great genius first exhibited itself: on the assembly-line. Although assembly line jobs did not immediately switch to interesting and varied work, Ford began putting in place means of listening to workers. Employee involvement has shifted from being one of the "programs of the month" to becoming institutionalized. For example, employees began to be involved in substantive changes, such as how to set up the assembly line (Shook 1990). Ford also increased its training of front-line workers substantially. Training in problem solving, statistics, and teamwork spread down to front-line workers, not just managers and engineers.

Just as important, Ford changed its relationship with the UAW to become better partners in problem solving. Many of the important initiatives concerning training, profit sharing, safety, and new technology were implemented jointly with the union.

At first, the threat of job loss provided strong motivations for employees to contribute ideas. In addition, Ford implemented a variety of pay policies to reward continuous improvement. Most important during the turnaround decade of the 1980s, the union and management established a profit-sharing plan to reward all employees for the company's success. In the first six years of this program, the average eligible employee received $12,200 (Shook 1990).

Get Incentives Right for Partners

In the early 1980s Ford came to understand that its traditional adversarial relation with suppliers, where price is the predominant factor, was creating more problems than it solved. Evidence was mounting that long-term, information-rich relationships between suppliers and customers lead to faster product development, increased flexibility, and higher quality. Many studies found that Japanese supplier relationships play a key role in the automakers' performance. For example, Kim Clark (1989) estimated that in the mid-1980s, supplier contributions accounted for one-third of the Japanese automakers' advantage over their U.S. counterparts in total engineering hours required to develop a new car. The reason is that, typically, a Japanese automaker will not itself design a part that it requires for a new model. Instead, it will specify exterior dimensions and performance characteristics and allow a specialist supplier to design the part to best match its process (Smitka 1989; Nishiguchi 1990; Cusumano 1985; Helper and Levine 1992).

The example of Japanese supplier relations has inspired American auto companies to move to more flexible, learning-oriented, and cooperative supplier relations. Instead of telling suppliers precisely how to make a part, they are beginning to outline goals for suppliers (for example, the size, power consumption, and cooling capability of an air-conditioner) but permit the supplier to decide how to achieve these goals.

In the Japanese automobile industry, suppliers and automobile companies are highly committed to the relationship. Suppliers know that as long as they make a good-faith effort to perform as they should, the assembler will ensure that they receive a reasonable return on their investment and on the relationship continuing indefinitely (Womack et al. 1990). If the supplier experiences a problem with cost or quality, the automaker will attempt to work things out before switching to another supplier.

Over the last decade, U.S. automakers have been moving to increase their levels of commitment. In the five years between 1983 and 1988, average written contract length doubled, as did the percentage of suppliers who said their customers would help them, rather than switch if one of their rivals came up with a superior product (Helper 1991a).

This deregulation by the Big Three and the move to high-trust supplier relations has two important preconditions. First, it does not apply until suppliers have a record of success. That is, the Big Three continue 100 percent inspection until the supplier has a record of high quality.

Finally, Ford certified the process of its suppliers. Although Ford no longer specifies how to produce a part, they do require their suppliers to implement policies for continuous improvement. Gaining Ford's coveted "Q-1" certification (now QS 9000) indicated a skilled supplier that always collected data on problems and was trying to solve them.

In short, the auto companies followed the advice Ronald Reagan applied to arms negotiations when he quoted an old Russian proverb, "Trust, but verify" (quoted in Graedon and Graedon 1996).

In some ways Ford *reduced* its reliance on markets, at least on the arm's-length market relations it had relied on frequently in the past. As part of this strategy, Ford has moved to single or dual sourcing of most components for each car or truck. In the 1970s, for example, Ford had twenty-seven wiring harness suppliers. By the late 1980s it had four or five—typically only one for each model (Helper 1991b).

Create Customer-Focused Solutions

The success of the Japanese at developing new models with the cooperation of all departments, partners, and workers caused Ford to fundamentally rethink its stovepipe arrangement. For each new car project, Ford created a cross-functional project team that brought together engineers, purchasers, and manufacturing managers at a single site. Importantly, key suppliers were also involved early on in the process (Carbone 1994). Workers were also consulted about how to make the car easier to assemble.

The result was a halving of the time it took to develop a new model.

Moreover, by involving suppliers and workers early, the resulting cars have been easier to manufacture and have had higher quality.

Ford wants customer-focused solutions when it is a customer also. Although suppliers are often large organizations, Ford requests a single telephone number to call with problems.

"Build-in" Continuous Improvement

Perhaps the biggest change in the outlook at Ford was its incorporation of the quality movement's principles of continuous improvement. By constantly collecting statistical and qualitative data about what works and what does not, Ford ensures that it is always learning. Although many bugs remain in the system of collecting and analyzing data, motivating people to implement changes, and institutionalizing continuous improvement, Ford has had some impressive accomplishments. By requiring suppliers to implement similar data-oriented quality programs, Ford has reduced its defect rate on incoming parts dramatically. More generally, auto plants that have moved to these closer supplier relations have experienced the highest levels of quality and productivity (MacDuffie and Helper 1997).

Save Money in the Long Term

Ford's turnaround did not come for free. Each portion of its reinvention required long-term investments: investments in training employees, investments in improving the capabilities of suppliers, and investments in reorganizing itself to focus better on customer needs. As Ford's chairman of the board at the time, Philip Caldwell, explained, "During the first two years after we started our quality program, we couldn't see any improvement whatsoever" (Shook 1990, 79). Nevertheless, the company persisted in making these investments (as well as billions of dollars of investments in plant and equipment) to improve the organization's capabilities for the long term.

By the end of the 1980s, Ford had returned to profitability. In 1987, earnings surpassed those of General Motors for the first time since 1924 (Holusha 1988). "From 1980 to 1988, Ford showed the biggest gains in domestic corporate loyalty among buyers—from 35% to 47%. In addition, Ford's car market share increased from 16.9% in 1982 to 21.3% at the end of the 1988 model year" (Englander 1989). The improvements in financial outcomes appear to have a fairly solid foundation (considering the very cyclical nature of the auto industry): a more highly skilled workforce, more competent suppliers, and higher quality.

The New American Workplace

The combined changes that leading workplaces in the United States and overseas have implemented turn upside down many of the basic foundations of traditional American management. Similarly, they turn upside down many of the traditional foundations of American public administration. Recall that it was within this century that Max Weber (1946) wrote his great essay on the wonders of bureaucracy, as the only fair and rational system.

The new workplace, with its customer focus, empowered workers, high levels of skills, incentives for all employees to solve problems, and so forth, has shown a new model for successful large organizations. This section reviews the evidence that these new work practices, although relatively rare, can increase organizational effectiveness.

Although it is difficult to obtain reliable nationwide data on the extent of employee involvement in decision making, the evidence is that employee involvement and other plans spread rapidly during the 1980s and early 1990s. By the early 1990s, the vast majority of very large U.S. companies had experimented with employee involvement in at least a portion of their organizations, and many smaller companies were experimenting as well. At the same time, however, only a minority of companies reported widespread implementation of an integrated set of high-performance workplace practices.

The effects of the new workplace systems can be impressive. Although measuring the effects of changes in work organization can be difficult, a number of recent studies provide a collage of evidence that a coordinated change in work organization can pay handsome rewards. (This evidence, and the difficulties in research in this field, are summarized in Ichniowski et al. 1996.)

For example, a multiyear study of steel finishing lines identified four distinct human resource management systems. The more innovative production lines had introduced problem-solving teams, higher levels of training, innovative incentive compensation systems, and higher levels of employment security, while the most traditional lines had few or none of these practices. The more innovative lines enjoyed significantly higher productivity. The most innovative lines ran 98 percent of the scheduled time, while the untransformed plants ran only 88 percent of the scheduled time. Plants intermediate in their introduction of innovative human resource policies were also intermediate in productivity (Ichniowski et al. 1997). Plants with more innovative practices also produced higher-quality steel. A separate study of steel minimills found that high-involvement plants not only excelled in quality and productivity but also enjoyed lower turnover (Arthur 1994).

These results have been replicated in a number of other industries, including automobile assembly (MacDuffie and Kochan 1995), apparel (Berg et al. 1996; Dunlop and Weil 1996), and flexible machine system operation (Jaikumar 1986; Kelley 1996). Several studies find that these innovative workplace practices are associated with financial gains, such as higher cash flow and stock market value (Huselid and Becker 1996; Hendricks and Singhal 1996, 1997; Jarrell and Easton forthcoming).

Changes in the Public Sector

The public sector has many differences from the private sector, including accountability to voters, not owners (and customers), and the replacement of a profit motive with a harder-to-define notion of the public interest. Nevertheless, many of the solutions in the public sector echo best practice in the private sector: improve incentives for citizens, improve incentives for partners such as businesses and states (and, whenever possible, use these incentives to replace detailed regulations), focus on customers, adjust to changes in the environment, and invest in high expected-value projects. Importantly, the experience of the public sector implies that these practices can improve results there just as in the private sector. This principles laid out in this section form the outline of the proposed solutions in the chapters to come.

These ideas are not a panacea. The problem of powerful interest groups redirecting public-sector resources to selfish ends is more of a problem than in the private sector. These "good government" prescriptions will not solve political problems of powerful and selfish groups. Nevertheless, although good management is not sufficient for good government, it is necessary.

Get Incentives Right for People

Just as Ford has tried to create training, incentives, and structures for improvement by its front-line people, the government must get incentives right for people.

Much of the current discourse in Washington concerns important problems of a fundamentally moral dimension, such as crime, divorce, drug use, and bearing children out of wedlock. On the one hand, it would be a complete misreading of the evidence to think that government programs will ever be able to solve such deep-seated problems. Ultimately, only a remaking of American families and communities can address all the profound sources of these social ills.

On the other hand, governments often provide very undesirable material incentives. Thus, there is ample scope for even narrowly economic solutions to help. Further, because we understand monetary incentives much better than cultural ones, narrow technocratic analyses should be considered seriously, even as policymakers should remember their severe limitations.

For the government as employer, front-line federal employees must face positive incentives for doing a good job. Budget cuts and downsizing should not follow from productivity or quality improvements that require fewer workers.

For workplace regulations, we must provide positive incentives for employers who involve their workforce in improving safety, solving disputes, and carrying out other functions normally reserved for regulators. The advantage of workforce involvement is that workers have good incentives to ensure that the system is fair and effective.

In the welfare and disability systems, we must make sure nobody is ever made worse off by working. In welfare, this means providing some benefits that are not phased out when recipients work; possibilities include guaranteed child support and health insurance for children. Time limits can help increase recipients' motivation, but the facts of the low-wage labor market imply that a substantial fraction of welfare recipients will never be able to earn enough to keep their children out of poverty. Thus, some government support or employment of last resort will always be necessary.

Get Incentives Right for States and Service Providers

Just as incentives matter for recipients of government aid, incentives matter for each level of government. We must reinvent our relations within the federal government and between the federal government and the states, local governments, and direct service providers. The goal is to match flexibility and deregulation with accountability, incentives, and continuous improvement.

Two simple solutions are often proffered by those who distrust big government and try to learn from the private sector: privatization, and block grants that return decision making to states. Each of these strategies has an important role in reducing outmoded command-and-control regulations. At the same time, the simplest versions of these approaches will often not achieve their goals.

Moreover, the simplest versions of privatization and block grants are quite different from what best-practice private-sector companies are doing when reinventing relations with their suppliers and other business partners. At Ford, for example, deregulation of suppliers (for example, permitting them to perform more design work, and halting 100 percent inspections of incoming materials) is conditional on good performance. Moreover, even when a supplier has an excellent track record, Ford requires it to have plans in place to ensure continuous improvement. Similarly, any deregulation via privatization or block grants should also be conditional (that is, include measures of accountability) and should require suppliers to have plans in place for continuous improvement.

This volume often stresses a third mechanism to reinvent government: vouchers. While privatization tries to capture the power of the market, it still leads to a monopolist providing the government service. Competition arises only in choosing who will be the monopolist—a government agency or a private company. Fortunately, the federal government can often use vouchers that give purchasing power directly to people who need services, completely bypassing intermediate layers of bureaucracy. Carefully designed vouchers hold the promise of both privatization (harnessing market forces) and block grants (decentralizing decision making). Importantly, well-designed vouchers provide a better test of effectiveness—consumer choice in a competitive market—than either blithe decentralization through block grants or potential monopoly via many forms of privatization.

Trust (but Verify)

While markets can solve many problems, the auto companies have reinvented how they relate to their suppliers. Following the example of Toyota, the auto companies have moved to more flexible, learning-oriented, and cooperative supplier relations. As noted earlier, they are moving away from command-and-control instructions to suppliers. Instead, they hold suppliers accountable for hitting design specifications but permit the supplier to decide how to achieve these goals.

As noted earlier, this "deregulation" by the Big Three automakers occurs only after suppliers have a record of success and after suppliers have implemented policies for continuous improvement.

These strategies of conditional deregulation apply to government as well. As detailed below, regulators should give more detail as to the goals of regulations, but less detail concerning how to achieve those goals. In dealing with grants to states or other levels of government, detailed rules can be replaced with block grants, but only if appropriate accountability mechanisms can be found. That is, the federal government's deregulation of agencies, state and local governments, and companies should be conditional on records of success (or well-conceived plans)

Furthermore, when the government replaces command-and-control regulations, it must ensure that suppliers have in place quality improvement practices that will improve whatever processes they choose. That is, the federal government does not know how best to process a welfare claim in every situation, but the federal government should reward welfare offices that are sure of improving over time whatever process the local office has chosen.

The standard should be flexible as to how suppliers demonstrate their capabilities for continuous improvement, but certification in this standard ensures that state and local agencies are measuring customer satisfaction and have in place a never-ending cycle of techniques for evaluating their current processes, identifying weaknesses, researching alternatives, and experimenting until the processes show improvement.

The Role of Privatization

Privatization is already an important strategy at all levels of government. The federal government alone spends approximately $1 trillion each year purchasing from outside suppliers. Privatization holds the promise of competition for government business, which can reduce costs and increase quality.

The advantages of privatization must not be overstated. The first time the contract to run a formerly government-run operation is put up for bid, competition is the rule. Bidders may bid very low in order to gain a toehold in the market.

Unfortunately, the next time the contract is put up for bid, the market is usually no longer very competitive. The service provider who won the first round now has experience, political clout, and connections to put in a bid that is very likely to win renewal. Given the advantages of the current provider, new entrants may not even compete.

Because bidders expect profits in future rounds of bidding, they have an incentive to bid artificially low prices in the initial round. Thus, in franchise bidding, a substantial portion of what appears to be savings is often just a portion of the value of future monopoly profits the bidder expects when it is able to jack up the price in future years. (The entire value of the future monopoly profits will not be incorporated because the bidder is unsure that it will be able to jack up the price in the future. For example, after the initial low-cost bid, the government might return to direct service provision before the high monopoly price has been paid. Moreover, companies usually discount future incomes quite heavily and usually act risk-averse. All of these reasons lead typical future price increases to be larger in present value than the discount on the initial bid.)

In short, the "savings" during the first contract often yields a misleading picture of the future costs of privatized services. For privatization to bring all the benefits of the market, it must create a truly competitive market, and creating such markets is a very difficult undertaking. The Republican governor of California, Pete Wilson, recently issued a report on privatization that indicates that even strong proponents of privatization are familiar with this problem. Nevertheless, the report uncritically cites estimates of savings that come from the first year or two of a new contract—precisely when we expect large savings, even if the near future holds large costs (Wilson n.d.).

Improving Procurement

When the government does purchase from the private sector, it should learn the lessons of best-practice private-sector purchasing: deregulate how things are done but require or reward processes that ensure continuous improvement. This approach is beginning to take hold in federal procurement, where some agencies are paying more attention to buying from suppliers certified to have excellent quality-improvement practices.

In some procurements, for example, the federal government is giving preference to suppliers who have achieved the widely accepted National Process Certification Standard (ANSI-EIA/599) (American National Standards Institute/Electronic Industry Association 1992). These standard states that "the supplier is responsible for demonstrating continuous improvement of processes ... and customer satisfaction" (pp. 7, 8). The standard is flexible about how suppliers demonstrate their capabilities for continuous improvement, but certification in this standard ensures that suppliers are measuring customer satisfaction and have in place a never-ending cycle of evaluating their current processes, identifying weaknesses, researching alternatives, and experimenting until the processes improve.

Block Grants: Devolution to and Deregulation of the States

An enormous portion of what the federal government does is actually implemented through the states. Everything from processing applications for Social Security to running the welfare system to performing safety regulation (in many states) is some form of state-federal partnership. For example, in 1995 the federal government ran more than 500 grant programs to the states. One popular political movement focuses on devolving responsibility for an increasing number of programs to the states. (Although this agenda is sometimes associated with conservatives, much of it can be found within the Clinton administration—Clinton, after all, is a former governor. Conversely, many conservatives push an agenda on issues such as banning abortion and federalizing a number of crimes that involves reducing the power of the states.)

Devolution is often desirable because localities have information Washington lacks. For example, the training offered in school-to-work programs should match local employment opportunities. Local control can also be desirable because the federal government has difficulty writing rules that respond to different regions' needs and preferences.

At the same time, federal control may be preferred when state governments have preferences that are unconstitutional or otherwise problematic. Before civil rights legislation, for example, some states provided inadequate services to blacks. Similarly, states, because they are smaller than the federal government, may be more easily "captured" by a special interest.

Just as citizens need a safety net, so do states. A key federal role is to perform redistribution across states, either to help poor states or to counteract regional shocks. For example, federal food stamp payments automatically rise in Louisiana if oil price declines lower employment, or in California when military spending declines. Block grants that are not indexed to need can reduce this valuable federally provided insurance.

On the good side, local control promotes learning from experimentation—states can act as the "laboratory of democracy." Because research is a public good, the federal government has a role in promoting systematic evaluation of these experiments and in disseminating information on best practices.

The benefits of local control are amplified as local governments compete to provide attractive mixes of public goods and taxes to attract new residents. Conversely, federal control is preferred when the federal government has comparative advantages, perhaps because of economies of scale or scope. For example, the federal government is very efficient at disbursing Social Security checks and other forms of cash transfers.

This competition between jurisdictions is not always desirable; it can sometimes lead to a "race to the bottom" in which no state or locality can afford redistribution. For example, the majority of the citizens of a state might like to raise taxes and fight poverty within the state, but they all recognize that many businesses and jobs will go elsewhere if they do so. Even if all states would be better off if all redistributed more, each individual state will find it in its interest not to redistribute. This problem is particularly serious because state taxation of the relatively wealthy to aid the poor will not succeed if the taxes lead the wealthy to move to nearby states and the poor to move into their state.

The key to achieving the goals of the federal government while deregulating states and implementing block grants is adding accountability. The accountability should be for outcomes whenever possible. When measuring outcomes is difficult (as it always is), accountability that rewards states' processes of improvement and states' efforts can also alleviate some problems.

Accountability for outcomes coupled with block grants works best when there are easily measured benchmarks that capture the primary dimensions of the goals. In the antipoverty example, goals fall short if they give incentives to reduce unmeasured aspects of performance (teach precisely what is on a test, at the expense of more useful skills), miscount the number of homeless, and shift problems to neighboring states (give homeless people bus tickets to other states).

Accountability also works better when the performance measures are reasonably related to matters within the control of the states, and the measurement and reward occur at the same pace at which state programs can have an effect. Thus, it is often useful to adjust performance measures for demographic and industrial shifts outside the states' control. For example, it might be desirable if performance measures on lowering poverty rates were eased in states with falling demand for their main industries.

Finally, accountability can work well only when the federal government can commit to follow through on adjusting funding according to results. Because states can always claim extenuating circumstances, the federal government often has difficulty carrying through commitments to pay for performance. This difficulty is particularly serious because it is appropriate for the federal government to redistribute to states that have been subject to bad luck outside their control. Finally, imposing accountability is made more difficult by the unwillingness of both Congress and the White House to punish governors or mayors of their own party.

Accountability can be implemented in a flexible fashion by permitting the states to set their own targets and then holding them accountable to those targets. For example, a state might be exempted from a set of regulations if it submits a plan with goals chosen by the state. The federal government then grants additional waivers to states with excellent plans and challenging goals. In the following years, states are evaluated on their achievements, and funds are added (and sometimes subtracted) based on performance. This management by objectives has the advantage of higher commitment from the states to hitting goals and a higher probability that the goals will be realistic. The downside is that states might set easily achieved goals.

Accountability for Process

In the ideal world, the requirements for accountability for results would be satisfied, and the federal government would not need to concern itself with process. In the world we live in, the difficulties in measuring all dimensions of performance imply that a role continues to exist in requiring states and service providers to implement plans for continuous improvement. Thus, the federal deregulation must follow the model Ford has with its suppliers.

That is, while the federal government does not know how best to process a welfare claim in every situation, it should still reward welfare offices that are sure of improving over time, whatever process the local office has chosen. Because one of the key goals of deregulation is to learn what works, the plans that lead to deregulation must include careful benchmarking and evaluations. Only with such evaluations can we be sure that five years from now we will have a better idea of how to make work pay in a cost-effective fashion. Finally, the deregulation should maintain the matching provisions of the current system—just because a grant moves from detailed rules to block-grant form does not mean it must lose the good incentives that matching grants provide in order to avoid the race to the bottom.

Accountability for Effort

When outcomes are difficult to measure, it is often fruitful to pay some attention to effort as well. For example, in switching federal funding from a matching grant to a block grant for job training or welfare, the federal government might require the state to maintain all or most of its current total spending in the area. Such rules for maintenance of effort can help reduce the problem of a race to the bottom, at least in the first years.

Unfortunately, just as measurement of outcomes leads to game playing, measurement of inputs such as rules for maintenance of current effort leads to game playing. For example, a rule that required or rewarded states for spending money on alleviating poverty would lead states to reclassify many expenditures as "antipoverty spending," just as a tax credit for research and development motivates companies to send extra janitors to the lab for ten minutes a shift. These rules also increase transaction costs because states must track categories of expenditures. Such rules also reduce flexibility for states that would like to place poor people into mainstream programs (for example, for training). Maintenance-of-effort rules can also be unfair, as currently ungenerous states receive permission to be ungenerous forever, while currently generous states are stuck with a permanently higher burden. Such rules also do not account for cyclical recovery of a regional economy.

For these reasons, maintenance-of-effort rules have diminishing effects (as states learn to game-play them) and rising costs (as state flexibility is diminished and the original level of effort is less relevant to the current situation). One possibility is to use maintenance-of-effort rules for the short run and phase in outcome-based measures for the longer term.

A variation of maintenance-of-effort rules is to continue some matching of certain forms of state contributions to antipoverty programs. The 1995 formula for Aid to Families with Dependent Children (AFDC, the largest cash welfare program) was a state–federal partnership. The federal govern-ment, in essence, "sold" a dollar of welfare to the states for between twenty and fifty cents. The 1996 welfare reform bill moved to a block grant with no accountability. The result is that states now pay the full price of each marginal dollar of welfare spending, raising the benefit governors receive from cutting welfare usually from fifty cents per dollar cut to one dollar per dollar cut. Just as incentives matter for welfare recipients, they also matter for governors. It is not an effective poverty-fighting strategy to provide governors incentives for massive cuts in aid to poor children.

Letting Citizens Choose and Monitor

In many instances, government can unleash the power of market forces much more directly than with privatization. The key is to identify cases where markets can achieve true competition, with informed consumers and multiple suppliers. When these conditions can be approximated, giving citi-zens vouchers for services can often lead to more efficient provision than can direct government provision of the service. This logic applies for a range of services, from schools for children to vocational rehabilitation for the disabled, from housing for the poor to job placement and training for those laid off, and to the entire range of goods and services a disabled person might need to assist work. (In most cases, refundable tax credits have identical advantages as vouchers. For simplicity, in this volume I refer to vouchers, but both are usually possible.)

The appeal of vouchers is some confidence in the wisdom of citizens to choose (on average) pretty well, at least compared to command-and-control regulations. Some people lose their jobs and need training; others have physical and mental disabilities and need a variety of services; while still others are poor and can use some help affording housing. In each case the status quo involves multilevel bureaucracies, federal-state-county-social-service-agency partnerships, myriads of regulations, and one-size-fits-all rules by the feds for states, by states for counties and local service provid-ers, and by everyone for citizens. What underlies all these rules is a fear (often legitimate) that lower levels of the bureaucracy will misallocate re-sources from the upper-level's intended mission of serving certain popula-tions. While mistrustful of lower levels of the hierarchy, the current system ironically is so mistrustful of *other* potential service providers for training, vocational rehabilitation, or housing that they are not permitted to compete for federal dollars at all.

Fortunately, a group of citizens has a strong incentive to ensure federal dollars are well spent—those they are intended to benefit. The voucher-based alternatives proposed here permit the citizens themselves to choose how to allocate the resources. Ineffective service providers will be sanctioned not by the federal government but by voucher-laden consumers who no longer choose to spend their voucher there.

For example, the market for adult education functions well with junior colleges, private trade schools, and public and private four-year colleges. The federal government has no need to fund a parallel adult education system when it can give purchasing power directly to unemployed or otherwise disadvantaged adults and let them make the decisions that they expect will best increase and ensure their standard of living. The GI Bill that helped nearly 8 million veterans after World War II operated under this model, and the Clinton administration has proposed replacing a hundred or so targeted retraining programs with vouchers for further education.

Markets work much better when consumers are well informed. Thus, the federal government has an essential role in creating report cards for training providers that indicate which programs actually raise participants' earnings and employment. (Some efforts along these lines are proposed by ALMIS 1996.)

A voucher system will also be subject to some fraud and abuse. Currently, some schools sign up students with promises of an education leading to a job and then provide no valuable training. The students are left with loans they are unable to pay off, leading to high default rates. Providing students with information on graduation, placement, and wage rates can greatly alleviate the problem caused by this kind of fraud.

To enhance their effectiveness further, the vouchers' value can increase when enrollees have higher earnings—in part, sharing the savings from unemployment insurance, disability insurance, and other programs the government enjoys when people work. Performance-based rewards for service providers also provide market discipline to discourage fly-by-night service providers and promote the growth of those with successful track records. Even with these incentives, some oversight concerning the outcomes will still be needed, just as the federal government establishes rules limiting loans to students attending schools with extremely high default rates on student loans.

Although pay for performance has good effects on incentives, it also leads to problems. When performance is imperfectly defined, then the incentives produce the wrong forms of performance. For example, when training providers paid by the Job Training Partnership Act had their performance measured by job placement, some training providers ensured a week or so of employment for their students, but the jobs ended quickly.

Performance incentives also lead to the problem known as "cream skimming," "cherry-picking," or (by less poetic and/or food-obsessed economists) "adverse selection." All three terms refer to the incentive that service providers have to serve the easiest to serve. This incentive can lead to three problems. First, the government may, on average, overpay for services, especially when those least in need of service can take care of themselves. In one recent case, a health-care provider was interested in selecting healthy senior citizens to enroll in its Medicaid program. Thus, it signed up people at a dance—a clever mechanism to identify the relatively healthy among the eligible population. When the government is the service provider of last resort (as in Medicaid), the government will end up serving the most costly cases; thus, total costs can increase substantially when moving to a voucher system. Alternatively, when there is no service provider of last resort, the most disadvantaged can be left with no services.

In the worst cases, a job placement or training service provider might search for voucher holders who found their own jobs and then receive payment when no valued services were rendered. This undesirable outcome occurred with the targeted jobs tax credit, which worked similarly to a voucher for companies that employed disadvantaged youth (and some other groups). Several companies specialized in identifying disadvantaged youth who had found their own jobs and then informing employers (for a fee) that they were eligible for a special tax credit. In this situation, the employment-inducing effects of the credit are guaranteed to be minimal (Bishop and Kang 1991; Bishop and Montgomery 1993).

In some settings, where virtually nobody is being successfully served today, cherry-picking is not a problem. For example, virtually no disabled people who receive Social Security disability insurance leave the rolls to return to work. Thus, cherry-picking (at least initially) would be desirable to begin returning disabled people to work. Cherry-picking also may not occur if well-meaning service providers attempt to serve those most in need, as James Heckman and others (1996) found in one job training program even after performance incentives were instituted.

In general, it is often useful to alter the value of the voucher based on the expected difficulty of the case, altering the payment schedule as certain classes of people (for example, young vs. old, rural vs. urban) become easier or harder to serve.

Related to the problem of adverse selection, vouchers encourage the wealthy and powerful to exit from publicly provided services. These are the groups that are most likely to have access to alternative providers, if only because they are typically better informed about alternatives. In terms of school vouchers (discussed in more detail in chapter 5), when parents who are prosperous and/or care the most about education leave a public school district, the voice for improving schools for the rest of the population is weakened (Hirschman 1970). (In fact, most school districts are already often relatively racially homogeneous. When a neighborhood includes both rich and poor or both black and white, the wealthy typically already have exited from the school district. For example, D.C.'s population is almost 30 percent white, but the public schools are 4 percent white [U.S. Department of Education 1996b]).

Any voucher system provides flexibility to meet local conditions. Importantly, market-based systems encourage experimentation, unlike command-and-control regulations. Finally, vouchers permit service providers to customize their service according to the needs of the citizens and permit citizens to choose the service mix they expect will help them most.

Vouchers are often touted as an alternative to direct government provisions of services. In fact, in many cases, government service providers perform very well. In these cases, vouchers merely become a means for them to measure and be rewarded for their success. For example, under the status quo, a training provider's funding is determined by bureaucratic and political means, with some attention paid to past performance. Under a voucher scheme, successful public-sector training providers will automatically find their budget expanded and will automatically be able to serve more clients.

Most privatization or voucher schemes will lead to some job loss within the current public-sector service providers. To the extent services are provided at lower cost merely by paying similar workers lower wages, because private employers are more likely to break employment laws or for other non-efficiency-related reasons, the social gain to the lower cost is less than the private gain. That is, the gains to citizens are matched by losses by workers, so total social welfare may not be enhanced much. One partial solution is to make the value of the voucher larger when used by service providers who provide these social benefits. (This partial solution runs immediately into the practical problem of measuring these social benefits, particularly when each service provider will claim that it is the most socially beneficial.)

More generally, competition does not mean only profit-maximizing service providers will exist. Vouchers should lead to a resurgence of the "third sector" of nonprofit organizations. Any service provider can potentially flourish, but only if the services provided are ones that clients value.

Vouchers versus Cash Grants

A basic result of microeconomics is that the recipients of government assistance would never prefer vouchers to receiving an equal amount in cash. On the one hand, if they intend to buy as much housing, education, or immunization as the voucher provided, then they are indifferent. In this case, vouchers work just like cash. On the other hand, if they intend to buy less of the product the voucher covers, then they would prefer the cash. In this case, vouchers add less to their utility than does an equal amount of cash. The textbooks conclude that unless the government has paternalistic reasons to affect how disadvantaged people spend their money, the government should just dispense cash, not vouchers.

However, vouchers have several advantages over cash grants. Most important, vouchers can target those goods that are often underprovided by a free market. As noted below, free markets may underprovide outcomes as diverse as training for the unemployed to immunizations to the education that makes youths into capable citizens. In addition, most Americans believe that all members of our society are entitled to a certain minimal living standard. Many people find that it both violates their norms and causes them discomfort when fellow Americans starve or go without valuable preventive medical care. It may be paternalistic in an individualistic sense to hand out vouchers instead of cash, but it can be in a community's self-interest to reinforce and protect its notions of what it means to be part of a community and what human beings deserve.

Vouchers have an additional advantage in terms of self-selection. Any scheme to assist the most needy gives the almost-most-needy an incentive to perform poorly in order to become eligible for the services. Vouchers or other service-oriented redistributions are often less attractive for these groups than are cash grants, reducing the incentives to game the system.

Vouchers also have higher administrative costs than distributing cash or checks. These costs will decline as more transfers are handled electronically (as several states are already doing with food stamps). The administrative overhead of vouchers is partly offset by the lower costs of preventing fraud—a person can receive multiple checks, but will rarely receive value for multiple vouchers for immunizations.

In short, vouchers have almost all the advantages in terms of flexibility and incentives that cash grants provide. In addition, they improve targeting on the people, goods, and services where society's interests are most at stake. For these reasons, vouchers and refundable tax credits, in spite of their higher administrative costs and in spite of (or due to) their constraints on choice, can often be a more cost-effective means of providing assistance.

Federal Standards Can Improve Local Accountability

Direct government provision of services often works well. For example, public schools in prosperous districts tend to be quite good. The keys to such quality appear to rely in large part on the local oversight provided by well-informed parents (Putnam 1993). Such local oversight permits schools to operate with a high level of flexibility and still maintain often impressive results. (To be clear about my biases, I am a product of public K–12 education.)

Oversight can be enhanced if all schools are measured according to common metrics. In this fashion, parents can tell whether, in fact, their schools are educating students at the desired level. Establishing voluntary national education goals is one way to achieve this increased monitoring without federal compulsion or regulation. Controversy exists over what national goals make sense, particularly for fields such as history.

One possible solution is to have a core set of goals and permit a menu of additional goals from which states and local school districts can choose. They would then measure their success against those schools with matching goals. (For example, all schools must hit baseline levels of knowledge of American history, with some knowledge of the effects of factors such as technology and racism. Beyond this baseline, if one school wants to empha- size the history of immigrant or nonwhite groups, while another wants to focus on the history of technology, auxiliary goals can measure success on these topics relative to other schools stressing these topics.)

More generally, the federal government has an appropriate role in creat- ing standardized "report cards" on schools, training providers, and other service providers to enhance clients' and students' ability to pick well and the public's ability to monitor its employees.

Overview of Improving Partners

No single mechanism for providing services is always appropriate. The federal government relies on a combination of direct provision of services, categorical grants, block grants, private-sector suppliers, and vouchers that provide purchasing power directly to citizens, and will continue to rely on a combination of these in the future. The question how best to meet the goals of government is fundamentally a practical one, and the key is combining deregulation with accountability either by creating markets or by condition- ally deregulating.

Create Customer-focused Solutions

In each realm of interaction with government, citizens should not need to know how government is structured. The solution for government is to create one-stop interfaces with citizens. A number of states have begun this process for dealing with citizens who are searching for a new job. These states have created one-stop reemployment centers that combine applications for unemployment insurance, help in searching for a new job, and access to training providers. The creation of caseworkers and one-stop interfaces should also be carried for other groups of citizens.

For small businesses, a single regulator should help them create safe, fair, and well-run workplaces. For welfare applicants, a single office, application, and set of rules should apply for cash assistance, medical insurance, housing assistance, child-care assistance, training, food stamps, and so forth. For disabled people, a single application and assessment procedure should apply for vocational rehabilitation, Social Security disability, Medicaid or Medicare, housing assistance, and other forms of assistance ranging from food stamps to personal assistants.

To achieve this customer focus, congressional committees and federal agencies must forego the detailed rules that limit the mingling of different funding streams so that service providers can create integrated solutions that meet their customers' needs. This "reengineering" (as it is known in management jargon) must begin at the source of the problem—multiple congressional subcommittees optimizing their own agendas—and continue through the incentives for agencies, for states, and ultimately for local service providers.

The federal government (in partnership with other regulating entities such as states and local air-pollution-control boards) must create an integrated information system for each set of users. Businesses should not provide wage and employment data separately to Social Security, state and federal unemployment insurance offices, the IRS, and the Equal Employment Opportunity Commission. Instead, a single form should suffice. Citizens should be able to fill out any government form and apply for any government benefit ranging from food stamps to hunting licenses over the Internet. Businesses should be able to find the regulations that apply to them without knowing whether the regulator is state or federal. (The Fedworld site on the Internet [http://www.fedworld.gov/] is a good start, permitting users to search data from multiple federal agencies. Unfortunately, as its name implies, Fedworld does not yet have a customer-focused view that combines information from all regulatory agencies, including those from the states.)

In the welfare and disability systems, the various tax rates plus benefit reduction rates from cash, housing, nutrition, medical, training, and other forms of assistance must be treated in a coherent fashion. Specifically, people should always keep at least forty or fifty cents from each incremental dollar they earn (that is, the combined marginal tax rate plus benefit reduction rate should remain less than 60 percent). A vast array of research indicates that tax rates in this range have only small effects on discouraging labor supply (e.g., Moffitt, 1992).

Institutionalizing Continuous Improvement

Best-practice management in the private sector requires each organization and its suppliers to gather and analyze data so that quality and productivity are always rising. Similarly, government programs must be designed so that in five years they work better than they do today. We need to institutionalize mechanisms for learning and continuous improvement to ensure that the programs are always serving their customers better.

There are many means by which learning occurs and many questions that knowledge can shed light on: for example, which programs work versus how to make a given program work better. Each of these forms of learning needs to be institutionalized. If program proponents cannot find appropriate metrics that show when a program (either new or old) works well, then that program should be given lower priority.

The goal should be that "every service creates data." That is, the agency should automatically collect follow-up data on those it serves and should be able to track which policies are effective and which are not. Data collection should emphasize not just the performance of those served but comparisons of those served with their previous performance (the agencies' value added), and how that value added compares to agencies serving a similar population.

Many of the needed data are already collected by Social Security, the IRS, and state unemployment insurance systems as they record wages and employment. The Department of Labor is working with the states to create a Labor Market Information System. The new system must be designed so that it automatically collects the data needed to evaluate our major social programs. (The new system must also reduce the number of forms employers must fill out to report these data to various government offices.)

Experiments

In the last decade the Department of Labor has financed a series of experiments concerning the unemployment insurance system. In these experiments, unemployed people are randomly assigned to one of several systems of unemployment insurance and reemployment assistance. Through these experiments, we have learned valuable lessons concerning the effects of employment bonuses on unemployment durations, the costs and benefits of permitting people starting new businesses to continue receiving unemployment insurance, and the costs and benefits of screening people at intake and directing them to different services. The Department of Labor is now using these lessons to redesign the unemployment insurance system (U.S. Council of Economic Advisers 1995, 1996).

In many cases, an experiment required special legislative authority. A number of federal departments currently sponsor randomized experiments, usually funded out of legislatively earmarked funds for demonstration projects. It makes no sense that a law is needed for an agency to perform an experiment. Moreover, the legislation often retains barriers to flexible use.

We must institutionalize experimentation so that at any given time even more experiments are being carried out. Past randomized experiments were often large-scale and very expensive. In fact, randomized experiments should be built into the work of most service providers. In many instances, service providers with a waiting list can easily perform a randomized experiment by selecting randomly from the waiting list and comparing outcomes of those served with those who remained in line. In other cases, a service provider can randomly allocate clients to different subunits or programs and compare results.

In any region with more than a minimal number of people receiving services, local governments can monitor the performance of subcontractors by randomly assigning clients to them. The relative performance of each contractor's clients can be used to determine the value added of services. This knowledge can then be used both for improving services and for allocating performance-based pay. The Upjohn Institute is currently implementing such an experiment with three welfare-to-work service providers in Michigan (Bartik 1996).

Rewarding Excellent Improvement Plans

The current best practice for large companies in the United States is to require their suppliers to implement policies for continuous improvement. Similarly, the federal government should reward states, education systems, social service providers, and agencies within the federal government that have put in place policies to improve quality continuously. (Along these lines, the Office of Federal Procurement Policy recently encouraged agencies to reward suppliers that achieve high ratings on public- and private-sector quality improvement awards and certifications such as the Baldrige National Quality Award and the auto industry's QS 9000 quality certification.)

Disseminating Best Practice

No single school district, welfare office, or even state captures all the gains from new knowledge that is widely applicable. Thus, a key role of the federal government is to help evaluate innovations and to disseminate information on those that work (Hanushek 1994).

The Commerce Department has greatly expanded the Manufacturing

Extension Partnership to promote the introduction of best-practice work organization and technology. Ironically, the government has no effort on a similar
scale to assist a similarly sized sector of the economy, the state and local
governments. The federal government should support efforts to disseminate the
best practices currently known; encourage experimentation to improve on the
best-known practices; assist local governments and service providers in
designing evaluations of those experiments; and disseminate innovations from
the originating sites to all sites that are likely to be able to use the innovation.

For any given measure, ranging from the number of days to process of
disability insurance claim, to success in teaching adults to read, to minutes
of waiting time in urban unemployment insurance claims lines, there is
often variation between and within states of more than 100 percent. Thus,
the federal government should subsidize and disseminate benchmarking
studies that determine what the best agencies are doing. The federal government should work with existing institutions that disseminate best practice
ranging from occupational associations and unions to schools of education
and public administration to the National Governors Association to create a
seamless delivery service for technical assistance. Service providers should
have available one-stop assistance concerning what works and how to build
in continuous improvement.

Budget Decisions

When choosing among programs to support or expand, we must focus on
what works. We should shift resources from programs whose careful evaluation indicates lack of success to programs whose careful evaluation indicates success. Furthermore, if programs have been in existence for many
decades and have minimal supportive systematic evaluations, they should
be candidates for scaling back. We can no longer afford to spend on programs that might work, when we are accumulating knowledge about programs that do work.

Adjust to the Changing Environment

The challenge for government is to adapt to the many changes we have seen
in the American economy. Many of these changes have already begun, and
further changes are described below. For example, schools are moving to
teach the new skills needed in the high-skill workplaces of the next century.
Government regulations and (slowly) private-sector benefits such as pensions and health plans are changing to acknowledge that lifetime employment with a single employer is the exception, not the rule. Regulations must
also be changed to promote, not inhibit, high-skill workplaces.

Save Money in the Long Term

After a generation of well-meaning government programs and social science research on social problems, it is clear that government has no magic bullet to solve all social problems. Nevertheless, just as we can no longer afford ineffective government programs, we cannot afford to allow the government to ignore the problems of crime, poverty, or unemployment.

A generation ago, the distinguished liberal economist Arthur Okun (1975) illustrated the dilemma he and other liberals faced with the image of the "leaky bucket." He wanted to transfer resources to the poorest in society but was worried that each dollar taxed from the wealthy lowered their incentives, while each dollar given to the poor lowered their incentives. The result was that each dollar of income the wealthy lost provided less than a dollar to the poor, just as carrying water in a leaky bucket led to some losses. He was distraught concerning how to resolve some difficult issues when equality and efficiency were so often opposed.

Although Okun's image is powerful and often illuminating, the nation is in luck. We are fortunate to have opportunities for investment that can raise efficiency and equity. To see the possibility of efficient redistribution, consider the social cost of high school dropouts.

The average high school dropout earns 49 percent less than high school graduates with no additional education, and 68 percent less than those with at least some college, leading the average high school dropout to pay less in taxes over the course of his or her working life than the average high school graduate. Dropouts are also more likely than graduates to end up on welfare or in prison. For example, on any given day in 1992 almost one-quarter (23 percent) of all males between the ages of eighteen and thirty-four who had not received a conventional high school diploma—but only 3 percent of those who had—were either in prison, on probation, or on parole. The typical young female high school dropout receives on average more than twice as much in food stamps and public assistance payments as high school graduates and almost five times as much as those with at least some college.

The present value of total welfare, prison, and parole costs averages about $70,000 over the course of an adult lifetime for each individual who does not graduate from high school, but only about $30,000 for each high school graduate who does not attend college, and only $15,000 for those who attend college. (These figures are calculated as the net present value at age eighteen of the costs of criminal justice and welfare incurred between the ages of eighteen and fifty-four, using 1992 data. Costs are discounted at a 4 percent annual rate.) Thus, ignoring differences in taxes paid, a program capable of influencing young people who would otherwise drop out of high school to graduate and behave like other high school graduates would reduce spending on welfare and the criminal justice system by about $40,000 in present value terms for each youth induced to graduate. These figures are almost the reverse of public spending on education and training: the typical college graduate is the beneficiary of more than $25,000 in public spending between the ages of sixteen and twenty-four, while the typical high school graduate receives about $11,000 and the typical high school dropout less than $6,000.

Nevertheless, because high school dropouts differ from graduates along many dimensions other than the fact of dropping out, these calculations do not directly translate into potential gains for society whenever a student is kept in school to graduation.

Investments are key, however. Today the poor make up a large percentage of our children. In twenty years, today's poor children will be a large part of our working population (or our prison and welfare populations). If we make poor children's lives much harder over the next five years, we will make them less productive citizens in 2015—and will make the rest of our lives much harder in 2015 as well. Alternatively, if we wisely invest in our children, we can increase equity and efficiency at the same time.

Programs that appear to be pure redistribution actually have a substantial amount of social insurance built into them. As inequality widens and incomes become more variable, the "safety net" starts to cover a major portion of the population, at least in each family's bad years. For example, the earned income tax credit (EITC) provides a subsidy for families with low earnings. Two in five prime-age adults who had children would have been eligible for the earned income tax credit in at least some part of the 1980s had the EITC rules of 1996 been in force. Moreover, while 22 percent of all children are poor in any given year, 35 percent are poor for at least one year during their childhood (Mishel et al. 1997, 307).

To put it in personal terms, most of the readers of this book are from the upper 15 percent of the income distribution. Nevertheless, often following a divorce, most extended families (including cousins, nieces, etc.) will have or already have had at least some members struggling for at least a few years. In short, social insurance programs are not paid by "us" to "them," but can provide a crucial safety net for many American families having one or more bad years.

The policies described in this volume often require up-front investments. The good news is that wise investments can address these social problems, raise Americans' living standards, and at the same time create a nation with lower inequality.

Capital Budgeting

In the short budget environment of the 1990s, a tremendous amount of top-level executive branch attention is focused on working with and around the budget rules imposed by Congress. The intent of these rules was noble—to ensure that the government spent within its means. Unfortunately, the problem of the deficit measures used by Congress implied that the rules led to many inefficient decisions.

One problem with our current deficit measure is that it declines if the government sells a building and immediately leases it back from the new owners. Just as bad, our current deficit gets worse if the government invests in a computer system that will reduce tax fraud. Thus, we must improve our measure of the federal deficit by correctly accounting for investments.

Suppose the CEO of a major corporation were to stand up and say that, even though revenues were $1 billion more than the cost of goods sold last year, the firm lost $500 million because it spent $1.5 billion making new net investments for the future? We would think that such a CEO was insane. In corporate accounting systems, investments are not subtracted from profits in a single year. Instead, long-lived investments are subtracted from profits over their lifetime. Unfortunately, many politicians follow this insane method of accounting when they decry the deficit without paying attention to whether the money is spent or invested. About $50 billion or so of the measured deficit is the federal government's net investment. No private-sector firm would ever consider such investments above and beyond depreciation as a "cost."

Capital budgeting in the government (as in the private sector) will lead to many difficult issues concerning the appropriate rate to depreciate various assets (that is, how long will the returns from current expenditures last?). One of my colleagues summed up this problem with a quip:

> *Question:* How many Office of Management and Budget staffers does it take to change a lightbulb?
> *Answer:* Two: one to change the light bulb, and the other to notify the White House press office so they can add the cost to the administration's "investment budget." (Halsey Rogers, personal communication, 1996)

Although these problems are serious, they have been addressed sensibly by most of the states and several other nations (most notably New Zealand). While not a panacea, even capital budgeting where the depreciation rates on some expenditures were subject to political manipulation would be better than the current assumption of instant depreciation for all expenditures. Only with capital budgeting can the government sensibly measure its deficits and sensibly decide which programs are worthy of investing in, and which are not.

Conclusion

For too long conservatives have (often correctly) emphasized the problems of government, while liberals have (often correctly) noted how inequality of opportunity saps the economy of both equity and efficiency. It is time for both groups to agree that some government interventions can potentially increase efficiency. These programs are particularly likely to be cost effective if they build up the capabilities of the most disadvantaged in society. Conversely, they are particularly likely to fail unless they move beyond the archaic command-and-control model we see all too often.

It is simplistic to copy mindlessly what managers believe is best practice from the private to the public sector. Much of one decade's "best practice" is the next decade's memory of a management fad. In addition, the public sector has a responsibility for due process, and a role in creating and shaping both our public sphere and citizens as they participate in the public sphere. In spite of these important cautions, government can serve all of us better if it follows the simple goals outlined here.

First, we must improve incentives for people and for partners. Following private-sector practice, this improvement in incentives must not just rely on deregulation. Instead, we must remove command-and-control regulations and improve other means of accountability. Often measuring results and rewarding good processes for improvement will suffice. In other cases, providing citizens with good information and permitting them to choose service providers can increase accountability.

Then we must create customer-focused solutions and ensure that they will exhibit continuous improvement. Continuous improvement can involve anything from a quality program to randomized experiments; what these have in common is a commitment to learning so that however a good or service is produced this year, it will be done better a few years from now.

Finally, we must invest for our future. Part of this investment involves better measurement. The federal government, like the private sector and most states, must measure investments correctly so that it no longer favors short-term spending over long-term investments. Another key goal of investment is to focus programs on children and youth. Although they do not vote, they are the source of higher living standards for the next century.

This recipe for improvement can be applied to programs for all groups of citizens. The following chapters show how to apply these lessons to create a life cycle of learning that begins in childhood and lasts throughout a career.

5

A LIFE CYCLE OF LEARNING:
THE SCHOOL YEARS

Increasingly, Americans "earn what they learn." This chapter outlines policies to prepare students to learn before they arrive at school, and to improve schools once they arrive. The proposals build on the principles of flexibility, good incentives, and accountability described in chapter 4.

Until recently, a high school diploma was all many workers needed to support a traditional middle-class standard of living. Increasingly, however, a high school education is not enough. Fewer high-wage jobs remain for high school graduates, and even many workers with college educations face the prospect of stagnant wages. This is a fundamental change in the economy. Although government is not the cause, it has the ability and the responsibility to improve the way Americans are educated and trained so as to mitigate this adverse trend.

Education should be a lifelong process for all workers, particularly in the changing economic environment of today. Creating programs to promote lifelong learning is difficult because of the intensely decentralized nature of our educational system: education is primarily the province of states and localities, and training is provided primarily by employers. Thus, the federal government's most effective role is often to serve as a catalyst for change.

This chapter begins by describing the problems of burdensome regulation, limited accountability, and slow improvement we see in many of America's schools. As in other spheres of public policy, the challenge is to deregulate judiciously; increase accountability; and improve incentives for students, teachers, and schools. Schools must also address the challenge of teaching the skills needed for the new economy. Jobs of the next century require not just readin', 'ritin', and 'rithmetic but also teamwork, managing diversity, and solving real-world problems.

This chapter lays out a conceptual framework of powerful incentives, continuous improvement, and cost-effective investments. It then compares this framework with current efforts of school reform: often taking place under the rubric of "Goals 2000." It next analyzes variants of a more dramatic school reform: school choice. As part of the focus on lifelong learning, the chapter also covers policies to help the citizens of the next century to arrive at school ready to learn and to move smoothly from school to careers.

The Problems of America's Schools

America's school system is vastly complex. Public schools educate 44 million students and employ 2.6 million teachers at 84,000 schools in over 14,000 districts. The system costs about 3.5 percent of GDP (Hanushek 1994, 26). Almost all (93 percent) school funding is from state and local governments. Thus, any reforms will need to be highly decentralized.

Public schooling in America largely grew up in the era of mass production. It is, thus, unsurprising that the methods and curriculums of most public schools are highly influenced by the logic of production once emphasized by America's largest employers. For teachers, this has meant layers of hierarchy writing detailed command-and-control regulations that specify many aspects of their tasks. For many students who will not attend college, this system has emphasized the importance of compliance with instructions. A smaller set of students who are destined for higher education receive more training in creative problem solving.

The result is that the problems of American education are familiar: poor incentives for students and teachers, poor incentives for schools and districts, a clutter of programs with too many rigid rules and not enough coordination, and mediocre results.

Poor Incentives for Students

In many American schools, the teaching methods and curriculums are little changed from a generation ago. Students sit in rows of desks, while teachers stand at the chalk board. Students (with varying levels of enthusiasm) raise their hands to answer questions, but most of the education is still transmitted as if the teacher were a pitcher of knowledge, and the students empty vessels waiting to be filled. The material is also not engaging, with each subject (math, reading, spelling) separated from anything that connects to the student's life. This model of passive students fit well when most employees were expected to obey instructions and follow rules. Thus, the intrinsic motivation of learning is often low, especially for students who are not expected to attend college.

To a large extent, the incentives for students to work hard in school comes from family members and classmates. In addition, for a small minority of students (although a much larger subset of this book's readers), the college admissions process provides incentives to work hard. Unfortunately, for the vast majority of students, grades in high school do not appear important: employers do not look at them, and they do not help find a good job. Thus, these students face little material incentives to do well in school (Bishop 1992a; U.S. Council of Economic Advisers 1996, 206).

Poor Incentives for Teachers and Schools

Although local control of schools is gospel in America, it is often absent from the classroom. Schoolteachers are subject to a myriad of rules concerning everything from the textbooks they can use (often set at the state level) to their treatment of students caught with weapons (bizarrely, set by federal law) to the order of topics they teach (often set at the district level). The federal government, states, and districts have all emphasized command-and-control regulations to restrict what teachers do.

The problem is that nobody in the federal government, state government, or even the district office actually knows the best action to take in a given situation. This statement is not intended to insult these education officials' intelligence; it merely reflects the dual problems of limited information about what teaching methods are effective in general, and the inevitable fact that teachers always have better information about what is going on in their classrooms than anyone else.

Many teachers receive enormous satisfaction from teaching well. At the same time, most teachers, like students, receive minimal material incentives concerning the learning that occurs in their classes. Teachers' material rewards are typically unrelated to good teaching.

To see the problems with creating such rewards, consider the performance measurement system in California, a fairly typical state. Current incentives in California come in part through "report cards" that rank schools based on how well their median student does on a standardized test. These scores are useful for parents and permit parents to track the school's progress relative to others in the state. Nevertheless, they suffer from at least two key failings.

First, the tests are sensible measures of certain skills, but their "multiple guess" format implies that they leave out enormous areas of learning, ranging from written communication to social interaction to problem solving. This incompleteness, in turn, gives schools incentives to stress the subset of skills on the tests, at the expense of a well-rounded education.

Second, the tests do not reflect the value added of a school because they do not measure learning during the students' stay at that school. Schools with well-prepared students will almost always have higher scores than schools with poorly prepared students, regardless of the quality of instruction at the school. (The test scores in California are also reported relative to schools whose students have similar family backgrounds, which is an attempt to control for how well students would have performed in the average school.) It makes no sense to punish teachers for poor preparation that occurred before students entered their class.

Designed for a Different Era

Patricia McNeal, assistant secretary for vocational and adult education, described the problem succinctly:

> Most high schools in America today were designed for the industrial age. Teaching practices, organizational structures, and the use of time pretty much reflect industrial practices of much of the 1900s (McNeil 1996).

Students at risk of doing poorly in school are often punished for their problems: given remedial classes that stress repetitive and boring drills and worksheets, instead of finding ways to engage them in the process of learning (Levin 1997). For example, a generation of people (and almost a dozen generations of computer technology) after computers were first heralded as revolutionary technology for classrooms, most computers are still used for fairly routine tasks. The top three uses of instructional computers in elementary and secondary schools were learning math (primarily routine drills), learning how to type, and learning to use a word processor (*Statistical Abstract of the United States* 1995, table 259).

Most schools have begun the process of transformation. Many stress the importance of problem solving and group work, but few have redesigned classrooms, rethought curriculums, or retrained teachers in the needed skills.

Slow Improvement, at Best

The rigidity of these rules are part of why the educational system in the United States improve so slowly. As one important recent study put it: schools teach, but they do not learn (Hanushek 1994).

importantly, a successful innovation often can be useful to many different schools and districts. Thus, the federal government has a role in subsidizing advances in education. Unfortunately, the track record of our education research establishment suggests only slow progress in identifying key principles for education. A combination of weaknesses in the research and poor incentives of schools makes for an even worse record of disseminating improvements to America's millions of classrooms.

Results: The Uneven Quality of American Education

By many measures, the quality of education in the United States has improved in recent years. Test scores in reading, writing, mathematics, and science have generally risen over the past decade for almost all ages and racial and ethnic groups. As noted earlier, dropout rates have fallen for all racial and ethnic groups and income levels since 1980, declining most sharply for black and low-income students. Enrollments in both preschool and postsecondary school have increased. Preschool enrollment rates have risen since 1970 from 14 percent of children ages three to four years to one-third. The percentage of high school graduates who enrolled in college following graduation increased from 49 percent in 1980 to 63 percent in 1993. Few other countries have postsecondary enrollment rates as high as those in the United States.

The United States still has far to go, however, to ensure that all its young people are acquiring the knowledge and skills they need to obtain high-paying jobs and adapt to future changes in the economy. High school dropout rates, for example, are still too high: 13 percent of the eighth grade class of 1988 had dropped out of school by the spring of 1992. The rate for Hispanics is roughly twice as high.

Comparisons of U.S. and foreign test scores give additional cause for concern. Although test scores are imperfect measures of school quality, and scores of U.S. students have generally risen in the science and math portion of the International Assessment of Educational Progress in recent years, the United States remains among the industrialized world's laggards. In math, for example, U.S. students at both the nine-year-old and thirteen-year-old levels not only trail their Taiwanese and Korean counterparts—the world leaders in this area—but also lag behind students in every other major nation participating in the test.

The Implications of Rising Returns to Education

Numerous studies have established that workers with more education earn substantially higher wages than workers with similar characteristics, such as age, experience, race, and sex, but with less education. But this relation does not necessarily imply that raising the educational level of those who are now undereducated will lift their earnings substantially. It may be that those students who obtain the most schooling are those who start out with greater ability. Nevertheless, a number of innovative studies that address this problem still support the conclusion that, on average, students at all skill levels gain substantially from additional education (e.g., Ashenfelter and Rouse 1997). (See box 5.1.) These results are consistent with the thesis that, for many students

---

Box 5.1. Straightening Out *The Bell Curve*

The Bell Curve by Richard Herrnstein and Charles Murray (1996), is probably the most reviewed work of social science since the Kinsey Report. This massive volume addresses many of the issues addressed in this book, so it is worth reviewing several of the main points of difference.

The Bell Curve argues that the cognitive abilities measured on standard achievement tests are fixed at a fairly early age by genes and early household environment. These abilities are the primary determinant of a number of social outcomes ranging from poverty to crime. In other words, people largely "win" in American society because they are smart, not because of their family background. In what Murray claims is "perhaps the most important section of the book," (p. 567), the authors present original research on this topic

The authors conclude that because cognitive abilities are largely fixed at a young age, social interventions such as compensatory education, job-search assistance, or subsidized prenatal care for poor mothers will not raise cognitive abilities. Because cognitive abilities are so important in determining who gets ahead, the fact that the policies are ineffective in making people smarter implies that they will primarily distort incentives but will have little positive affect on outcomes for children or parents.

Herrnstein and Murray manage both to ask the wrong question and to answer it incorrectly. They answer it incorrectly because they make several basic mistakes. A number of replications of their analysis, using their data set as well as others, have corrected these mistakes. All these replications find that measures of family background are more important than test scores in predicting all or most outcomes (Fischer et al. 1996; Korneman and Winship 1996; Dickens et al. 1997; Levine and Painter forthcoming).

Even worse, Herrnstein and Murray's policy conclusions would not follow even if their analysis were correct. Test scores predict only about 10 percent of the variation in most outcomes we observe. Thus, policy has plenty of scope for effectiveness, even if it does not affect cognitive abilities. Social interventions should be retained if their benefits outweigh their costs, regardless of their ability to influence test scores.

Finally, Herrnstein and Murray claim that their evidence shows discrimination against blacks is over. Thus, affirmative action that promotes minority access to higher education or to good jobs is neither fair nor efficient. Instead, they claim, affirmative action merely leads to enormous levels of reverse discrimination, promoting blacks who are much less competent that whites left behind.

In fact, direct experimental evidence indicates discrimination against blacks, Hispanics, and women remains important (see chapter 2). Conversely, the analysis of reverse discrimination in *The Bell Curve* has serious flaws (Dickens et al. 1997). While affirmative action programs have several important critiques, Herrnstein and Murray's analysis does little to contribute to this debate.

growing up in low-income households, limitations on access to information and to funds for paying for education, not lack of payoff from further schooling, are major causes of their lower average years of education.

Principles for Improving Our Schools

The solution in education, then, is to move away from detailed rules, whether these rules are promulgated by principals, districts, states, or the federal Department of Education. What can replace these rules in education is the same as in other spheres: getting incentives right for teachers and school administrators; creating student-focused solutions; and building in continuous improvements so that schools become as effective at learning as they are at teaching. Finally, the start-up costs of new programs can be substantial, and we must be willing to invest both in well-designed new ideas and experiments and in our most disadvantaged children.*

Accompanying these changes in process must be a change in focus away from the skills needed by the routinized factory and toward the skills needed for the workplace of the next millennium. Our schools must re-create themselves with more learning that occurs when students work together in groups to solve interesting problems, where students learn not only the basics but also the tools for continuous learning (U.S. Department of Labor 1991).

Such a change can take advantage of one of the (rare) instances where the interests of students, businesses, and society all agree. Students want more engaging schools, where they can get out of their seats and do interesting things. Businesses repeatedly emphasize teamwork and problem solving as priorities in their hiring. Society also wants these skills to create informed voters and good citizens. Thus, the new focus can alleviate the difficulties schools have in everything from retention rates to school-to-work transitions.

The question then becomes, how can we transform schools to teach not just basic skills but also these higher-order problem-solving skills? The key to this strategy is to align the various dimensions of schools, including designing new curriculums, creating richer assessments, giving teachers the training to work with the new techniques, and providing teachers and schools incentives to experiment in teaching new ways.

Because we want to move away from rigid rules and toward rewarding

---

*Many of the arguments in this section can be found as well in Hanushek (1994). For a review that a similar set of principles underlies the successful Accelerated Schools project, see Levin (1997).

education value added, we must create richer assessments that go beyond the multiple-choice tests most schools currently use. These richer assessments must measure how well students communicate, cooperate, and creatively solve problems, as well as their ability to fill in vocabulary and math problems with #2 pencils. The assessments must also identify the value added of the schools. Teaching disadvantaged students is already challenging—we must not further punish teachers in such schools by failing to measure their successes in adding value.

Getting Incentives Right for Students

The curricular changes away from "chalk and talk" and toward teamwork and solving real-world problems will inherently make education more interesting for most students. Moreover, as the material taught in schools becomes more practical and useful in the world of work, students' incentives based on long-term material self-interest also increases.

The move to a new curriculum and set of assessments has several interacting effects on how businesses treat students' school records. Given the weak relationship that school performance has on getting a job, one potentially important change is for high schools to report grades and attendance on a standard transcript and make it promptly available for employers. High school transcripts can help predict future job performance (Bishop 1993, 361). The new assessments for students must express results in clear language that employers can understand; for example, in terms of nationally recognized skill certifications. In addition, schools could make transcripts available by e-mail on the Internet when students request them. Employers, conversely, must begin to examine transcripts in making their hiring decisions. As schools teach more of the skills that businesses need, employers' incentives to examine school records also increases.

Some states are moving toward "high-stakes" exams, where students must pass an exam to graduate. Such exams provide incentives for students who are near the margin of failing. In contrast, the test provides no incentives for those who, regardless of effort, are sure to fail or are sure to pass. A variant of this idea would provide certification of multiple levels of mastery. This would provide marginal incentives for all students.

Moreover, having states coordinate exams would make the certifications more valuable for students and employers. Such coordination would lower employers' costs of learning about certifications and raise students' stakes in studying hard.

Any meaningful assessments must move away from the nation's almost exclusive reliance on multiple choice. The typical problem outside the classroom is poorly defined and must be solved by a group. The analysis involves sifting through far too much data. The solutions typically involve tradeoffs among goals and must be tested after implementation. None of these elements can be easily incorporated into a multiple-choice exam.

In fact, even modern approaches such as assessing a portfolio of a student's best work often fail to capture the richness of real problems. Thus, although creating new assessments is crucial, it is equally crucial that the assessments subject themselves to a process of continuous improvement—are they, in fact, measuring the critical skills that future citizens need?

Getting Incentives Right for Teachers and Schools

Teachers and schools deserve to be rewarded when they do a good job. These material rewards should build on the intrinsic satisfaction of good teaching. At the same time, with good incentives and accountability, teachers should be freed from the tyranny of federal, state, and district rules that currently burden them.

Improved incentives will not suffice unless participants in our educational system have the skills they need to move to the new curriculum and teaching methods. Teachers' education and certification must broaden to include these essential skills, if the next generation of Americans will be prepared to work in the twenty-first century.

All analysts agree that any effective school reform requires increased parental involvement. Thus, at least as important as material rewards are the roles that assessments can make in improving accountability to parents. Importantly, assessments that are comparable across regions can promote accountability to parents. (Schools can promote parental involvement in many other ways. Examples include writing formal contracts between schools, parents, and children, creating homework hotlines for parents and children, and contacting parents promptly concerning truancy.)

As with students, poorly designed reward systems will not promote incentives. Any material rewards must be based not on absolute scores (or the percentage passing), but instead must compare schools to relevant benchmarks that adjust for the privileges and disadvantages of the students. Past performance and the performance of school districts with a similar composition of students and families both make sensible comparison groups. Moving to assessments that no longer grade students in comparison with their classmates also has the benefit of promoting cooperation among students and giving teachers and students a shared goal to achieve.

Continuous Improvements at Schools

As we decentralize the control of schools, we must institutionalize continuous learning. As in other spheres, much of this learning will occur by evaluating current practices. Much of this evaluation capability should be concentrated at the state and federal levels because no school district can capture the entire benefit of any successful new idea it generates or learns how to implement. The state and federal governments also have a key role in designing and validating assessments because, again, a well-designed assessment is useful for thousands of teachers.

Assessments with common elements are also important for promoting accountability. In the California case, for example, the use of identical exams permits school rankings. Even with their substantial problems, these rankings give parents more information to measure schools' success and hold schools accountable. To some extent, high test scores raise real estate values. Thus, even nonparents may tolerate higher resources for education, knowing they will recoup some of the expenditures in higher property values.

Invest in Schools

Almost all calls for school reform are accompanied by calls for additional funding, and this one is no different. At the same time, the investments called for here are much more selective than in some recent writings.

Specifically, by "investment" I do not necessarily mean across-the-board increases in teacher salaries or reductions in class sizes or lengthening the school day or year. Each of these interventions is extremely expensive. At the same time, to the extent evidence exists at all, each has been shown to have only a modest effect on children's educational attainment.

In some cases, each of these high-cost interventions may be called for. (For example, some inner-city schools have class sizes over forty-five, and horrific facilities.) Nevertheless, in general we should permit local districts and schools to experiment with how to spend their current funds. At the same time, some new money is appropriate for two crucial purposes: experimentation and helping our most disadvantaged children.

Funds are needed for experimentation because the start-up costs of new programs can be substantial. For example, if we move, as many have proposed, to schools that teach problem solving and working together in groups, schools will need new curriculums, teachers will need additional training, and some schools will need to buy new facilities. States will also need to produce new assessments that measure schools' value added at creating these skills.

Some of the new funds must be channeled into evaluating the new programs. Any funds for innovation should be conditional on schools cooperating in the design and execution of the evaluation of the program.

Assistance to help our least advantaged children should include providing access to new technologies. According to a recent report, in 1995, 50 percent of U.S. public schools had access to the Internet. This percentage was up from 35 percent just one year earlier.

Unfortunately, access is not evenly shared. "Only 31 percent of schools with large proportions of students from poor families have access to the Internet, compared to 62 percent of schools with relatively few students from poor families" (U.S. Department of Education 1996c). Funding from the Technology Literacy Challenge Fund and the Universal Service Fund established by the 1996 Telecommunications Act, may help both to improve the quality of all schools' access and to equalize access for less advantaged schools. It currently remains unclear how these funds will be raised or the level of services they will support. However the details work out, it is crucial that (at a minimum) schools and libraries have high-quality connections. (For additional suggestions on improving the use of computers in school, see the Appendix to this chapter.)

Are We Just Throwing Money Away by Spending It on Schools?

A number of studies, beginning with the influential Coleman Report in 1966, have found only a weak relationship between school resources such as class size and standardized test scores (Hanushek 1986). Thus, a number of commentators have questioned whether additional funding for schools is useful. There are several reasons to doubt the results of the Coleman Report.

First, the weak evidence on the payoff to school resources is not too surprising because schools with less-advantaged students (e.g., in poorer neighborhoods) often need to spend more on everything from metal detectors to attracting teachers, yet still show below-average test scores or other results. Studies must control for the need for funds, not just the supply.

Second, more recent evidence finds that more generous school resources have beneficial effects on student test scores. An important recent study reanalyzed previous research and concluded that the literature had too many statistically significant findings to support the view that school resources have no effect on test scores (Hedges 1993). In addition, the only large-scale, randomized experiment on class size and student achievement ever performed in the United States—the Tennessee STAR experiment on grades K–3—concluded that students performed slightly better if they were assigned to smaller classes. Smaller class size had especially beneficial effects on test scores for low-income students and for black students.

Third, most studies that look directly at the relationship between school resources and students' subsequent income or years of education (instead of at test scores) find a positive association. Because test scores have only a weak relationship with economic outcomes, such as subsequent income, it is important to look at the relationship between school spending and economic outcomes. A recent review article concluded that on average, a 10 percent increase in school resources leads to a 1 to 2 percent increase in students' annual income later in life (Card and Krueger 1996). Other studies, however, have raised methodological concerns with this literature and have argued that there is an insignificant relationship between school resources and students' subsequent income. This remains an unsettled issue, but a strong case can be made that school resources lead to higher income for students down the road.

Finally, high-income parents voluntarily locate to high-tax cities that spend more per student and have smaller class sizes. These parents, at least, believe resources matter. It is disingenuous to suggest resources matter for children from wealthy families, but not for children of the poor.

Federal Support for Disadvantaged Children

This approach to setting standards runs the risk of harming our least-advantaged citizens: poor citizens. If we set high goals and do not give poor schools resources, then few of their students can achieve those goals. Graduates from disadvantaged families or those attending troubled schools will have their almost-valueless diploma depreciate further. Thus, any move to a goal-based system must be accompanied by substantial increases in resources targeted on schools with high concentrations of hard-to-serve children.

The federal government promotes education of our most disadvantaged children primarily through a system of grants to districts with poor children, known as Title I of the Improving America's Schools Act of 1994. These grants suffer from several problems. First, districts receive some funds even if they have far fewer poor children than the average district. The 1994 reauthorization of these grants targets a small proportion of its grants to districts with high concentrations of poor children. A sensible system of federal grants should focus grants on those schools and districts with concentrations of poverty and avoid spreading aid to virtually every district in the nation.

Even with well-targeted federal funding, the problem remains that for goals to motivate, they must be difficult but also be attainable. When measuring school progress, rewarding teachers, and rewarding students, it is valid and legitimate to adjust the goal to take into account the privileges or disadvantages of the students. This disadvantage-based "affirmative action" can both increase equity and, by increasing incentives for those without resources to hit extremely high goals, can increase efficiency as well. (Conversely, by lowering goals for the most talented among the apparently disadvantaged, this form of affirmative action can reduce a few students' incentives.)

State Support for Poor School Districts

Many school districts with low property values have both high property tax rates and low revenue per child. This situation is widely perceived to be unfair. Moreover, the majority of states have been subject to lawsuits that question the constitutionality of this situation.

A solution that several states have tried is for the state to make up for lower property values so that similar property tax rates raise similar (or at least a minimum) levels of revenues. (This is known as "power equalization.") This solution retains local control of spending levels, but increases equity, and has been intended to increase spending at poor schools.

Unfortunately, in some states (most notably California) this solution has mean that districts are able to increase school spending by less than a dollar when they raise a dollar of property tax revenues. The result of these unintended and perverse incentives is that states often "equalize down" after implementing power equalization (Hoxby 1996). Thus, in designing "fixes" to the financing of education, it is important that local districts retain benefit when they tax themselves or improve their school quality. In many cases, subsidies based on the characteristics of the residents of a district, such as the percentage who are poor, avoid the problems of tinkering with the property tax system.

Policies to Promote Improve Schools

Learning must be thought of as a lifetime endeavor. Thus, this section starts with programs to improve readiness to learn for very young children, then moves to schools from ages five to eighteen, and closes with a discussion of the transition from school to career. (The following chapter picks up with policies to promote learning after age eighteen.)

Importantly, these principles can be implemented with widely different mechanisms. This chapter first describes and analyzes current efforts of school reform based on Goals 2000. In this model, authority is decentralized to the school and classroom levels, and parents are involved through improved assessments that promote accountability. It then describes an alternative (sometimes complementary) means based on school choice. As noted below, emotions are high, and evidence is surprisingly thin, on the merits of these two visions of school reform.

Goals 2000

The current efforts at school reform follow many of the precepts laid out in this chapter. The heart of this reform movement is in the Goals 2000: Educate America Act, enacted in 1993. This act sets eight ambitious national education goals to be achieved by the end of the decade:

- *School readiness.* All children will start school ready to learn.
- *Improved student achievement.* All students will demonstrate competence in challenging subject matter in core academic subjects.
- *Best in math and science.* U.S. students will be first in the world in mathematics and science achievement.
- *Safe, disciplined, and drug-free schools.* Every school will be free from violence, disruptive behavior, and illegal drugs.
- *Increased graduation rate.* The high school graduation rate will improve to at least 90 percent.
- *Teacher education and professional development.* All teachers will have the opportunity to acquire the knowledge and skills needed to prepare their students for the next century.
- *Parental involvement.* Every school will promote parent-teacher partnerships that will increase parents' involvement in the social and academic enrichment of their children.
- *Adult literacy and lifelong learning.* Every adult will be literate and possess the skills necessary to compete in a global economy.

These goals establish a framework for a lifetime of continuous learning, from preschool to college and throughout adulthood. The Goals 2000 act provides a framework for comprehensive state and local efforts to improve both teaching and learning, based on clear and challenging academic standards for all students. The framework of Goals 2000 is meant to encourage the alignment of various aspects of the educational system including curriculum design, student assessments, teachers' professional development, and instructional materials. These systemic reforms are voluntary, and their design in each state will be a group effort including parents, businesspeople, educators, and others. (See box 5.2.)

The reforms embedded in Goals 2000 and its related legislation, the

---

Box 5.2 What Works (So Far): Kentucky School Reforms

The 1991 reforms adopted in Kentucky are an example of the type of alignment Goals 2000 is intended to promote in other states. Kentucky adopted six broad goals and further refined these in sixty-two specific academic expectations. One of the goals, for example, is that students should be able to apply principles from mathematics, science, social studies, and other disciplines to real-life situations. In science, this goal translates into such concrete expectations as that students should be able to recognize and use patterns such as cycles and trends to understand past events and make predictions. The state's major employers have been involved throughout the reforms, helping to ensure that the schools' expectations match the needs of employers and future graduates.

The state's new goals are accompanied by new assessment procedures that combine traditional multiple-choice questions with tests requiring students to solve practical problems, and with evaluations of each student's best classroom work collected throughout the year. This new assessment better measures the full range of each student's progress. The assessment is also used to evaluate a school's success in improving student performance. Schools that do well receive monetary rewards, while unsuccessful schools are required to develop plans for improvement. Coupled with the increased accountability, Kentucky is decentralizing decision making to school-based councils of teachers, parents, and principals on matters such as curriculum and assignment of staff. In addition, resources for professional development have been increased, and family and youth service centers have been established at low-income schools to provide and coordinate services for families such as child care, family counseling, and referrals to service agencies.

Results in Kentucky are preliminary so far, but encouraging. Average test scores in core academic subjects increased markedly after two years at all grade levels tested. On average, scores on the new assessments in 1995 and 1996 were approximately 15 percent above those of 1993 and 1994. Although there was substantial variation, these results were on average equal to the schools' goals for improvement. Time will tell if these results are sustained and translate into better careers and life chances for Kentucky's graduates.

Improving America's School Act, attempt to move away from rigid rules to a new model in which the federal government provides seed money and technical assistance for states and local school districts to engage in their own reform efforts, keyed to high standards. The acts enhance local flexibility by providing states and local school districts with the opportunity to coordinate better the activities of federally funded programs in their areas. Both acts allow states and school districts to apply for waivers of federal rules that impede their plans for school improvement. The objective is to create a system in which highly skilled teachers can focus on achieving clear, widely agreed-on goals, assisted by parents and the community, who in turn can look to a set of well-defined standards by which to hold educators and school systems accountable.

Ensuring Readiness to Learn. The first goal is to ensure that all children start school ready to learn. Even good schools will have trouble educating children who come to school unprepared to learn because of poor nutrition at home or for other reasons. Some of these children will always find themselves struggling to catch up. We should expand two programs that promote early cognitive and physical development and help prepare children for school. The first is the Special Supplemental Food Program for Women, Infants, and Children (WIC), which provides food supplements and health education to 6 million low-income pregnant women, new mothers, and their children up to age five annually. The WIC program has been shown to save the government money as well as increase children's health (box 5.3). Nevertheless, WIC serves only approximately 72 percent of those who are eligible.

The second program, Head Start, also has a proven track record. Head Start is an intensive preschool program that has significant beneficial effects on the cognitive and social functioning, health status, and school readiness of low-income youth. In spite of its fairly positive track record, only about one in three eligible three- to five-year-olds participates. Moreover, Head Start currently emphasizes part-day programs, making it much less useful to working parents than it could be.

Goals 2000 in the Schools. The first goal, that all students enter school prepared to learn, is difficult. At the same time, we have sensible policies that can make progress to achieve this goal. The other portions of Goals 2000 are often more problematic.

For example, the list of objectives in the Goals 2000 legislation is difficult to argue with but not always realistic. When Congress pronounced the goal "U.S. students will be first in the world in mathematics and science achievement by the year 2000" they were, as one pundit observed, at risk of being accused of using some of the controlled substances that schools are supposed to be free of. In general, to maximize their effectiveness goals should be difficult but attainable (Locke and Latham 1990). In 1990 when President Bush endorsed the goal, and in 1993 when President Clinton signed the goal into law, American students were two grade levels behind the world's best in their age group. Nobody expected the Americans would catch up by the year 2000. Moreover, several of the goals, such as school safety and

---

Box 5.3. What Works: Preparing Students to Learn

Both the health-and-nutrition program WIC and the preschool program Head Start have been subject to numerous evaluations. A 1990 study of five states compared WIC participants with nonparticipant mothers with similar demographic characteristics and prenatal medical-care usage patterns. In each state the WIC program was highly effective in improving the health status of infants. In addition, WIC appears to be a money saver: for every dollar spent on the prenatal WIC program, approximately $3 is saved in Medicaid and other costs due to lower incidence of low-birthweight births and improved health. To the extent that poor prenatal care and infant health are associated with future behavioral and academic problems, the benefits of WIC are even greater.

Head Start and other preschool programs have also demonstrated their ability to improve preparedness for school. Numerous studies have found that participation in Head Start produces immediate gains in health and in scores on tests of intellectual ability, emotional maturity, and school readiness.

Most of the benefits of Head Start (including lower rates of being held back a grade) appear to persist at least past the end of elementary school. At the same time, one of the most consistent results in the many studies following up the effects of Head Start programs is that the early improvements in test scores usually fade before the children have finished elementary school. Pessimists have acted as if the lost gain in test scores indicates Head Start's failure. Optimists have noted that this effect may reflect failure to measure the low test scores of students in the comparison groups who have been held back. Moreover, even if the fading is real, a few quarters of preschool should not be expected to accomplish lifelong changes. Disadvantaged students may need enrichment of their K–12 schools to avoid losing the gains of Head Start. So far, this debate is unsettled, although the need for additional research is clear.

Moreover, more intensive preschool programs, most notably the oft-cited Perry preschool, have shown very large positive benefits well past the end of high school. Although the sample was small, this intensive early childhood intervention led participants to have higher earnings, lower dropout rates, lower involvement with crime and drugs, and lower rates of out-of-wedlock births than a control group (Schmidt 1996).

---

parental involvement, concern issues where the federal government has virtually no role to play.

In addition, the goals were written with an emphasis on providing productive workers for businesses, without enough emphasis on the goals needed for a good society and for good citizens. To see the contrast, consider the Vermont Common Core attempt to write state-wide education goals. These goals were written with the help of 4,000 citizens. The Common Core describes twenty "vital results" in four categories: communication, problem solving, personal development, and social responsibility. These vital results are to be played out in three fields of knowledge: mathematics, science and technology; arts and humanities; and social sciences (Mills 1995, 27).

Although businesses as well as society at large are interested in the skills of critical thinking and working in groups, many of the benefits spill over into society in the form of better-informed voters and better citizens. Thus, the optimal level of these skills for society is probably larger than what businesses desire. It is, therefore, unsurprising that the bottom-up Vermont goals stresses "communication, problem-solving, personal development and social responsibility" more than the Goals 2000 approach.

A further problem with the Goals approach as most states are implementing it is the lack of interdisciplinary focus. Problems outside the classroom typically require integration of interpersonal skills, math, reading, writing, and technical knowledge. Some mixture of these skills is required for fixing a car, teaching a friend how to bake a soufflé, solving a quality problem at work, or understanding the costs and benefits of an environmental policy. In part because of the segmented nature of curriculums today, few of the goals that most states are developing require much integration. This lack is unfortunate because this integration is a crucial part of the education of a well-rounded citizen.

Finally, the Goals process permits states to set their own standards for performance. This approach maximizes experimentation and adaptation to local conditions, but it is not always beneficial for students. To a large extent, the United States is a single national labor market. Roughly one in ten Americans moves to a new state over a five-year period. For youth, rates are roughly twice as high (Borjas et al. 1992). Students want credentials they can carry to labor markets different from where they went to high school. Employers want certifications that they understand, even if their employees did not all grow up nearby.

Consensus goals are also crucial because no school, district, or even state can afford to pay all the costs of developing and validating new assessments and curriculums (Mills 1995, 26). Experimentation is important. At the same time, it makes no sense for each state to decide how to measure problem solving, or how to teach teachers how to run a classroom that encourages teamwork. Nor does it make sense for textbook writers to have to produce multiple versions of a text. These costs should be spread among the many states striving to achieve related goals. Finally, the goals cannot inform universities about how to train teachers unless they are similar across much of the nation.

Thus, the Goals process will meet students' needs only if the national goals-setting board can establish high-quality consensus benchmarks that most states adopt. Such a consensus standard should be modular, with "merit badges" that students can earn and employers can understand. Furthermore, states and communities should be able to add content to the consensus standards. This solution would permit a state to remove a portion of a goal (for example, not to put some modules into its goals and assessments) or to add custom content that it found more important than other states. At the same time, the consensus standard would meet the needs of students, employers, textbook writers, states, teachers and teacher-training institutions.

Unfortunately, that is not what is happening. The fifty states are not coordinating their goals. Instead, they are producing literally tens of thousands of pages of "standards," "goals," "themes," "strands," "outcomes," and what not. The creation of these documents involved endless reinvention of the wheel, with sufficient inconsistency of phrasing to make meaningful comparisons quite difficult (Council for Basic Education 1996). Assessments for similar concepts are being created dozens of times, and only minimal economies of scale are being realized.

School Choice

Ever since the writings of Adam Smith, the notion of providing vouchers that permit parents to purchase education for children has had some appeal. Ideally, vouchers could offer increased flexibility for schools and parents while providing powerful market incentives for teachers and schools. At the same time, critics have expressed concerns that school choice would destroy the public schools; they fear that the prosperous and politically powerful would switch to elite schools, while the public schools would lose their political support and become the primary "choice" for the children of less prosperous families. It remains to be seen whether carefully designed school vouchers can enhance choice and potentially improve school quality while maintaining equality of access.

Thirty years ago, Milton Friedman described a school voucher scheme that provides market-based incentives to schools (Friedman 1962). He proposed school vouchers worth a fixed amount that could be used at any school. Moreover, schools would be permitted to choose as well—to choose which students to admit and choose to charge tuition above the value of the voucher.

This proposal would maximize choices for the prosperous, who would have the choice of any public or private school. It would also provide market incentives for schools to satisfy parents and children or lose their market share and funding.

At the same time, Friedman's vouchers would create a number of the difficulties. Chapter 2 pointed out several common problems with vouchers, such as incentives for "cherry-picking": private schools would select easy-to-serve students and those of wealthy families, leaving hard-to-serve students (for example, the disabled) for the resource-strapped public schools. As prosperous families exit the public school system, it will lose both economies of scale and political support, further harming the disadvantaged. Moreover, under Friedman's proposal, parents choose with little information (other than potentially misleading advertising). The result is a school voucher without meaningful choice for a high proportion of families.

An alternative school voucher system can provide the advantages of parents' choice without most of these problems. A voucher that maximized choices for the majority of families would limit the use of vouchers to schools that did not charge extra tuition, that accepted all students (and had a lottery to choose if oversubscribed), and that agreed to share information and assess students using standard methods to permit informed choice.

Under Friedman's scheme, the ability of schools to charge tuition above the value of the voucher has two important implications. First, the wealthy will disproportionately segregate into elite schools. Most other families will not find that a market-based system adds affordable choices. (Parents with modest amounts of financial resources and with sufficiently high concern for their children to supplement the value of the voucher will also prefer Friedman's version of school choice.)

Given the disproportionate political power wealthy people have, improving schools requires their involvement and participation in universally accessible schools.

Friedman's vouchers also suffer from poor targeting, raising costs to the government. Specifically, wealthy people who are willing to pay $10,000 for an elite private school would now receive a voucher for $5,000—reducing their out-of-pocket costs and raising government costs. This transfer leaves fewer resources for education of the nonwealthy. The vouchers proposed here have this problem, but to a lesser extent because those who choose schools that charge extra tuition will not receive government vouchers. Thus, the targeting of educational funding at the margin is better with the vouchers proposed here. The converse of this poor targeting is that families sending their children to private school will no longer pay for education once with taxes and a second time with tuition.

Permitting schools to select students also leads to adverse selection—private schools will select cheap-to-educate students, while leaving students with special needs to public schools. This gives an unfair cost advantage to selective private schools. Requiring open admission will also make it more difficult for schools to discriminate on the basis of race and religion.

As a further encouragement to schools to serve a diverse group of students (and avoid sticking public schools with all costly-to-educate children), the school voucher's value should be adjusted based on the special needs of the student. As a further enhancement to choice, vouchers should include some value toward transporting students so that poor parents are not restricted to local schools. Instead, even parents who do not own a car should be able to pay for a van or public transportation for their children.

Charter schools can increase the supply of schools among which families can choose. Charter schools are typically chartered and funded by a school district but are freed from most regulations. Funding is proportional to student enrollments. Any group of parents and students can start a specialized charter school. The majority of states now authorize charter schools.

Friedman's vouchers also provide choice, but no information. Choice without information greatly diminishes any advantages the market may have. Thus, a choice-oriented voucher would require schools to give "report cards" on the achievements of their students.

Schools should be free to teach however they prefer, and have the right not to teach some topics. Nevertheless, parents should be aware of what knowledge is being transmitted in the classroom. Report cards should be based on well-rounded assessments (described above) to minimize the problems of teachers teaching to the test.

To avoid penalizing schools whose students come from disadvantaged backgrounds, the assessments should be reported both in absolute scores and relative to other schools with a similar mix of student advantages and disadvantages. Alternatively, for students who transfer to a different school, scores can be presented in terms of learning since arrival.

Thus, a choice-focused school voucher scheme exists that avoids most of the problems of Friedman's voucher scheme. It ensures that choices increase for all families, not just for the wealthy. Even with guaranteed increase (or at least not decrease) in choice, it is likely that these choices will be used more often and more carefully by well-educated and prosperous families—families with the time and resources to investigate school quality and transport children to and from school.

At the opposite extreme of Friedman's vouchers is a version of school choice that provides vouchers only to disadvantaged families in poorly performing school districts. This has recently been tried in several cities; the Milwaukee experience is described later in the chapter. Because the vouchers are targeted to low-income families, it is unlikely that they will increase racial or class segregation. Because the nonpoor largely have effective school choice by choosing where to live, this form of choice maximizes the increment to effective choice for each dollar spent on vouchers.

Problems with Any Version of School Choice. Even the best-designed voucher scheme for schools has one important problem: by promoting market-based choices, it weakens parents' incentives to work together to improve neighborhood schools. Unlike most of the other government services discussed in this book, schools can help build strong neighborhoods. Having a network of strong local institutions appears important in creating the cohesiveness that promotes local public goods (Putnam 1993).

That is, because parents can reward one another by helping at the school, they are more likely to interact positively in local politics, nonprofit organizations, and social services. As one thoughtful critic of privatization explained:

> Public schools are a principal motivation for the participation of parents in local elections; the vitality of local government depends on their involvement. Privatization of the schools would weaken the foundations of local democracy. (Starr 1988)

Evidence. So far, the evidence on school choice is mixed. The preponderance of evidence suggests that choice can increase student achievement (although the effects do not appear large). In two recent studies, Caroline Minter Hoxby (1994a, 1994b) has found evidence that within the range of competition currently observed between public and private schools and between neighboring districts can improve school quality for some students without harming any identifiable group. In contrast, Grosskopf et al. (1995) find conflicting results in Texas. At the same time, the evidence is largely consistent with critics' fear of cherry-picking and increased segregation and sorting.

Most private schools have lower tuition per student than the government pays for public schools. In addition, private school students have better academic records on average than do public school students. Thus, some commentators suggest that it is clear that private schools are more cost effective and that choice will cut costs and raise quality.

This reading of the evidence is too simplistic. Families that choose private schools are typically above average in their resources, their concern for education, or both. Complementing this self-selection, most private schools engage in selection. They can choose not to admit high-cost students, they can expel troublesome students, and they typically do not have as many high-cost disabled students. Thus, a fair comparison is difficult to make.

Nevertheless, some careful research that attempts to control for at least some of these problems finds that Catholic schools do a better job of educating non-Catholics (but not Catholics) than do comparable public schools (Sander 1996). Levin (1998) summarizes opposing evidence.

Complementing the public-private comparisons, most evaluations find that school choice improves students' learning. (West [1997] reviews the evidence. Stecklow [1997] provides anecdotal evidence concerning the problems of public school choice in Arizona. Many of the problems he describes are specific to the start-up stage of new schools.) Unfortunately, the lack of appropriate control group in most of the studies reduces our confidence in the results.

The largest experiment with school choice to date, in Milwaukee, has led to conflicting studies. Parents who place their children in private schools are pleased with the new schools (Witte et al. 1995). Those placed in private schools have not increased their test scores more rapidly than apparently similar students who remain in public schools. At the same time, the plan was targeted to disadvantaged children, so it is possible that these disadvantages would have led these students to perform worse than the comparison public school students.

An alternative study design took advantage of the fact that some schools had lotteries to select at random students into oversubscribed programs (Peterson et al. 1996). Thus, the losers of the lottery create a random comparison group. Compared to those not selected into the private schools, it appears that lottery winners did in fact win—their test scores grew more rapidly. Unfortunately, even this result is not completely convincing because it does not appear until after three years. The delay in finding positive results may reflect the time it takes to adjust to a new school. Alternatively, the delay may reflect the more troubled youth leaving the school, so the positive results are due to selective attrition, not learning.

The Milwaukee experience with school choice also indicates some evidence of the cream-skimming problem that opponents of choice fear. Parents of children applying for the choice program had somewhat higher education and involvement with schools than did parents who did not apply for the program. (Contradicting the cream-skimming hypothesis, students did not have high test scores [Witte and Thorne 1996].) Research in other nations is typically consistent with some cream-skimming when school choice is introduced (Rothstein 1993).

In conclusion, the Milwaukee program provides some evidence that school choice can improve student achievement. At the same time, the study does not help us understand whether the prod of competition will, on balance, improve public schools or whether the loss of resources and of engaged parents will hurt them.

From School to Work

The various reforms of schools will not work unless they succeed in motivating students. Unfortunately, students, especially those not headed for college, spend little time or energy on schoolwork. As one study concluded:

> High school students in 1980 spent an average of 3.5 hours per week on homework, far less than the 10 hours per work devoted to a part-time job and the 25 hours per week watching television.
>
> Low motivation is most acute among non-college students, who see little immediate gain from working hard in high school. They realize that earning a high school degree will affect their access to jobs, but they see little connection between their specific performance at school and their chances for good jobs or careers. High schools typically do not have elaborate job placement services; employers rarely rely on the recommendations of high school teachers; and those hiring new students generally do not request academic transcripts (Lerman and Pouncy 1990).

The School-to-Work Opportunities Act of 1994 addresses the increasingly poor job prospects of high school graduates by providing states and localities with venture capital to build systems that prepare young people to pursue a variety of options after completing high school: a good first job, career-oriented training, or college. The school-to-work initiative funds partnerships among businesses, labor representatives, and educators to offer young people learning experiences in both school-based and work-based settings that will help provide them with the knowledge and skills they will need to make a smooth transition into the world of work.

The school-to-work initiative creates the opportunity for students to learn in a setting that connects academics with problems in a real workplace. The program integrates classroom instruction with work experience, structured training, mentoring at job sites, and matching students with participating employers. Whenever possible, students are paid for their work. School-to-work opportunities bring the workplace into the classroom, combining quality course work at school with hands-on learning and training in a work environment. By the end of a course of study, students will have received a high school diploma, an industry-recognized skill certificate, and, for some, a diploma for completion of one or two years of postsecondary education. The experience of the industrialized nations of northern Europe with apprenticeships indicates that school-to-work programs can potentially dramatically improve results for high school graduates (box 5.4).

By 1996, all fifty states were developing school-to-work systems, and a number were implementing comprehensive systems. More than 100,000 students at over 2,700 schools were participating, along with roughly 40,000 employers (Leonard 1996). In most states, employers are directly

Box 5.4. What Works: The German Apprenticeship System

Germany has created a system that smooths the transition from school to work in that nation. About half of all high school graduates enroll in apprenticeships during their final years of high school. (Many of these youth enroll in college at some point after completing their apprenticeship.) During the last years of high school, they combine paid part-time employment with part-time schooling. Exams that are supervised by employer and union representatives certify the achievement of skills in each occupation.

About half of all trainees end up working at an employer different from the one where they spent their apprenticeship. Many employers also appreciate the ability to screen potential future employees during their apprenticeship. Nevertheless, the training appears to create value for the entire industry.

To reduce the market failure related to the creation of transferable skills, union and industry federations help pressure employers to create apprenticeship slots. Schools and the government also provide subsidies for apprenticeship training. The result is that local employers cooperate in the provision of training relevant to their sector; that is, independent firms are willing to share the costs of investing in training and other services that are to their common benefit.

The results of the system have been impressive. Young high school graduates earn wages equal to roughly twice the U.S. level. Until German reunification and the political decision to set wages in the East very high, these high wages for young workers were coupled with relatively low rates of youth unemployment—an indication that the high wages were accompanied by high skills.

The German apprenticeship system is not perfect. Before the apprenticeship, the system requires choice of occupation at a very young age. During the apprenticeship, the skills in some sectors are not kept up to date with changing technology. After the apprenticeship, the German system has not created institutions that are nearly as strong at providing continued training.

Finally, some German metalworking firms, historically among the greatest supporters of the apprenticeship system, are now seeking alternative sources of skilled labor. It is possible that the same set of institutions that encourage managers to invest more in the skills of their existing employees (by raising the costs per worker and strengthening the employment relationship) may also discourage companies from making incremental hiring because of limits on managerial flexibility.

For more detail, see OECD 1994b and den Broeder 1995.

contributing to the development of industry-based standards in broad clusters of occupations. To the extent that school-to-work programs are successful, they should benefit many students by connecting academic learning with problem solving in an actual workplace, thus making learning more relevant. The programs should also provide valuable labor market experience and connections. These programs should also benefit businesses by increasing the number of trained workers with experience in specific fields.

For example, California's Partnership Academies, which combine high school education with career-focused training and work experience, have apparently been quite successful in reducing dropout rates among program participants (Hayward and Tallmadge 1993; Stern et al. 1989). More definite results are available for established programs targeted at high school dropouts, such as the highly successful Center for Employment Training in San Jose. Study of such programs has shown that a key element (and one that is at the core of the school-to-work effort) is contextual learning—that is, providing a "real world" context in which students can learn academic skills (U.S. Department of Labor 1995c).

Both employers and students gain if the school-to-work program improves job matching, so employers are training workers who are interested in the field, and students are receiving training and experience in a field in which they are likely to stay. Thus, providing good information to students on different careers and industries can help school-to-work programs add value to employers and students. This information can be provided by guest speakers, site visits, mentoring, and other means. Without such help, it is unlikely that sixteen- and seventeen-year-olds can choose the occupations they will enjoy and fit well with for many decades to come.

Although school-to-work programs have much potential, they suffer from a serious problem. Preparing students to work requires the cooperation of employers to provide mentors, visits, and (most expensively) internships. In these programs, employers often have incentives to use the employees as cheap labor, not as trainees (Roditi 1992). To the extent the schools can hold the employer to a training program, costs for the employer rise, and incentives to work with the schools decline. Thus, school-to-work programs face the problem that employers do not want to invest in youth and hire apprentices or other co-op students in anywhere near the scale of supply (Stamps 1996).

Schools will be more successful at attracting employers to the extent that they can customize their courses to the needs of the employers, ensuring that students have adequate preparation for their internship. An incentive for employers to cooperate with schools, then, becomes the ability to help design a curriculum suited to the employer's needs. The downside is that overly customized training benefits the employer but not the long-term interests of the majority of students. (A partial solution for some of the nation's most troubled schools can be found in chapter 10, where I propose federal funds for employers and schools that can create an integrated school-to-work system in neighborhoods where the schools and labor markets work worst for youth, and where failures are most costly to society.)

A related dilemma appears in attracting students. If school-to-career programs focus on the noncollege bound, both academically talented students and employers will shun them as they currently do many vocational education programs. Too often, the alternative to the college prep track is, as one parent put it, "nowhere prep" (quoted in Stern et al. 1995, 125). Thus, many of the most successful school-to-work models integrate college and career preparation. Unfortunately, when programs are focused on everybody, then employers have even weaker incentives to invest in the youth because many will go on to college and leave the industry (Stern et al. 1995, 126).

A partial solution to the problem of lack of engagement by employers is to separate the two main components of school-to-work programs: exposure to the world of work to facilitate good job matches, and real-world experience in problem solving. Employers are clearly needed for the former goal. Although apprenticeships are useful, extensive mentoring, field trips, and shadowing of employees can provide students with a wide array of exposure without expensive internships. Conversely, school-based enterprises can permit students to use and advance their "book learning" in an applied setting. The downside of these enterprises is that loss of occupational experience and lower student engagement may occur without a paycheck. This is partly compensated for by the lower cost and higher control that the school has to make sure the students are not merely pursuing menial tasks. Thus, some preliminary evidence suggests that students perceive higher teamwork and more complex problem solving at school-based enterprises than at internships (Stern et al. 1995).

Conclusion

Most Americans endorse the goal of sufficient equality of opportunity so that every child has a decent chance to achieve a middle-class standard of living. Americans also favor efficiency in the provision of government services. These two goals sometimes conflict. Happily, a series of policies concerning education hold the promise of increasing equality of opportunity as well as efficiency.

The key is creating a system of lifetime learning. For children and youth, that system has three elements: preparing children for school, improving K–12 schools, and helping students move from schools to careers.

Preparation for school requires that all children arrive at school with adequate health care and readiness to learn.

American public schools educate tens of millions of students each year, often with remarkable success. At the same time, the system is incredibly decentralized, implying that students do not graduate with skill certifications that are meaningful for employers. The advantage of decentralization is the ability to innovate, but many American teachers find themselves surrounded by innumerable command-and-control rules and regulations that limit innovation.

One model of school reform builds on this decentralization with school choice. Some versions of school choice emphasize choice for the prosperous; others limit subsidies for expensive private schools and maximize choice for a broader group of society. Both versions attempt to use market incentives to promote innovation and flexibility in meeting the needs of students and their families. The first version, but also the second to some extent, runs the risk of isolating the least powerful in declining public schools.

A less dramatic (although potentially complementary) approach to decentralized school reform uses clear goals to create accountability to parents and employers. By having agreed-on goals, the schools can be freed to experiment in meeting those goals. By having meaningful assessments, parents can monitor school effectiveness. Unfortunately, the current movement to create goals is so decentralized that employers and future employees will not be able to benefit from the presence of meaningful certifications.

Importantly, the reformed schools and school-to-work programs also redirect their energies away from passive student learning. Instead, students learn the skills of teamwork and problem solving that employers want, students find more interesting, and future employees and citizens will find most valuable. With such a system, students finish high school with much better preparation, with skill certifications, and with some experience to begin their careers.

APPENDIX

WHAT MIGHT WORK: THE INTERNET AS JUST-IN-TIME TEACHER

A Story: A group of students are playing a video game that confronts them with a series of problems. They need to analyze data to solve the problems, and they need to collaborate to bring all the pieces of the puzzle together in one place. The tools they use to communicate, collaborate, and analyze the data are general-purpose tools such as spreadsheets and e-mail that they can use for real problems. As the problems become more difficult, the players receive assistance from an embedded help system that leads them through increasingly sophisticated problem-solving techniques. In short, while they are playing a game, the players are also learning both techniques and computer-assisted tools that will make them more successful employees and citizens.

This fictional anecdote outlines a model for active learning that holds great promise. The government should encourage the creation of learning tools to teach such skills as systematic problem solving and teamwork. Ideally, such tools should have three elements: engaging simulations, computer-assisted tools that also work for real problems, and embedded training. The goal is to have just-in-time training available to anyone who needs to learn new problem-solving techniques.

Engaging Simulations

To make learning enjoyable, the tools should include simulations of interesting problems that are interesting to solve. Many current computer games simulate interesting problems ranging from landing a rocket on the moon to running a city, but they rarely couple these problems with systematic problem-solving skills. To be concrete, the example presented below discusses a game that teaches problem solving by running a simulated factory. The same principles of design can be integrated into games that range from saving a rain forest to exploring new worlds.

Integration with Computer-Assisted Tools

The simulations should be integrated with computer-assisted tools that decisionmakers use for real decisions. For example, tools to teach teamwork should build on existing groupware capabilities of standard software such as Internet browsers. When users interact simultaneously, the simulation should permit them to talk simultaneously, view and edit documents, have private conversations and bulletin boards, and write on a collaborative whiteboard.

The simulations move beyond these capabilities that are already standard features in browsers to promote systematic problem solving. The program should step the group of plays through a structured problem-solving process, explaining the reasons why each step is important. That is, it should help users organize their priorities, gather data on the problem, brainstorm possible solutions, and so forth. At each step, the simulations should rely on software tools to automate steps in the problem-solving process. For example, the simulation should interact with participants' calendar programs to put "next steps" they have agreed to on their calendar, and remind them when they should be taking an action before the next meeting.

Embedded Training

Finally, each program should include embedded training that provides tutorials for each operation and provides step-by-step guidance through difficult operations. For example, consider a program teaching the problem-solving tool of statistical process control by analyzing a simulated stamping machine. The software should lead novice users step-by-step through the process, showing how data moves from measurements of defects of the simulated stamping output to the graph of defect rates. Users could alter the "dials" on the simulated machine and see how the defect rates change. Intermediate users would have to choose the parameters to measure, based on their previous analyses of which problems are most important.

Importantly, the training should also explain to interested users the reasoning, principles, and evidence supporting the usefulness of each step. Thus, in the example of the stamping machine, advanced users would have access to explanations of the statistical principles underlying statistical process control.

While many students learn well in classrooms, a large number learn principles more easily when they are embedded in actual problems. For such students, embedding principles of statistics within a simulation can teach the distinction between the standard error and the standard deviation more effectively than hours of lecture and dozens of formulas. The enjoyment of watching videos of tons of large presses crash down on a piece of metal is an added bonus.

One goal should be breadth of learning opportunities. Ideally, when an employee or citizen encounters a new problem, whether it is buying a new car, planning a family budget, or running a small business, they should be able to play a game or simulation to learn many of the skills needed for the task and to learn how to use helpful software.

A second goal should be depth of learning opportunities. The government should promote efforts to embed conceptual training in all popular software. With such training, users can become experts in their spare time. Ideally, each common program would have training not just in running it, but also in the principles behind its operation. The goal should be a network of training topics that can create a variety of career paths and enhance occupational mobility. A clerical worker should be able to advance from writing simple macros in a word processor to understanding principles of programming such as data structures and algorithms. The goal is to have enough embedded training that a user can use standard software packages to learn how to become a meeting facilitator, a teacher of decision making, a graphics designer, or an expert in advanced decision-making techniques such as experimental design.

6

A LIFE CYCLE OF LEARNING:
AFTER HIGH SCHOOL

Most Americans will hold many jobs in their careers. This chapter describes a reemployment system based on portable health benefits, highly automated information systems concerning job openings and applicants, and simplified training grants. This system holds the promise of permitting a flexible labor market while reducing the human cost of job changing.

A Story: John had wanted to attend college but could not afford the tuition. Fortunately, during the four years he had worked at his first job, he had taught himself to be an excellent graphics designer. Then, like 2 million other Americans that year, John was the victim of job loss due to no fault of his own. John was shocked at the downsizing and did know how to deal with the unexpected bad news.

A trip to the local unemployment office helped him apply for a few dollars a week in unemployment insurance and required him to fill out some paperwork promising to search for work. John received no help in identifying strategies for finding a new job. Other than reading the want-ads and asking his friends, John had no way of knowing what jobs were available in his city. Although he was willing to move for a good job, he had even less information on job openings elsewhere. In fact, John could not even get information on what training programs he might be eligible for—he did not even know what office to visit to ask.

For six long months, John was unemployed. During this time, he was without health insurance. John would have liked to attend classes at the local junior college to improve his graphic design skill. Unfortunately, unemployment was precisely the worst period in which to pay the fees and materials expenses. Moreover, he had no information on which courses were useful or whether a proprietary school might be worth the extra cost. Even worse, the hundreds of hours he had already spent learning graphics design were almost useless in landing his next job. Employers had no way to measure his skills.

When he found his next job, he was pleased that his benefit package included health insurance. He was less pleased when he found out the coverage would not include payments for continuing therapy on an injury he had experienced two years previously—the insurance did not cover pre-

existing conditions. He was also displeased when he realized that the pen-
sion benefits that he thought he had accumulated at his previous employer
were lost when that job ended.

Although this scenario is fictional, the problems outlined are all too real. For far too many Americans, lifelong learning is impeded by lack of access to funds for college, lack of access of funds to upgrade skills after job loss, and lack of information about which educational programs lead to labor market success. When employees do acquire skills, both they and their future employers suffer because they lack the means to certify their skills. In addition, unemployment spells between jobs are often lengthened by lack of information about job openings, lack of information about available services to help the unemployed, and lack of help in searching for a new job. Finally, every American is at risk for loss of health insurance, lack of coverage for preexisting conditions with new health insurance coverage, and loss of the value of their pension benefits.

Fortunately, each of these problems can be ameliorated. This chapter outlines a set of policies to promote lifelong learning and reduce the costs employees face when they move between jobs.

Better Access to Education After High School

Because our capacity for learning does not end at age eighteen, we must improve access to education after high school. Similarly, our capacity for learning does not end at age twenty-two, so we must improve access to educational opportunities throughout people's careers. Thus, we must create opportunities for education after high school, not just via the traditional path of an immediate college degree, but also through continuing education and training for those who have jobs or are between jobs.

Improving Student Loans

If capital markets functioned perfectly, any student for whom the returns to education were greater than the interest rate would be able to borrow enough to cover tuition and living costs. Thus, low- and high-income students with similar abilities would be expected to enroll in college at similar rates. But in practice, future earnings tend to be far less effective as collateral than are assets such as houses or parents' wealth. As a result, students cannot necessarily borrow enough to cover the costs of education. In practice, college costs matter more than they should: even when costs are low enough to make education a good investment for a low-income student, they may be too high for him or her to stay in school. A variety of evidence suggests that by easing the borrowing constraint, government can in fact substantially increase the amount of education students receive.

For example, lower college tuition leads substantially more students to enroll in college. The net cost of college education appears to have a substantial impact on the likelihood of college enrollment for low-income students. One recent study has found that students from states with low public university tuition levels are more likely to attend postsecondary education than apparently similar students from other states (Kane 1994).

Government aid can also play an important role in driving down the cost of college and thus inducing more students from low-income families to attend. There is a substantial amount of evidence that for low-income students, the availability of grant aid strongly increases the likelihood of participation in further education (McPherson and Shapiro 1991; Jensen 1983; Leslie and Brinkman 1988; Manski and Wise 1983).

The low levels of educational attainment of low-income students (caused both by borrowing constraints and by other risk factors) are costly in terms of lost future productivity. For poor children, rates of school completion and advancement to postsecondary education are much lower than for other children. For example, children who experience poverty between the ages of six and fifteen years are two to three times more likely to drop out of high school than are students who never experience poverty. A recent study commissioned by the Children's Defense Fund, which added up the costs of low educational achievement for the 14.6 million poor children in 1992, estimated that each year that these children spend in poverty costs the economy somewhere between $36 billion and $177 billion in reduced future productivity and employment. (Again, these estimates assume that the productivity benefits of a year of education are as large for poor students as they are for the average student.)

Reformed student loans will reduce the burden of borrowing for college and for continuing education. Under the new Federal Direct Loan Program, individuals can borrow money for college directly from the federal government and can tailor their repayments to suit their financial circumstances. Borrowers will be able to choose from among several repayment plans and to switch plans as their needs change. The standard plan, the one most widely used today, will continue to allow students to repay their loans in fixed monthly payments over ten years. The most innovative plan has income-contingent loan payments; that is, payments depend on the borrower's actual income. This choice of plans makes it easier for graduates to start businesses, work in their communities, or meet other family responsibilities by better matching their loan service to their varying incomes.

In addition to lightening the burden of loan repayment, the Student Loan Reform Act restructures the federal student loan program itself, phasing in direct lending to students over the next few years. Direct lending will significantly reduce the costs of the loan program by eliminating middlemen, thus streamlining the system. The savings are estimated at approximately $6.8 billion over a five-year period.

One crucial aspect of income-contingent student loans is that they reduce the risk for students. This element can be critical for low-income students because their families' experience with debt is more likely to involve either loan sharks or high fear of default (U.S. Council of Economic Advisers 1996, ch. 7).

Income-contingent loan repayment, where the present value of payments is lower for people with low incomes, also provides a way of means testing financial aid based on the student's income (while working), instead of on the parents' income and assets, as is traditionally done. Means-testing based on parents' assets can imply high penalties for parental savings, so it is desirable to means-test based on students earnings as well.

As is often the case, the new system is not without its problems. First, the insurance properties of the income-contingent loan can also weaken incentives. That is, the government effectively taxes graduates' earnings in the form of higher loan repayments. Thus, students face incentives to choose lower-paid careers, and they face lower incentives to earn high salaries at their job. These problems are probably not too severe because, as noted earlier, labor supply is not very responsive to reasonable tax rates. In addition, to the extent the lower-paid careers provide positive externalities, such as working for many nonprofit organizations, the incentives for low-wage career choice can provide benefits for society.

A more important problem is that self-selection among loan applicants can raise the costs of the income-contingent loan program. Consider a system where the repayment schedule is set so that the typical student will repay his or her loan. In this case, students who think they will earn substantially above-average wages will have an incentive to take out a traditional fixed-payment loan. Conversely, students who intend to enter low-income professions will choose the income-contingent loan and make payments that, on average, are below that of the average student. To the extent that low-income professions are working for charities or otherwise helping society, this subsidy is not a problem. Nevertheless, the repayment options must be carefully designed to avoid costing the federal government an unexpectedly large amount.

Facilitating Retraining

Needs for increased training are not well matched with the current complicated system of dozens of government-assisted training programs, each with its own rules, regulations, and restrictions. One sensible proposal of the Clinton administration has been to replace this complex system with a single coherent, choice-based system for adults, in effect creating a GI bill for the current workforce. (See box 6.1 on the original GI Bill.) This proposal will consolidate nearly seventy current training or related programs. Dislocated or low-income workers would be eligible for "skill grants" of up to $2,620 per year for two years, enough to cover tuition, supplies, and fees at a typical public institution. Unlike the current system, in which government agencies often choose what training workers will receive and who will provide it, the new skill grants could be used at any eligible training provider, including community colleges and private technical schools.

The current system of student loans has a problem concerning schools that talk students into taking out loans but provide no education. Often such schools saddle the students with high loan repayments, but the students do not find the classes useful (or, in some fraudulent cases, never attend any classes). The worst schools have default rates of over 50 percent. Any move to an education and training voucher system will worsen some of the incentive problems because fly-by-night schools can offer to pay students (perhaps with services such as "educational" vacations) to turn over their vouchers. Thus, a move to a voucher system would still require some government oversight and quality control. Standards on class completion and on wage or employment improvements may be needed (standardized for the disadvantages students face when entering the program).

Helping Choose a Training Provider

Consumers in the market for adult education face a bewildering array of choices, ranging from junior colleges to universities to private schools that train in everything from computer repair to dental receptionist. This broad array of choices is a great strength of the market but can also be a confusing weakness.

An important element of the proposed new system will be a labor market information system in which users have access to the track records of local education, training, and job placement providers. The system should provide "report cards" on training providers so that students can choose schools with strong records of placement in related fields and of wage

---

Box 6.1. What Worked: The GI Bill

At the end of World War II Congress was concerned that there might not be sufficient jobs for all of the returning servicemen. Thus, they set up the GI Bill to pay for veterans to attend college. Consistent with the principles of vouchers proposed here, students were given the purchasing power to chose their own school—no bureaucracy decided for them. Although some of these students chose programs with little value, on the whole the experience with the GI Bill strongly supports the importance of providing consumers with purchasing power and choices, not command-and-control regulations.

In all, almost 8 million young Americans were given the purchasing power to go to college or other educational institution after World War II. While we do not know how many would not otherwise have attended, we do know that college enrollments shot up by 71 percent between 1939 and 1947. Some of this increase was presumably due to returning soldiers making up for college years they had missed while in the service, but the GI Bill appears to have played an important role in improving the educational attainment of this group.

---

gains. With this information available, the power of the market and of informed consumer choice should work to weed out ineffective programs and reward those that help workers get the skills they need.

Promoting Learning on the Job*

Training on the job or in a work-related setting tends to be especially well tailored to the requirements of the workplace. One study of work-related training, while not fully capturing the vital but hard-to-measure effect of informal on-the-job training, showed that the impact of such training on wages is of similar magnitude to that of more traditional schooling. (As with measures of the returns to education, these measures of the returns to training may be over- or understated if there are other, unobserved differences between those who do and do not receive training.)

Provision of on-the-job training is skewed in favor of those already relatively well educated. Among young college graduates 35 percent received training from their employers between 1986 and 1991, whereas only 19 percent of high school graduates and 19 percent of high school dropouts received any training during that time period.

---

*This section draws on Finegold and Levine (1997).

Formal on-the-job training is considerably less common in the United States than in other industrialized nations. Large Japanese companies train their workers far more than do their U.S. counterparts, partly because employees there are much less likely to switch employers. In Germany, high levels of training take place in formal apprenticeship systems that are supported by the government as well as by powerful industry and union federations (see box 5.4).

Skill Standards

Skill standards can play an important role in increasing the supply of highly skilled workers and smoothing their transitions between jobs. The United States is unique among its major competitors in lacking formal mechanisms for national certification of most worker skills. This diminishes the portability of training and reduces the incentives for employees to invest in increasing their skills.

The National Skill Standards Act creates a framework for voluntary development of workforce skills standards in broad clusters of occupations. The law promotes standards that include both the skills needed in the high-performance workplace (such as problem solving and teamwork) and industry-specific skills. Many industry groups are already at work designing their standards for occupations in their industries. A blue-ribbon National Skill Standards Board is being established to stimulate the development and adoption of the new voluntary skill standards.

Skill standards can also help alleviate imperfections in the market for training. Often training provided by one employer is useful to another. Thus, when trained workers change employers, the benefits to the first employer of its investments in training may be captured by the second. This reduces employers' incentives to train. Skill certificates developed in cooperation with industry leaders should reduce this market imperfection, since employees would be more willing to pay for training if it leads to a certificate that another company recognizes and will pay a premium for. These payments to employers for training may take the disguised form of lower wages during the training period, just as they do for traditional union apprentices or medical residents. Because of this implicit or explicit payment, employers would take less risk when they provide training.

Some economic theory predicts that making general training more visible to the market will increase turnover. That is, when employees can show their next employer how skilled they are, the cost of moving to a new job declines. In fact, turnover is *lower* at many companies that pay for publicly certified training. The reason for the divergence of theory and evidence is unclear, although it may be that company-sponsored education increases worker loyalty, or there may be a selection effect, whereby hard-working employees are both less likely to quit and more likely to take advantage of company-sponsored education.

In the computer industry, the saying is, "Standards are wonderful, there are always so many to choose from." Certifying what our students and workforce have learned is becoming as complicated as standards in the computer industry. Currently the electronics and retail industries (among others) and a number of states are each creating separate standards that measure skills in problem solving and working in groups—the key skills employers say they need. Thus, someone who has good skills at solving problems in one industry might receive no credit for these skills when he or she moves to another industry. Moreover, as noted in the previous chapter, the national skill standards for K–12 education differ by each state. This chaos does not permit school-based certifications to integrate with industry-based skill certifications.

Our skill standards should be created from a common set of building blocks that measure these key skills. Standards for measuring how well students work together in groups and solve problems have the additional benefit of helping schools. Clear standards in these areas would help schools understand what they need to do in their move away from "chalk and talk" toward making education both more interesting and more relevant.

Some opponents of skill standards resent federal intrusion into issues of curriculum design that have traditionally been the domain of state governments and local school boards. To some extent this position is difficult to defend because the nation already has de facto skill standards for the college bound, the SAT and related college entrance exams. Current proposals involve enhancing the SAT with tests that measure more complex and relevant skills than a multiple-choice exam can cover. More important, well-designed skill standards should permit increased levels of local flexibility in how to teach, and (to some extent) in what to teach. The standards would merely permit parents to see how these schools succeed in their goals compared to similar schools.

Building a Reemployment System

As noted earlier, each year more than 2 million U.S. workers permanently lose their jobs through no fault of their own, when plants close or there are mass layoffs. In addition to these involuntary job losses, voluntary job changes are common. In total, most American workers will work at more than seven jobs during their career. Millions of Americans who lose their jobs also lose valuable pension benefits. Even worse, in many cases they lose health insurance, and when they next receive health insurance the new policy may not cover existing conditions. Our economy must make job changes as painless as possible and promote effective job matches that enhance worker satisfaction and productivity.

Just as education policies must focus on smoothing the transition from school to work, labor policies should focus on smoothing the transition from work to work and on increasing skills to avoid job loss. Workers often find the path from one job to the next beset with hurdles. Many do not know what other jobs are available, and having found out, discover they lack the skills to fit into any of them. And some who clear both those obstacles find that their new jobs do not work out because, for one reason or another, employee and employer do not fit together well. These bad matches can increase turnover and reduce satisfaction and productivity.

One-Stop Career Centers

To address these problems, the nations's unemployment system is undertaking a transition of its own—to a reemployment system. A key element of the new system is one-stop career centers for all workers. The federal Department of Labor is working with the states to create a nationwide network of local centers, offering job counseling and allowing workers to apply for jobless benefits and sign up for training programs all in one place. The goal is for a single site to provide unemployed people with all the information about available services, regardless of who funds the services, and regardless of whether the service is inccme support, job search assistance, or training funds. The one-stop centers will also provide help in searching for a new job.

An important element of the reemployment system is an easily accessible store of labor market information. The one-stop centers will contain information on training providers such as junior colleges and proprietary schools, as described above. The centers will also provide information on job openings; on local employment trends, including the wages and skill requirements of occupations in greatest demand locally; and on relevant federal, state, and local programs.

The Extended Unemployment Compensation Act, passed in 1993, requires that all states establish and utilize a system for profiling all new unemployment insurance claimants in order to identify, and refer to job search assistance, those who are likely to exhaust their regular unemployment benefits and are at risk of experiencing long-term unemployment.

Unemployment insurance can also be improved by removing the incentives some companies now face to lay off employees. As noted earlier, in most states employers that repeatedly lay off workers pay less in unemployment insurance than their employees receive; the difference is paid by employers that do not lay off employees. A more sensible system would remove the subsidy by raising the unemployment insurance rates of companies that repeatedly lay off workers. (The system should retain some insurance so that employers that hit unexpected bad times do not see their unemployment insurance rates skyrocket.)

As one-stop centers, improved training and assistance between jobs, and improved labor market information come together to create a national reemployment system, movement between jobs should become smoother, and the economy should be able to operate at a lower rate of unemployment without the risk of pushing up inflation.

A Labor Market Information System

A key element in improving our labor market policies is improving out labor market information system. Much progress has been made in permitting individuals to use government-provided computer resources such as computerized want-ads and résumé banks voluntarily to circulate data about themselves. The Department of Labor has built a national job bank on the Internet that can be searched by region, occupation, and other attributes of the job (box 6.2).

Conversely, the federal government is creating America's Talent Bank to collect job-seekers' résumés and to help employers identify possible candidates. (In fall 1997 the site was just opening up [http://atb.mesc.state.mi.us].)

Importantly, the labor market information system will receive real-time information on hiring patterns. Ideally, each new hire should be entered into the system a single time, with this information then forwarded to the IRS (that is, W-2 forms), the Social Security Administration, the child-support parent-locator system, the system for collecting both delinquent and income-contingent student loans (see chapter 6), and the states' unemployment insurance systems. The labor market experience of the graduates of education, training, and employment service providers should also be summarized into reports for their potential clients.

As the labor market information system expands to become a real-time census based on data from employers, the need for some labor market surveys diminishes. This can lower response burden. In addition, the government's ability to understand the present state of the economy and to forecast the near future should be enhanced.

A key element to enjoying these benefits from modern information technology is an integrated approach to federal data collection. The key must be

Box 6.2. **What Works: America's Job Bank**

The federal government and states collaborate to run the nation's Employment Service. The Employment Service's goal is to help people find an appropriate new job, and to help employers find an appropriate new employee.

In the recent decades, the Employment Service has helped fill an ever-shrinking proportion of jobs. While in the early 1960s roughly 20 percent of jobs were filled with referrals from the Employment Service, by the late 1980s that proportion had declined to under 5 percent (Bishop 1993, pp. 380–382). Moreover, the quality of jobs, as measured by pay and occupational status, has also declined over time.

The decline of the Employment Service has many causes, but it is unfortunate. Nations with more effective labor exchanges and job search assistance appear to enjoy lower average rates of unemployment, largely by helping people find new jobs more rapidly. Moreover, increased information on both job openings and the qualifications of job applicants has the possibility of improving the matches between new workers and employers. Improved matching can reduce unemployment (as fewer people change jobs due to a poor match), raise productivity, and increase earnings.

The Department of Labor is responding with an Internet-based national job search service, America's Job Bank (found on the Internet at http://www.ajb.dni.us/). Providing a national job search service is an appropriate role for government, in part because of the government's interest in reducing unemployment. Moreover, a job bank exhibits increasing returns to scale. That is, employees want to post their résumés once and have them easily found by all potential employers. Conversely, employers want to post their job openings once and have them easily found by all potential employees. Finally, the programming costs are identical regardless of the number of cities or regions covered.

In its current (1997) version, applicants can search a nationwide pool of job openings. In August 1997, the job bank had over 1.1 million job listings. For some employers, applicants can apply for the jobs online. Future versions will permit employers to search a nationwide pool of résumés.

Ideally (although this is not currently planned), employees should be able to access their high school and college transcripts as well as records of any skill certifications they might hold. Employees should then be able either to post these records to the Internet or to forward certified copies of these records to employers they select.

to create a system that requires the private sector to enter data only once but permits the government to use the data multiple times. At the same time, the system must increase the privacy protections in current law and practice. Some of the needed changes are outlined in the Appendix to this chapter, "Improving the Federal Statistical System."

Protecting Benefits When Jobs End

In most industrialized nations, pensions and health insurance are provided by the national government. In contrast, the United States has a decentralized system that typically links these benefits to employment. The U.S. system maximizes flexibility to adjust to individual company or workforce needs, and (with distortions noted below) is more likely to bring market forces to bear to induce the benefits to be provided in a cost effective fashion. The downside is that these essential benefits are often lost when jobs end. This section outlines means to enhance coverage and improve the cost effectiveness of these benefits.

Incremental Improvements to Health Insurance

The health insurance system in the United States has two enormous problems: too much and too little.

The system provides too much health insurance; people with health insurance often overspend on medical care because they pay little or none of the costs. This incentive for overspending, in turn, has spawned ever-more-expensive technologies for marginal improvements in health care. Conversely, the system has provided weak incentives to provide cost-effective preventive and other treatments, and weak incentives to research cost-effective prevention and care (Weisbrod 1991).

Moreover, the employer-provided health insurance in tax deductible. The tax deductibility of health insurance provides incentives for people to over-insure themselves, buying more complete insurance than they would in a free market. The tax deduction is open-ended, implying a growing subsidy from the government regardless of how much insurance a person buys. The current tax subsidy costs the federal government almost $100 billion per year (Pauly and Goodman 1995). Both of these forces raise the demand for medical care and increase costs. The tax deduction is also regressive, worth more to high earners than to low earners, and worth nothing at all to the third or so of all Americans who earn too little to pay income taxes.

The health-care system provides too little insurance because about one in seven Americans (over 40 million) are without insurance in any given month. The proportion rises to one in four who are uninsured at some point over the course of a thirty-two-month period (*Statistical Abstract of the United States* 1995, table 171). This lack of insurance implies that people sometimes go without cost-effective treatments and preventive measures. In addition, it means that families' standards of living are much more variable than they would be with a well-working insurance market.

The lack of insurance has many sources. To some extent, the forces described above that raise costs induce some people who expect to have low health-care costs not to insure themselves. (They often know that if they become truly ill, they will be receive care paid for by government or charity.) The exit of these people with above-average health from the insurance pool raises the costs for all those with insurance—potentially leading other people who expect to be healthy to go uninsured.

Insurers typically do not cover preexisting conditions. Thus, anyone who has a chronic condition and has lost insurance (perhaps as the result of changing jobs) can never receive full insurance. Because ill people often must stop working, this situation deprives those most in need of care of their insurance.

For historical reasons, most health insurance is provided through employers. Employer-provided health insurance is somewhat surprising because most Americans buy most of their goods and services directly. Only a small percentage of employees receive meals or housing from their employers, but most with health insurance receive it from their employers. Employer-provided health insurance is also unusual in a global sense because almost all other industrialized nations provide health insurance through the government.

The problem with employer-provided health insurance is that when people lose their job, they often lose their health insurance. In recent years, approximately one-fourth of those displaced from their jobs had not regained health insurance (Mishel et al. 1997). Insurance companies are leery of selling individual policies because they reason that people going out of their way to buy health insurance probably expect above-average health-care costs. (This problem is known as *adverse selection.*) Thus, individual insurance policies cost much more than adding a person to an employer's plan. Employer-provided insurance has an additional problem even when people change to a new job that provides insurance—the new insurance policy usually will not cover preexisting conditions.

A Partial Solution

Thus, the resulting system provides inefficiently high health-care expenses for the insured, but does not insure enough Americans. The causes, in turn, can be traced in large part to the lack of coverage of preexisting conditions and the tax deductibility of employer-provided health care.

A simple alternative can reduce the overinsurance of some Americans, thus reducing some of the upward pressure on health-care costs while greatly expanding health-care coverage. This alternative replaces the tax deduction on health insurance with a refundable tax credit or voucher for purchasing health insurance. (The vouchers proposed here lead to almost exactly the same incentives and costs as a refundable tax credit for health insurance, as proposed by David Kendall and Mark Pauly [1996]. Preference for one scheme or the other, or for a combination of the two, depends on which is less expensive to administer.)

To keep the proposal cost neutral, the value of the health insurance voucher would be set equal to the cost of the current health insurance deduction per capita, increased by the expected take-up rate. (A more politically palatable version for the current recipients of the tax deduction would set the value of the voucher equal to the typical value of the health deduction today. In that case, the subsidy for newly insured people would raise costs while expanding care.)

Because the insurance voucher is for a fixed sum, it removes the open-ended subsidy on health insurance that leads some Americans to overinsure themselves. Unlike the tax deduction, the voucher is progressive. Moreover, the vouchers, by inducing more of the relatively healthy to buy insurance, can reduce average cost and induce others to buy insurance.

Presumably, most employees whose employer currently provides health care would turn over their health insurance vouchers to their employers. This would reduce transaction costs and maintain continuity with the existing system. Employers, in turn, would report the value of health benefits as part of employees' taxable income.

Certain medical treatments have a higher social benefit than they do private benefit. One important example is vaccinations, where parents want all the *other* children in their child's school to be vaccinated. A second involves catastrophic health conditions, where most people will exhaust their private resources and require public assistance. Thus, the voucher should require that the policy cover catastrophic conditions and certain cost-effective preventive treatments, particularly vaccinations.

Families would receive more insurance vouchers for each child, making this a family-friendly policy similar to refundable child tax credits. Importantly, these child tax credits would be available only for families providing the socially valuable service of providing health insurance for their children.

Even with a voucher, some families will find it difficult to purchase high-quality insurance. Thus, the government should permit people to use their vouchers (supplemented with their own incomes) to buy into three existing federal health care plans: Medicaid, Medicare, or the federal employees' health-care plans.

Federal employees are currently given a choice of private health-care plans including health maintenance organizations (HMOs) and preferred provider organizations (PPOs) in each region. (PPOs are insurance plans in which the deductible and copayment are lower when subscribers use medical service providers who are part of the preferred provider network.) Employees pay more for high-cost plans, providing incentives for plans to reduce costs while maintaining quality of services.

Costs of the buy-in should be set so that Medicaid, Medicare, and federal government insurance plans do not lose money. At the same time, opening up these plans to citizens' buy-in increases consumers' choice—one of the goal of almost all the government reforms proposed here. Furthermore, opening up these choices ensures Americans will never lose their health insurance as a result of to job changes or even taking a job that might make a family or disabled person ineligible for Medicaid or Medicare. As a final advantage, guaranteed health insurance for children combined with a phase-out of the Medicaid subsidy and a Medicaid buy-in can greatly increase incentives for work while protecting children.

Preexisting Conditions

To reduce the problem of losing insurance after bad events, the federal government should forbid denial of insurance benefits for preexisting conditions for people moving between plans. The essence of insurance is that it covers bad events. The denial of benefits when people lose their job and move to a new insurance plan exactly contradicts the goal of a socially desirable health insurance system.

A move in this direction was made by the 1996 Kennedy-Kassenbaum insurance reform bill, which forbids insurers from denying coverage for people who had been insured within the previous twelve months under another plan. Unfortunately, this bill permits insurers to raise rates based on diagnosis. Under this system, the expected increase in rates should effectively deny seriously ill people the benefits of insurance.

Problems

As is usual with all voucher plans, ensuring that consumers make informed choices is difficult. It is appropriate for the federal government to work with large employers and with federations of small employers (who purchase health insurance) and health insurers to create standard "report cards" of the quality of care available from different insurers and health-care suppliers. (Enthoven and Singer [1996] describe in more detail the institutions to create this coordination.)

Consumers have particular difficulties when plans differ along a myriad of relatively minor dimensions. Thus, the federal government (in partnership with employers and health insurers) should define a modest number of standard insurance plans and encourage insurers to compete on price and quality of care.

Eliminating restrictions on coverage of preexisting conditions will raise insurance costs as more sick people receive treatment. At the same time, much of this increase in costs will be matched with lower spending by Medicaid, states, and charities and lower spending by insurance companies as hospitals quit shifting costs from insured to uninsured patients. Counteracting this force, as noted earlier, insurance costs will decline as the vouchers induce more relatively healthy people to buy insurance. (It is important that net insurance costs not increase because each increase induces more fairly healthy people to avoid insurance. This effect worsens the average health of those with insurance and can raise prices further [Akerlof 1970].)

Longer-Term Goals

The health-care vouchers proposed here can become the first step in creating true national health insurance (Pauly et al. 1992). The value of the vouchers can be increased over time for low-income families. This increase would be partly paid for by lower Medicaid costs, and perhaps also by phasing out the tax credit or voucher for high-income families. When the voucher plus family income become large enough for all families to afford health insurance, it then becomes sensible to mandate individuals to be covered by health insurance. (Most employed individuals would presumably remain covered by their employers.)

Such a mandate, coupled with appropriate subsidies, would achieve the goal of universal health coverage. Importantly, it would do so in a system where competition would continue to put downward pressure on health-care costs. Universal coverage would eliminate the free-rider problem, where people who expect to be healthy know that taxpayers and the insured will cover their medical needs in case of a costly emergency.

Reform of the Veterans Administration

Millions of Americans receive additional health-care subsidies from the federal government's Veterans Administration (VA) because they are veterans.

Unfortunately, these benefits are usually available only at VA hospitals. Thus, even people with severe disabilities must find a way to a VA hospital, even if closer facilities are much more convenient. It makes no sense that a veteran must make his or her way to a potentially distant hospital for eyeglasses when a commercial store can make them as well for less cost a few blocks from home.

Veterans' benefits should also be replaced with health-care vouchers that incorporate the value of services the government typically provides to veterans with that medical condition. As always, vouchers provide consumers with meaningful choices, choices often denied when only one portion of the government is permitted to provide services. These vouchers should continue to be accepted by VA hospitals so that veterans would not lose options they currently have. (As a complementary policy, VA hospitals should be permitted to accept nonveteran patients, if space permits.) VA vouchers should be particularly cost effective because the VA has detailed knowledge of the medical condition of its patients. Thus, the value of the voucher should be similar to the expected cost of each diagnosis under VA care.

Portable and Simplified Pensions

Good pensions are simple to administer, maintain their value when workers move between jobs, and provide good insurance against events such as unanticipated inflation. Unfortunately, pensions in the United States rarely achieve even two of these three goals. Improving coverage by pensions that achieve these goals is important because they provide a key source of retirement earnings. The growing number of retirees when the baby boomers hit their late sixties implies that the future value of Social Security benefits is likely to decline in real terms. This likely decline increases the importance of private pensions.

Pensions in the United States come in two basic flavors: defined-benefit plans and defined-contribution plans. In defined-benefit plans, benefits are typically a function of the employee's years of service with an employer and of his or her highest few years of earnings while working there. These plans implicitly index the pension for inflation during the employee's work life (assuming that wage growth roughly keeps up with inflation). Moreover, the employer bears the risk that the invested pension funds will not perform well. Thus, defined-benefit pensions provide important insurance, which is very valuable to the workforce.

Defined-benefit plans have several drawbacks. First, they are often not easily portable, reducing workers' pension wealth when a worker quits after job loss. During the first five or so years on the job, workers are not fully vested, implying that they will lose all or some of their pension if they change employers. Even after the pension is vested, because benefits often increase with years of service and (in real terms) decrease with the time between working and retiring, the real value of the pension often depreciates enormously for jobs that ended some years ago.

In addition, defined-benefit plans move the risk of fluctuations in the value of the pension portfolio on to the employer. The employer, in turn, must invest funds to pay for future benefits. If these invested funds offer low returns (due to poor investments or a weak stock market), the employer must increase its contributions. If the employer cannot pay, the pension fund can go bankrupt. Most pension funds are insured by the federal government, but bankruptcies add headaches to retirees and losses to taxpayers.

Because of these drawbacks, an increasing fraction of U.S. pensions are defined-contribution plans (Mishel et al. 1997, 159). Defined-contribution plans typically resemble tax-favored savings plans, where employers contribute to a pension account (sometimes supplemented by employee contributions). Retirees can often move their pension contributions between several investment funds.

Defined-contribution funds are portable, but move part of the burden of administering the investments on to the workers. Moreover, these pensions do not insure workers against unexpected inflation or against low or negative real returns on investments, both serious risks. Thus, employees cannot be sure of the future purchasing power of their pension savings.

Fortunately, the government recently began issuing bonds with interest payments tied to the rate of inflation. This important innovation can greatly simplify the life of individuals planning for retirement. People can buy these bonds at age thirty, and know that in forty years their purchasing power will have increased steadily. Such bonds greatly reduce the care that people must put into the pension planning. The combination of defined-contribution pension plans and inflation-indexed bonds provides both the portability and insurance that a pension plan should deliver.

Complementing this public-sector innovation, a private-sector innovation greatly reduces the transaction costs of holding a diversified stock market portfolio. Specifically, several funds now offer diversified indexed stock funds for the United States; several indexed funds also exist for foreign markets. These funds hold a broad array of stocks and do not trade them actively. Holding an index fund makes sense because actively traded accounts must arithmetically achieve the average return. An indexed fund also achieves the average market return, but does so with minimal transaction costs. The indexed fund also has lower risk than a portfolio that holds only a portion of the market.

Finance theory suggests that a diversified and indexed portfolio is ideal for the bulk of most people's retirement savings. At the same time, most retirement savings are not held in index funds. Apparently, many potential investors are not aware of the wisdom of holding a diversified and indexed portfolio. This lack of awareness partly reflects imperfect information, where investors are given biased information by brokers, investment advisers, and others who profit from sales. The problem in part also arises because investment managers mismanage funds to increase their incomes. Psychological biases that lead people to believe they are above-average investors may also play a role. (How many people believe they are below-average drivers?)

Regardless of the cause, the federal government has a role in providing education concerning sensible investment strategies for retirement accounts. Such an information campaign should stress the lower risk and higher expected return of well-designed indexed portfolios.

Downsides of Decreased Mobility Costs

The policies proposed in this chapter can greatly reduce the suffering and inefficiency associated with the loss of one's job. Although job loss is an increasingly large concern among Americans, most Americans have always faced the threat (and often the reality) of the loss of their job due to circumstances beyond their control.

Nevertheless, reducing the costs that workers face after quitting or being laid off has some downside. When employees face a lower cost of job loss, employers will sometimes find it difficult to motivate the employees and will sometimes be even less willing to invest in the workers' skills than they already are. (Empirically, employers frequently do pay for general skills, yet workers who acquire these skills but do not receive a raise do not appear more likely to quit [Krueger and Rouse 1996]. The reasons for the empirical failures are not well understood, but may be because the process of acquiring general skills self-selects for the motivated and intelligent workers.) Thus, any move to reduce mobility costs should also be sure to increase incentives for training, as these proposals do.

Conclusion

The stylized model of the large Japanese labor market emphasizes that many men enjoy lifetime employment. A single company trains workers, provides their health benefits, and provides their retirement benefits. The employer's central personnel office gathers information on the workers' skills and the company's job openings and shifts employees from job to job within the enterprise.

In the United States, almost all workers are employed at more than one company during their career, frequently more than ten employers. Nevertheless, many institutions in our economy are designed as if lifetime employment were the rule.

No government program can stop job loss from being a traumatic event. At the same time, numerous government programs and incentives for private programs can reduce the costs and frequency of layoffs while increasing the number of transitions directly from an old job to a new one.

To promote lifelong learning, this chapter proposes extending policies to provide flexible loans for college. In addition, citizens could better use flexible vouchers or scholarships for continuing education to upgrade skills after job loss, rather than access to the unwieldy complex of training programs that currently exist. Finally, consumers need an information system that tells them which educational programs lead to labor market success.

When employees acquire skills, both they and their future employers would profit from a means to certify these skills. These certifications must emphasize the generally useful skills such as problem solving and teamwork, and must be built of the same component modules we see in schools. To shorten spells of unemployment, citizens need information about job openings, information about available services to help the unemployed, and help in searching for a new job. Conversely, the system must provide employers with the information they need on applicants and on their skills.

Finally, in an economy where lifetime employment is rare, Americans need portable health insurance that covers preexisting conditions, and portable pensions. Health-care coverage could be further expanded if the current open-ended and regressive deduction for health insurance were converted into a progressive tax credit or voucher.

APPENDIX

Improving the Federal Statistical System*

The federal government collects statistics because a democracy depends on the flow of unbiased, timely information about the state of its economy and social institutions. The statistical programs of the federal government

---

*This section draws on collaboration with Paul Bugg, Martin Baily, and Katherine Wallman. These colleagues bear no responsibility for the opinions expressed here.

should be designed to inform the electorate and to provide accurate, reliable, and timely information for private and public decision makers. Statistical programs should improve their relevance, efficiency, and quality while protecting the integrity of statistical information products, respecting pledges of confidentiality, and minimizing the reporting burden on the public.

The U.S. statistical system is among the finest in the world. Within strict resource constraints, statistical agencies perform a wide range of tasks with professionalism, respect for respondent confidentiality, and a consistent emphasis on providing accurate and unbiased information.

At the same time, the statistical system must react to changes in basic economic and societal structures. The postwar decades have witnessed dramatic shifts in the pace and organization of these structures, including *economic shifts* from manufacturing and agriculture to services and from domestic to international markets; *institutional shifts* reducing reliance on regulatory information and increasing reliance on technology; and *demographic shifts* toward two-earner families, increased life expectancy, and less traditional attitudes about marriage and childbearing. Unfortunately, the current federal statistical system, intended to monitor midcentury America, has not kept pace with these structural changes.

Thus, many federal statistical programs, designed to provide data for a bygone era, no longer satisfy the demands of today's public and private decision makers. This diminution of relevant data has led successive presidential administrations to assess deficiencies in the system, to define conceptual and methodological changes that are needed, and to request increased support for improving statistical programs.

Issues

Federal statistical agencies were established largely to meet the needs of policymakers. It would be virtually impossible for the executive branch or Congress to make good economic, social, or environmental policies without accurate and impartial data. The range of consequences from policy errors are orders of magnitude greater than the costs of a strong statistical infrastructure.

Federal data also convey substantial benefits to industry and the general public. With accurate and timely data, markets operate more efficiently. For instance, companies need supply and price data to plan production efficiently. In addition, the public is educated by federal data, often through the work of academics and journalists. Finally, the public will only believe public decisions are well reasoned and fair if they perceive that the data used for public decision making are accurate and unbiased.

Although private vendors supply data for many needs, government has unique capabilities to establish comprehensive data collections and maintain the confidentiality such data require. A federal statistical system is also better attuned to providing the data federal decision makers require. Private vendors are themselves often dependent on federal data because such vendors more often repackage than generate data. States are often important partners in collecting data, but the need for national data precludes a completely decentralized statistical system.

In a rapidly changing world, the federal statistical system must adjust to new conditions. Statistical measures produced by federal agencies have been increasingly criticized both within and outside the government for their lack of relevance, accuracy, and timeliness. Some of the criticisms have been offered by the agencies that produce the statistics, whose experts know best the limitations of the current programs. Others have been levied by policymakers within the government whose interests may be sparked more by the impact of these data on government expenditures and the national economy. A number of resource, organizational, and legislative constraints have kept the federal statistical system from keeping pace with rapid structural changes in the domestic and global economies.

Statistical Confidentiality Protection Is Inconsistent

Statistical agencies need the cooperation of respondents to produce complete, accurate, and timely data. Response to privately sponsored surveys is at an all time low. Government surveys still enjoy a substantial advantage over private research, but this willingness to cooperate depends to a large extent on the public perception that information provided for government statistics will not be used to the detriment of respondents.

At the same time, the public is becoming more sophisticated and sensitive to the potential uses of statistical information for regulation and taxation. There is widespread suspicion that information provided to the government for statistical purposes will be shared with regulatory or tax authorities. For example, in at least one case, a federal law enforcement agency not responsible for the data collection attempted to overturn existing disclosure rules long after information was provided by respondents. To renege on a policy that protects respondents' legitimate interests would undermine one of the cornerstones on which public confidence in the federal statistical system is built. The complexities of the Freedom of Information Act and various confidentiality statutes have created substantial uncertainties about the meaning of confidentiality pledges. All statistical agencies need to be able credibly to commit that their data will never be disclosed for nonstatistical purposes.

Respondent Burden Is Too High

The current fragmented nature of our statistical system ensures that some respondents are asked for the same information more than once. Because they are housed in different agencies and laws limit sharing data, both the Census Bureau and the Bureau of Labor Statistics (BLS) must spend millions of dollars each year compiling lists of all the businesses in the United States. When other agencies would like to perform a survey, they must then spend their scarce funds to purchase similar mailing lists from private-sector companies. Each agency must separately survey the universe of employers to determine which employers own which establishments.

Some Statistics Lack Relevance and Accuracy

For many years, the inability of the nation's statistical system to keep up with changes in our economy and society has been a matter of grave concern to the business, academic, and policy communities. To remain competitive in the dynamic global economy, the United States needs to accelerate and facilitate the statistical agencies' efforts to address the shortcomings of federal statistics. These changes must focus on rapidly changing areas of the economy and society and must take into account how globalization, technological change, and the shift out of manufacturing affect our nation.

For example, the measurement of output and prices, and therefore productivity, in the rapidly growing service sector is seriously flawed. Improvement will require basic research to develop accurate measures of output for the service-sector. Current measures of construction and service-sector activity provide inadequate coverage and detail. Our basic classification system for domestic economic activity is outmoded and lacking in detail. These shortcomings extend to our corporate financial data as well.

In addition, accuracy can be a problem when statistical agencies are ordered to change methods or results to meet politician's goals. In 1993, for example, the Bureau of Labor Statistics was under great congressional pressure to reduce the measured inflation in the Consumer Price Index (CPI) as politically palatable means to cut Social Security payments. Although (as the BLS has long explained) the CPI has several measurement problems, it is doubtful that permitting politicians to dictate the solution will improve accuracy, relevance, or credibility.

Federal Data Are Often Difficult to Access

Our decentralized statistical system has no single "place" where a user can go for information. For example, someone interested in the health of secondary school students and its effect on their suitability for employment would have to make separate inquires to the National Center for Health Statistics, the National Center for Education Statistics, and the Bureau of Labor Statistics. In addition, each agency has different dissemination policies, computer systems, and formats for the release of information. The extent to which online information is provided—and the standards for gaining access to these online systems—also vary across agencies.

Users want a single interface to government statistics. They no more care which agency produced a statistic than the typical car buyer cares which engine plant produced their car engine. (That is, a few users find information concerning the source useful, but not many.)

Statistical Agencies Face Barriers to Coordination

The problems with inconsistent confidentiality protections, too-high respondent burden, inaccurate or conceptually outdated statistics, and difficult access all stem in part from barriers statistical agencies face when they try to coordinate. By examining each program in isolation, without looking at how the system as a whole is serving its customers, the government has not undertaken research or implemented changes to adapt the system to changes in the nation. This failure greatly limits the statistical system's ability to produce high-quality data to inform public and private decisions. The statistical system as a whole has no means to redirect resources between major sectors of the economy or society, between agencies, or to priorities.

Furthermore, the laws protecting confidentiality have created barriers to effective working relationships between agencies. For example, the Bureau of Labor Statistics pays most of the cost for the Census Bureau to collect the Current Population Survey; nevertheless, the BLS never has full access to the actual data collected by Census. This has inhibited both analysis and resolution of errors.

In several cases, promising joint projects between major statistical agencies that would have made efficient use of unique expertise available in each agency have foundered because there was no legal way to share the data for statistical purposes. In a few instances, agencies have made the extraordinary efforts needed to perform limited data exchange under existing law. The large payoffs from these efforts indicate the importance of facilitating such data sharing. For example, limited comparisons that have been undertaken have shown large gaps in our ability to classify and report economic activity properly. Based on these experiences, it is likely that even modest exchanges of information will unearth and eliminate substantial errors in existing data series, permit substantial consolidation of overlapping programs (with comparable reductions in cost), and permit substantial reductions of burden imposed on the public.

For example, the Consumer Price Index (CPI) is measured within the BLS, while the inflation adjustment for gross domestic product (GDP) is made within the Bureau of Economic Analysis. Each agency has research programs to improve the separation of inflation and quality adjustments for specific sectors. Unfortunately, they do not jointly choose which sectors each should cover to maximize the value of their research.

Collection by federal agencies of related data bases would be far more useful if they were integrated. For example, data on productivity of enterprises are not matched with data on pensions, profit sharing, or pay systems. The lack of matching implies we cannot evaluate the effects of these practices on organizational performance.

As is usual in our federal system, states have a key role in collecting a significant portion of the data the federal statistical agencies use. Unfortunately, as we create the "report cards" for training providers, they are being calculated at the state level. Thus, the earnings and employment of any graduate who leaves the state will not be recorded. Given how frequently Americans move across state lines, such attrition from the sample can greatly distort our understanding of which schools and training programs succeed. The distortion is serious because those who receive distant job offers, or go on to college, or who do poorly and must move back in with their families may be the most likely to move. Thus, those remaining are not necessarily representative of all graduates.

Establish a "Virtual" Federal Statistics Agency

One organizational option that addresses the issues outlined above is to establish a "virtual" federal statistics agency. This would establish coordination mechanisms among the current agencies in the areas of long-range plans, budget priorities, data collection, data sharing, dissemination, and research. This plan builds on agencies' current efforts to increase coordination and improve data quality and is intended to facilitate their many ongoing efforts. This approach can improve quality, access, and public confidence in data security while minimizing cost and respondent burden. Creating a virtual agency, as opposed to consolidating into a single agency, also has the advantage of maintaining each agency's links to a host department. These close links will preserve responsiveness to policy needs. This set of improvements would achieve most of the advantages of consolidating statistical agencies while incurring few of the disadvantages and costs.

This approach requires effective coordinating structure and data-sharing legislation that permits integration. Coordinating structures, in turn, include a mission statement, an Interagency Council on Statistical Policy, and cross-cutting project teams.

A *mission statement* can give focus to the new virtual agency. A proposed draft mission statement would include:

- Create a statistical system that ensures confidentiality of statistical data.
- Create a statistical system that minimizes respondent burden.
- Create a statistical system that provides high-quality statistics responsive to the needs of policymakers and the private sector.
- Create a statistical system that is easy to use for all users in both the public and private sectors.
- Create a cost-effective statistical system with high levels of coordination and with no unnecessary duplication.

The Interagency Council on Statistical Policy

The central focus of the virtual agency would be the Interagency Council on Statistical Policy, as called for in the Paperwork Reduction Act of 1995. The council should direct the virtual agency. It should meet regularly and be responsible for preparing the background materials for the spring and fall reviews used to set governmentwide priorities.

The council should be large enough to represent the universe of government statistics, but small enough to function effectively as a management committee. Permanent members should include the heads of the larger statistical agencies, agencies with cross-sector responsibilities (i.e., the Bureau of Economic Analysis, which constructs the national income statistics), and the chief statistician from the Office of Management and Budget (OMB). Smaller agencies would serve on a rotating basis.

The council's staff should be professionally neutral with an institutional memory that will give continuity to the virtual agency. These staff characteristics will protect the integrity of the statistical system while helping the Interagency Council on Statistical Policy to take a long-term view of improvements in the statistical system. Some staff should be drawn from the statistical agencies on a rotating basis. Other career employees based in OMB would also serve on the staff to assure continuity and preserve institutional memory.

Cross-cutting working groups will be key elements in achieving many cross-cutting projects. Such teams will be chartered by the council and will contain members with the technical skills relevant to each topic. Membership will be drawn from the various agencies for short- and long-term projects that benefit multiple agencies.

Once these structures are in place, the virtual agency will need to be able to direct resources to its priority projects. To facilitate cross-agency prioritization, the OMB will perform budget cross-agency reviews. In preparing for the reviews, the Interagency Council on Statistical Policy should seek to formulate priorities for statistical activities for the government as a whole. This might involve identifying the best potential and worst current projects, and shifting resources appropriately, and identifying overlap in topics, surveys, or data with ways to consolidate and associated benefits and costs.

In addition, the Interagency Council on Statistical Policy will propose a list of projects that provide benefits for the statistical system as a whole. Agencies will then make proposals to complete these projects. Winning agencies will then be reimbursed by all agencies because all agencies will benefit from the results. Such reimbursements are common within the statistical system today, but the projects are chosen by each agency, not by an Interagency Council on Statistical Policy.

Statistical Data-Sharing Legislation

Confidentiality statutes that permit data to be seen only by employees of a single agency aid in maintaining confidentiality (e.g., Title 13 for the Bureau of the Census and Title 15 for the Bureau of Economic Analysis). At the same time, they often present a barrier to effective working relationships among statistical agencies, inhibit successful joint projects, lead to duplication of effort, and lead to inconsistencies among related data sets.

Virtually all statistical agencies agree that improvements in the ability of statistical agencies to share data for statistical purposes are needed. Such sharing should take place through "statistical centers." Statistical centers could—under conditions that would still guarantee confidentiality—share data for any statistical purpose.

Integrating the Statistical System

The virtual agency must move from being a number of discrete statistical organizations to an efficient coordinated statistical *system.*

Thus, it must create common definitions and common tools for data collection such as computer-assisted interview technology. It should improve coordination and search for duplication. Possible dimensions include consolidating lists of businesses (assuming the passage of data-sharing law) and searching for areas where multiple agencies analyze productivity in the same sector and opportunities to move resources to understudied sectors. A key goal must be to reduce respondent burden. For example, other opportunities for consolidation might include where the same data (such as corporate structure) are collected by different agencies, and where the same respondents are asked related questions (typically the BLS asks prices, Census asks quantities). Other forms of consolidation include where similar adjustments are made, such as when two agencies make quality adjustments for a good or service. Consolidation will also be possible where similar industry analyses are repeated, such as where the Bureau of Labor Statistics, Census, the Bureau of Economic Analysis, or industry-specific groups in the Department of Commerce research an industry.

Importantly, the new agency must create one-stop shopping for data users. That is, there should be a single place where one can go for information. Moreover, the information can be integrated and presented using standard formats and a standard user interface. The statistical agencies should nevertheless try to minimize the effects of decentralization on their customers by creating an integrated approach to disseminating information. To the maximum practical extent agencies should create common formats, graphical interfaces, and online access. Agency ownership of each data source would not be lost, and agencies would not develop a single physical data base of information products. Instead, the objective would be to make federal statistical information dissemination standards and practices more consistent and transparent for users. In addition, the virtual agency should allow users who have questions, and are not certain where to go, to approach a single access point and be treated as if they were dealing with a single centralized information dissemination organization.

The new virtual agency should investigate opportunities for consolidating field forces, especially if common definitions and computer-assisted interview interfaces facilitate training for multiple surveys. Efficient use of part-time workers has the potential to reduce the costs of collecting data. Along the same lines, it must reinvent the relation between statistical agencies and the states to increase access to administrative records for purely statistical purposes.

The virtual agency would benefit from a coordinated advisory board of experts both inside and outside government. The board could inform the Council on Statistical Policy of priorities in resolving statistical issues and offer ideas, technical advice, and informed criticism of current practices. The advisory board would include private organizations as well as government agencies and meet one to four times a year. Representatives from the

American Statistical Association, the National Association of Business Economists, and other professional organizations might be included.

Finally, the virtual agency can increase our ability to understand the economy and society. Our inability to link data sets limits the questions we can ask. Such linkages of collection and analysis often cost very little but multiply the return for our investment in statistics. For example, if BLS and Census could link data sets, a family of questions of interest to government policymakers, managers, and employees and their representatives could be addressed. What is the link between management practices such as profit sharing, employee stock-ownership plans, training, high relative wages, or employee involvement with organizational performance? Possible performance measures include managerial-oriented measures, such as productivity, earnings, and stock market returns, and worker-oriented measures, such as wage levels and growth, safety, and employment security. (Data sets could include the Census's Longitudinal Research Database for productivity; Compustat for earnings, profitability, and stock market returns; BLS Human Resources and Training Surveys for human resource policies; IRS Form 5500 and BLS benefits survey for data on profit sharing and employee stock ownership; the BLS or Census establishment lists for employment stability and survival, BLS safety survey for injury and illness data.) Similar gains in understanding could be achieved on issues ranging from health insurance coverage to the well-being of families and the aging population.

Evaluating the Proposal

The proposed virtual agency goes a long way toward achieving the goals in the Mission Statement.

With regard to *confidentiality*, the virtual statistical agency will impose uniform confidentiality protection and have data-sharing legislation to permit the exchange of statistical data among its component agencies that is essential to improve data quality, decrease duplication, and reduce respondent burden. Issuance of an Executive Order on Statistical Confidentiality and passage of data-sharing legislation will set the stage for the realization of the other benefits of the virtual agency concept.

With regard to *respondent burden*, a virtual statistical agency offers opportunities for coordination that support the goals of reducing respondent burden, as required by the new Paperwork Reduction Act reauthorization. For example, more integrated survey operations (such as coordinated sample selection and universe lists) would reduce the need for redundant identifier questions and minimize burdens.

With regard to *data quality*, a virtual statistical agency would bring together the information, expertise, and management focus needed to address important statistical issues. For example, it could encourage a more coherent approach to measurement issues involving capital investment, productivity, and service industries. The greater cost effectiveness, accuracy, and responsiveness to policymakers and other users should help build the statistical agencies' credibility. This increased credibility, in turn, should help ameliorate political pressures that might reduce data quality.

With regard to *availability and service,* a virtual statistical agency would provide statistical data users with a single focal point for many of their information requests, and their program advice.

With regard to *responsiveness to policy needs,* a virtual statistical agency would allow its component agencies to remain responsive to their host department concerns, as well as increase their responsiveness to overall national goals. The ability to create matched employee-employer data sets will open up research into new policy-relevant areas.

Creating a virtual agency avoids many executive and legislative branch hurdles compared to integration into a single statistical agency. To be effective, however, the virtual agency will need the active cooperation of its component agencies and their host departments, as well as legislation to permit data sharing and facilitate common data dissemination. Furthermore, the virtual agency will need the ability to allocate sufficient resources to optimize the goals of the entire statistical system, even if one agency occasionally loses out.

7

POLICIES TO IMPROVE WORKPLACES

> Customers want to buy from suppliers who solve their problems. Corporate headquarters wants to reward divisional managers who build up their organization's capabilities to solve customers' problems. Investors want to reward top executives who create incentives for managers to invest for the long term. All of these decision makers suffer because it is difficult to identify which organizations have the capabilities to improve continuously and to solve problems for customers. Improved measurement of organizational capabilities can help managers, top executives, and investors, as well as improve the administration of the public sector. Government should also help diffuse best-management practices. Most importantly, government must apply these lessons to its own operation.

Policies to increase the supply of skilled workers are important but may not be sufficient unless jobs are available that utilize the enhanced skills. Skills alone may not lead to high wages, high productivity, or even interesting work. We need labor market policies to enhance the trend toward workplaces that rely on high levels of skill, lifelong learning, and continuous skill improvement.

These workplaces typically are quite different from traditional ones. They have been transformed so as to give employees greater ability and the incentive to improve their workplaces. Workers' ability to generate good ideas is often strengthened by high levels of training and information sharing. Forms of worker empowerment vary widely but often include work teams and forms of representative participation such as elected committees of workers or union representatives. Incentive schemes vary as well but typically reward individuals for learning new skills, reward groups of workers for their collective success, and build cohesiveness and solidarity more than individualistic competition. Motivation is also supported when companies ensure that the efficiency gains achieved by implementing workers' suggestions do not end up costing them their jobs.

As described in chapter 4, new work systems with higher levels of employee skill and involvement in decision making have spread fairly rapidly in the past fifteen years. Moreover, such workplaces appear capable of improved performance compared to traditional workplaces.

This chapter outlines several important obstacles to diffusion of these new workplaces. It then shows how better measurement of investments in skills and in each organization's capability for continuous improvement and quality can help alleviate these obstacles. Because some of the obstacles reflect lack of information, government also has a role in disseminating good practices. Finally, the federal, state, and local governments employ roughly one-fifth of the workforce. These lessons must be applied to government workplaces as well. (Policies concerning workplace regulations are discussed in the next chapter.)

Obstacles to Diffusion

In spite of their potential efficiency, a number of obstacles slow the diffusion of high-skill, high-involvement workplaces. Some of these are market failures, as noted in chapter 3. (Porter [1992] and Levine [1995, 86–97] review the economic theory and evidence concerning these market failures in more detail.)

Many of the market failures concern the inability of decision makers to evaluate whether an employee or workplace has built up high capabilities. For example, employers cannot easily measure which employees have high skills. Customers cannot easily measure which suppliers have strong competencies in delivering high quality and in solving customers' problems. Executives cannot easily measure which divisions have built up their organizational capabilities. This problem is perhaps most severe in the federal government, where cabinet secretaries have short expected tenures on the job. Similarly, investors cannot easily measure which companies have lower observed earnings because they are investing in their capabilities. Finally, international investors cannot easily tell if a nation has high budget deficits because it is investing in building the skills of its workforce. In each case, the difficulty in observing the quality of investment in skills and organizational capability reduces the incentives to make those investments.

Improve Measurement of Worker and Workplace Skills*

It is neither possible nor desirable for the government to mandate how managers should manage. Instead, the government has the simpler role of working with the private sector to make it easier for employers, customers, and investors to see which employees and suppliers are constantly solving problems.

That is, both public and private accounting rules should put investment in people and in quality on a more even footing with investment in plant, equipment, or research. In the United States, organizations as varied as the

---

*This section draws on Finegold and Levine 1997.

American Institute of Certified Public Accountants, the Association for Investment Management and Research (which charters financial analysts), the Financial Executives Institute, and the Office of Economic Cooperation and Development (OECD) have issued recent reports emphasizing the need for better measures of nonfinancial aspects of investment. International organizations, governments, industry, and the accounting profession must work together to create standard measures of workplace investments that are comparable across time, across nations, and across companies. Only then can investors understand which companies are investing for the long term. Moreover, only then can international investors understand which nations have budget deficits likely to lead to future problems, and which are investing in the future.

This recommendation would provide coherence to the dozens of disjointed policies the government already has that affect the workplace, including accounting rules that fail to measure training as an investment, skill standards that define problem solving differently in different states or industries, and procurement policies that emphasize low bids over quality. The win-win approach of measuring who solves problems can foster the goals of government, business, and employees.

In the last decade, many governmental policies have taken important strides toward making the nation's implicit workplace policy more friendly to high-skill workplaces. These efforts range from the highly successful Malcolm Baldrige National Quality Award to creating a framework of voluntary skill standards that promote higher levels of training. Nevertheless, much more can be done.

Identify Reliable Training Measures

The current lack of a common definition of training and the fact that most firms do not measure training expenditures make it impossible to arrive at an accurate estimate of training investment within each country, much less to compare the levels of workforce development across countries (see OECD 1993, chapter 5, for more detailed discussion of methodological problems).

To illustrate the immense methodological problems in this area, consider one example taken from two concurrent workforce surveys in a single country, the United States (Zemsky 1994). The surveys—the Current Population Survey (CPS) and Survey of Income Program Participation (SIPP)—asked virtually identical questions regarding whether an individual had received training to qualify for his or her most recent job and whether she or he had undergone training to improve skills once on the job. The responses, however, were diametrically opposed: The CPS found that approximately two-thirds of individuals had received some form of training, while SIPP found that 75 percent of workers had no training. The CPS, like most other training surveys in the United States and abroad, found that individuals with the highest prior educational levels and income were most likely to receive training. In contrast, the SIPP revealed that more schooling did not lead to increased training. Indeed, it found that individuals with a college degree were less likely to receive training.

Zemsky (1994) attributes this discrepancy to the context in which the questions were asked on the two surveys that reflects a wider division between private and public training in the United States. While the CPS focuses on an employee's occupation and work history, the SIPP concentrates on federal programs for the disadvantaged, with training questions following a series of questions about food stamps, Social Security, and federal income maintenance programs. Thus, while the training questions themselves were virtually identical, the SIPP results reflected "the negative image most Americans attach to welfare programs, even though the respondents were being asked about job-related training that had little to do with welfare" (Zemsky 1994, 4).

This example also serves as a more general caution for researchers on the difficulty of interpreting even the most basic information on training in isolations from its surrounding cultural and institutional context.

Future measures should build, wherever available, on existing work, both to lower research costs and encourage comparability of findings. There has been a recent growth in the number of national individual and firm-level training surveys (e.g., Elias 1994 for a review of British survey data; for the United States, Lynch and Black 1995; Osterman 1994; Lawler et al. 1995). In a few cases, researchers have even attempted to coordinate similar training surveys across a number of countries (e.g., European Union labor force surveys, World Bank projects; see Tan and Batra 1995). Future research must ensure that measures of human resource policies are also linked to measures of organizational performance.

The training and workplace measures should identify training outcomes such as skills learned as well as training inputs such as hours in class or dollars spent. Such outcome measures typically involve skill standards. Unfortunately, rapid organizational and technological changes can rapidly make industry- or occupation-specific skill standards obsolete.

Fortunately, general problem-solving skills appear to remain useful for long periods of time. International organizations should work with member governments and the private sector to create a common set of building blocks that measure these general skills. Industries and nations could then voluntarily adopt these building blocks in future generations of skill standards. Having generic standards (and sample test instruments and training materials) would lower the cost of creating high-quality skill standards. Importantly, these skill standards would emphasize the skills of solving problems and working together in groups that are crucial for high-performance workplaces. Ideally, people moving between nations, industries, or occupations would only need to receiving training in those skills not already covered by the generic building blocks.

Moreover, international comparisons of skill attainment could enrich the current measures of literacy and of standardized test scores with measures of work-related general skills. Standard labor market surveys should include questions on whether employees are learning on the job. These questions should cover both work practices (enrollment in formal training programs, extent of on-the-job training) and the work itself (agreement whether "I solve problems on my job"; "I learn new skills on my job"). Both financial institutions judging which nations have sustainable growth-oriented policies and companies choosing where to site new facilities could use these metrics to help measure labor market quality. If two economies have similar wage and output levels, but one has more on-the-job learning at all levels (not just training), that one will probably have better long-term growth and income equality.

Validate Measures

Measures of on-the-job learning will be taken more seriously if they have been shown to predict important outcomes. For example, one cross-national study compared automobile assembly plants. The researchers found that plants with innovative work systems (including extensive training, work teams, and decentralization of responsibilities for quality control to line workers) manufactured vehicles in an average of twenty-two hours with an average of 0.5 defects per vehicle (MacDuffie 1995). In contrast, more traditional plants took thirty hours with 0.8 defects per vehicle. We need additional studies, particularly those that compare similar plants (perhaps with a single owner) across national boundaries. Employee-oriented outcomes (safety, wages, employment stability, job satisfaction, turnover) should be included in these studies, as well as employer-oriented outcomes.

Quality Certifications for Organizations

One means of promoting high-performance workplaces is through recognition programs, most notably the Malcolm Baldrige Quality Award

---

Box 7.1. What Works: The Baldrige Award

The Malcolm Baldrige National Quality Award measures companies' progress on a number of quality goals. The company (or division) must provide evidence that it incorporates a focus on quality into management practices, works closely with suppliers, trains workers in quality techniques, and meets customers' desires. The completed application must be less than seventy pages. The examination process begins with a board of examiners scoring the written application. The examiners are recognized quality practitioners themselves, whose feedback the contestants value. High scorers then have site visits led by a senior examiner, and winners are selected by a panel of judges.

The Baldrige Award has been an effective catalyst for managerial change. More than 1 million copies of the award criteria have been distributed, and the award serves as the model in many companies' internal evaluations of their move to high performance.

Although few companies have won the coveted award, its effects are more broadly felt. For example, one truck engine manufacturer that was having serious quality problems applied for the Baldrige Award as a way of "turning a harsh spotlight on itself." Although the company did not come close to winning, the feedback it received led to valuable new practices concerning worker training and listening to truckers' complaints. Defect rates plunged from 10 percent to below 1 percent in only two years.

(box 7.1). Unfortunately, companies face the same problem as employees when trying to certify the quality of their goods or services—a profusion of awards and certifications. A company that hires workers who solve problems and that collects data from its customers to improve its products and services is a good supplier. Nevertheless, it has to jump through different hoops to sell to a car company than to sell to an airplane company, and different hoops again to sell to different parts of the U.S. government.

The federal government must work with other large customers to create standard certifications that measure which companies offer products of high quality and are organized to improve their quality. The good news is that the federal government is already beginning to copy the private sector's best practice. Specifically, the government is starting to rely on existing supplier certifications as one factor when choosing suppliers. This move should improve the quality and lower the lifetime cost of the goods and services bought by our government. Suppliers of high-quality goods and services tend to rely on their workers for help in improving quality. Thus, buying higher quality should not only save the government money but also increase the quality of U.S. jobs.

Many companies are adopting the International Standards Organization (ISO) 9000 series quality standards. These standards require that companies maintain and follow documented procedures for almost everything they do. Unfortunately, the ISO standard has no requirement that procedures be improved continuously. An addition to the ISO standard can increase its usefulness for identifying excellent suppliers:

> *Improving Quality Plans.* The supplier shall establish and maintain documented procedures for continuously improving all documented procedures. The supplier shall ensure that this procedure is understood, implemented, and maintained at all levels of the organization. (Guidance on procedures for continuous improvement is given in ISO 9004-4, *Guidelines for Quality Improvement* [Dobb 1966].)

Because high-quality suppliers tend to rely on their workforce, a move to improve product and service quality will also improve the quality and skill of jobs. (A more complete proposal for improving ISO 9000 is found in Levine 1995, 140–141.)

The multi-industry Process Certification Standard (known in the United States as ANSI/EIA 599) is becoming widely accepted in the private sector. International standard-setting organizations must ensure that this standard and its successors identify employers where each employee has the incentive, ability, and authority and responsibility constantly to improve the workplace.*

Identify Benchmarks

To facilitate these comparisons further, public- and private-sector benchmarking organizations can provide cross-company and cross-national comparisons of best practice. For example, the cross-national study of auto assembly mentioned earlier found that in the mid-1980s newly hired auto assembly workers received 310 hours of training in Japan and 280 hours of training in Japanese-managed plants located in the United States, but only 48 hours of training at traditional American plants (Krafcik 1990). This

---

*Elsewhere I have described a number of market failures that can impede the spread of high-involvement workplaces (Levine 1995, chs. 5, 6). To the extent that these theories are supported empirically, it may also be appropriate to provide tax preferences for workplaces that provide these high-skill, high-involvement jobs (Levine 1995, ch. 8). Providing effective measurement of worker skills and workplace improvement practices is a precondition for such tax subsidies.

simple fact was a wake-up call for many U.S. employers about the gap between typical U.S. and best practice.

Improved Accounting Standards

Investors face the same problem as customers: how do they know if the company is investing in building a high-quality reputation or if it is depreciating its customers' and employees' goodwill? Unfortunately, current accounting rules do not measure the investment managers make in building a high-quality workforce and in producing high-quality goods. Instead, in the short run, such spending shows up only as lower earnings.

Accounting rules should not treat investment in training for a new computer system differently from the way they treat investment in the hardware. The government can work with industry and the accounting profession to create standard measures of workplace investments that are comparable across time and across companies. Only then can investors understand which companies are investing for the long term.

Improving Diffusion of Best Practice

The policy response to the problems facing high-performance workplaces should be to remove obstacles and to improve the quality and delivery of information that can facilitate private-sector initiatives.

The Clinton administration has attempted two strategies for improving dissemination. In 1993 the Department of Labor created a new Office of the American Workplace to reduce barriers that impede organizations from adopting high-performance work structures. Its initiatives included creating a clearinghouse of information on high-performance workplaces, creating educational programs for unions and for managers to learn how to work better together, and working with institutional investors such as pensions (collectively the largest owners of America's largest companies) so as to better measure which companies are investing in their people for the long run. It was closed at the end of 1995 due to budget cutbacks. (Some disclosure: I worked at the Office of the American Workplace for six months during 1994.)

Separately, the Clinton administration has expanded the Department of Commerce's Manufacturing Extension Partnership (MEP). The program began with three extension centers in 1989. In 1996, forty-two centers were operating in thirty-two states (Corporation for Manufacturing Excellence 1996). MEP centers provide small- and medium-sized manufacturers with access to public and private resources, information, and services designed to increase firms' use of appropriate technologies and modern manufacturing practices. Building workforce skill and a work environment that fosters a culture of continuous improvement is a major factor in companies' ability to benefit from these technologies. Thus, the expanded MEP program should be helping U.S. industry to move toward adoption of the high-performance workplace model. In the future, small manufacturers will be able to work with a local MEP center for needs ranging from new technology to redesigning the entire workplace.

Reinventing Government Workplaces

Reinventing Government: Not Just Longer Meetings, But More of Them.
            —Summary Statement of a Hard-Working Reinventor.

Reinventing the government workplace is crucial for creating a government that works better and costs less. One key element of this reinvention is to turn the federal government itself into a high-performance employer, one that relies on the skills and motivates the creativity of its employees (see box 7.2).

As discussed in chapter 4, there is an increasingly well understood "recipe" for high-performance workplaces. This recipe involves providing every employee with the ability, motivation, and authority to improve how work is done. Managers and union leaders must support the new work organization, and top executives must lead the change. (See references in Levine 1995, chs. 3, 4.)

There is also a well-understood list of obstacles to these high-performance workplaces, ranging from a history of distrust to incentive systems for managers that focus on the short-term, not long-term, success of the organization (Levine 1995, chs. 5, 6). Unfortunately, government workplaces are subject to most of the list of obstacles, and while reinvention has helped, many of the obstacles remain.

For example, high-skill, high-involvement work organization requires that all employees have the ability to improve the workplace, abilities often built on formal and informal training. This training, by its very nature, will be valuable for more than one year. Unfortunately, annual budgets and the lack of a capital budget implies that agencies and Congress have an incentive to skimp on training. A dollar cut from training today will permit that dollar to be spent on more immediately gratifying expenses this year.

Using the Internet to Promote Decentralization

The new high-skill workplaces require empowerment of front-line employees. Unfortunately, as has been noted repeatedly throughout this volume,

Box 7.2. **What Works: Empowering Civil Servants to Serve Citizens Better**

One goal of reinventing government is to empower government employees. Simply by listening to their good suggestions, the government can become a better provider of services. An example of empowered civil servants making good policy at the front line involves the restoration of the Santa Monica Freeway after California's Northridge earthquake of January 1994.

The Santa Monica Freeway is one of the most important transportation corridors in the United States, and for each day that it was shut down the local economy suffered about $1 million in lost output. Nevertheless, the highway administration often takes over a year just to develop a plan, solicit bids, review proposals, and award funding for a major project such as rebuilding the Santa Monica. Fortunately, the chief of district operations for the Federal Highway Administration in Sacramento had some ideas for improving the process.

The main ideas were to speed up the bidding process and to award large bonuses to contractors who finished ahead of the date proposed in their bid (and impose equally large penalties on contractors who missed deadlines). By accelerating the competitive bidding process and rewarding speedy completion, the chief of district operations and other empowered federal employees helped finish in about 140 days projects that would normally have taken 2 years. In addition, thanks to cooperation between groups ranging from Amtrak to the Army Corps of Engineers to the city's transportation department, traffic patterns were quickly rerouted, averting gridlock.

front-line empowerment is inconsistent with the command-and-control culture of government.

Of course, in many cases command-and-control has important good features. Specifically, it makes it more likely that people in different regions will be treated similarly. The puzzle for reinvented workplaces, then, is to permit decentralization while also permitting consistency in treatment for different people with similar cases.

The current efforts at reinventing government have no theory of how to achieve consistency across units or regions coupled with discretion within units. For example, nobody believes that each Social Security office should make up its own rules concerning who is disabled.

Fortunately, the private sector has encountered this problem many times and has workable solutions. The key to decentralization coupled with cross-office consistency is sharing information with a common database. A few strategies are possible.

In one scenario, current best practice is summarized into a database. Often, an expert system sorts though the masses of information to identify how the agency has handled similar situations in the past. The expert system should also explain the reasoning behind the past decision. The database, with or without an expert system, differs from detailed rules because the past is considered advisory; front-line workers can still use their own best judgment. In effect, workers are continuously writing and updating a "best practice" manual to advise themselves.

In some settings, front-line employees might need to justify major discrepancies from past practices, either to managers or (as at Xerox) to front-line experts. For controversial situations, groups of front-line employees (often with the support of managers and stakeholders) must convene to establish the new version of best practice that will hold until a better idea comes along. These new practices, in turn, should be entered into the database as the new recommendation for that situation. Workers should receive rewards for innovations that are widely applicable. In other settings, front-line workers should be able to ask other employees nationwide how they have handled similar tough cases.

This brief description covers only some ways to create bottom-up standardization. What many of these methods share is a reliance on information technology to help front-line workers share current best practice.

Partnering with Unions

The new work organization requires partnership with unions. Unions must take on new roles, helping to oversee issues that span multiple work groups, ensure the credibility of management's promises, and take on new roles in strategic decision making (Levine 1995, ch. 4).

Reinventing government, then, has a problem caused by the nature of public-sector unions. Within the federal government, union membership is voluntary, and nonmembers receive almost all the benefits of union membership. Thus, public-sector union members are often self-selected to be those who are least happy with management. Partnering with government employees who trust their managers least avoids cooptation, but can delay achieving the full benefits of partnership. Union leaders often naturally appoint union members to serve on joint projects, a process that selects against those employees who might be most enthusiastic about a partnership.

As government executives and union leaders make clear the key role that the union will have as a partner, more employees should realize that union membership and activities can be useful tickets to interesting work and important projects. This situation occurs at many employers in Japan, for example. In unionized settings there, many future managers work as union officials to gain exposure to top management and to become involved in larger-scale decision making.

Minimizing Job Insecurity

The new work organization also has a tension with the increased use of markets and competition for clients, as results from vouchers or from privatization. Specifically, high-involvement workplaces require long time horizons so that employees find it worthwhile to work hard, knowing their rewards will come, and managers find it worthwhile to invest in employees. When service providers can rapidly lose market share, it is hard to build long-term relations with employees. When government agencies have had a monopoly, the introduction of competition (that will reduce employment) can work at cross-purposes with the building of a high-trust workplace.

Effective high-trust workplaces require assuring workers that job loss will never result from higher productivity. At the same time, even high-performance workplaces may be subject to job loss following reduced demand from clients. While the latter rule is often cruel, at least both of these rules provide incentives to increase quality and productivity.

Currently, the job security incentives in the federal government are almost precisely wrong on both rules. Congress and the executive branch find it tempting to reduce budgets and head counts whenever an agency's effectiveness rises and it needs fewer employees to do the job. At the same time, the lack of competition in providing many services implies that clients cannot exit from even the most ineffective offices or departments; such a possibility of exit would provide additional incentives for high-quality service. Thus, the current environment often gives incentives to avoid improvements, instead of embracing them.

The only solution here is a difficult one: a credible commitment from Congress and the executive branch that high quality and low cost will be rewarded, not lead to downsizing. Furthermore, a commitment that downsizing, even in cases of declining demand (perhaps caused by competition from other service providers) will be a recourse of last resort. (In cases where downsizing is inevitable, the reemployment system described in chapter 6 will help reduce the cost of job loss for federal employees.)

Incentives for Managers

Finally, the government must create incentives for managers to focus on quality, employee empowerment, and satisfying customers. The Clinton administration's process for reinventing government made a sensible start by forcing agencies to define their customers and to set standards for customer satisfaction. Unfortunately, agency heads still face incentives to underinvest in quality programs and other workplace programs that may not pay off until after the next election. (That is, measuring outcomes is important but not sufficient as long as the measures are imperfect. Because we care about future outcomes as well as this year's outcomes, rewarding only single-year measures provides too little incentive for agencies to focus on longer term success.)

Congress and the leadership of the executive branch should, thus, monitor agencies' quality improvement efforts and reward those that are making the most progress on institutionalizing continuous improvement.

In the private sector, such monitoring is often performed by administering in-house quality audits of divisions. At AT&T, for example, each division competes in an in-house quality competition modeled on the Baldrige National Quality Award. Not surprisingly, three of the large-company national winners have been AT&T divisions.

We need a similar federal effort to monitor agencies' progress on criteria similar to those in the Baldrige award. These data should be benchmarked so that federal agencies know how they are doing. Moreover, agencies should set specific goals for improvement on the quality criteria and should be held accountable by Congress and the White House for progress toward their goals.

Other Sectors

Although this section has focused on the federal government, similar lessons apply to state and local governments. Many governments, often in partnership with the relevant unions, have engaged in successful reinvention efforts, typically using the "recipe" of workplace practices emphasized in this volume. At the same time, most civil servants remain in fairly traditional workplaces, with more regulations than empowerment to serve their customer-citizens.

Conclusion

It is neither feasible nor desirable for the federal government to mandate how workplaces should be organized. Nevertheless, employers want to hire workers who know how to solve problems. Similarly, consumers and downstream companies want to buy from suppliers that are constantly solving the customers' problems. Investors also want to reward managers who build up the organization's long-term capabilities to solve problems for customers. Finally, Congress and the executive branch want to reward government executives and programs that are continuously improving their service of customers.

What these many stakeholders desire are measures of investment in the individual's and organization's skills. The government has a role in working with the private sector to set standards that facilitate such measurement. The measurement can occur at all scales from individual skills to the competence of our largest corporations and cabinet departments. The government also has a role in subsidizing research to validate these measures, for such research is again a classic public good.*

These public-private partnerships should create a common language and validate a set of measurement tools. Such measurement tools for worker skills can increase incentives for workers to learn both at school and on the job, reward employers who provide training, improve employers' hiring decisions, and make life easier for schools in deciding what to teach. Corresponding measurement tools for organizations can improve their incentives to produce high-quality goods and services, improve customers' ability to identify high-quality suppliers, improve top managers' (including government executives') ability to reward divisions that improve their long-term capabilities, and improve investors' ability to reward managers who invest for the long term.

---

*Difficulty in measuring investments in problem solving and other capabilities is only one of the market failures that impedes effective workplaces. Levine (1995, ch. 8) discusses additional policies to promote high-skill, high-involvement workplaces.

8

REINVENTING WORKPLACE REGULATION

Workplace regulations typically are rigid and detailed, raising their costs for business yet reducing their effectiveness at protecting workers. This chapter argues in favor of giving employers the option of working with employees to solve the workplace's problems. Under this proposal, employers have the option of creating plans that achieve the goals of the regulations. If these plans meet minimum standards, the employer would be exempt from many detailed command-and-control regulations. A key element of this proposal is that the workforce (or its representatives) has the authority to ensure that each plan protects the employees.

In the United States, more than a hundred laws regulate everything from safety to discrimination to overtime rules (U.S. General Accounting Office [GAO] 1994). Unfortunately, workplace regulations often do not work well for employees, employers, or regulators.

This chapter outlines a reinvented regulatory system based on giving employers the option of working with employees to solve their mutual problems. That is, employers and employees can create custom plans that achieve the goals of the regulations and meet minimum standards. A key element of this proposal is that the workforce (or its representatives) must approve each plan. Furthermore, the workforce has the authority to cancel plans that are not protecting them.

The chapter outlines in some detail how the new model would work for safety and dispute resolution. It also discusses how the model applies to regulations ranging from overtime to employee stock ownership to training subsidies.

The advantages of this system include more interesting work and better jobs for workers, more productive workplaces for owners and managers, and more flexibility for all involved. In addition, this system can increase total compliance while permitting regulators to focus their efforts on the minority of workplaces with the most serious problems.

Overview of the Problem

Although typically intended to protect their interests, regulations often do not work well for workers. One problem for workers is that workplaces are not safe. At some point during their career, perhaps one-third of all employees will miss work because of an on-the-job injury or illness. Furthermore, although fatality rates have declined in the past twenty years, rates of workplace injuries (as best we can measure them) have not declined (U.S. Bureau of Labor Statistics 1994, table 4).

In addition, millions of workers are subject to discrimination and sexual harassment each year (Rowe 1990). Unfortunately, most workers who perceive discrimination have no meaningful recourse. The process of appealing to the Equal Employment Opportunity Commission (EEOC) is adversarial and costly, discouraging employees from using it. When an employee *does* pursue an EEOC claim, he or she joins a line almost 100,000 people (eighteen months) long (Duffy 1995).

Finally, the vast majority of employees also would like more involvement in decision making than they find at work. In one recent poll, 90 percent of respondents with opinions wanted more involvement at work (U.S. Commission on the Future of Worker-Management Relations 1994).

Regulations do not work well for managers, either. Although the total benefits of workplace regulation probably outweigh the costs, often the tens or perhaps even hundreds of billions of dollars spent on workplace regulations are not cost effective (U.S. Office of the Vice President 1993). Few regulations provide incentives for managers and workers to discover the most effective means to accomplish the regulations' goals. In addition, many federal rules assume "one size fits all," imposing similar regulations for different industries, regions, and company sizes (Howard 1994). Similarly, laws and regulations often require regulators to use similar enforcement strategies for companies with very different compliance efforts and records. The result is harassment of "good" employers and a lack of focus on "bad" ones (Clinton 1995). Regulatory agencies often create different definitions, inspection schedules, and paperwork requirements with no coherence to the system. Employers also resent laws that discourage employee involvement that might satisfy the goals of both workers and managers.

Finally, regulations do not work well for the regulators. Rules are difficult to modify even decades after the regulators realize they are out of date. For example, one agency used an eighteen-foot chart with 373 boxes to describe its rulemaking process (U.S. Office of the Vice President 1993). Inspections are rare, frustrating many regulators' desire to ensure safe, legal, and nondiscriminatory workplaces. For example, the federal government and states together employ about 4,000 safety and health inspectors to cover 6 million workplaces. In addition, rules often require regulators to play "gotcha" and count minor infractions. The resulting system often leads, as one author put it, to *The Death of Common Sense* (Howard 1994). Most regulators would prefer to use common sense so that they can assist those companies that want to play by the rules to comply, while focusing enforcement on the worst offenders.

An Alternative

Fortunately, an alternative exists, one based on creating incentives for companies and workers to solve their own problems. The proposed system is based on *conditional* deregulation, where companies with good records of compliance can choose to work with their employees to improve compliance and face fewer regulations, inspections, and penalties. To ensure the company does not reduce safety, increase discrimination, or otherwise worsen employees' lives, employees or their representative must approve each alternative plan.

When the system works, regulations will be more flexible and will achieve their goals more effectively (for example, providing more safety at lower cost). The methods used to meet these goals will be designed to meet the needs of each organization and its workforce, reducing the costs of compliance. In addition, more managers and employees will have the authority and the incentive to ensure that the company complies. The new system also will provide incentives for companies to be proactive in working with their workforce to search out and solve problems. Companies that provide good workplaces will be rewarded with regulatory flexibility. These positive incentives will be in addition to existing negative incentives such as fines, the costs of workers' compensation, or the threat of a union drive. The outcome should be safer, fairer, and less discriminatory workplaces that are both better places to work and more productive.

Importantly, regulators will be able to spend less time and energy at the majority of workplaces that intend to comply with the spirit of the law (even if they do not comply with the letter of each regulation). This change will free up regulatory energy to focus on the "bad actors." (At the same time, some fraction of regulators' resources will need to be redirected to providing training materials and other assistance to workplaces that are moving to the new system.)

The potential disadvantages of the proposed system are equally clear. Companies might merely go through the motions of setting up alternative systems, while reducing safety and ignoring statutory rights of the employees. In this scenario, a system of conditional deregulation will diminish the already-weak enforcement powers of the regulators. Self-regulation without oversight is not a recipe for compliance.

Employees Can Oversee the New System. Fortunately, one group has an interest both in effective regulation and in a flexible and productive workplace—

the workforce. A premise of the proposed system is that employees must collectively approve any plan for achieving a regulation's goal. For example, employees can provide oversight when considering new means to achieve the goals of a safety regulation; they might choose to exchange more flexibility in weekly hours in exchange for ending mandatory overtime; and they can approve an employee involvement group to improve working conditions or safety that might otherwise run afoul of labor law. In all these cases, if the workforce agrees, it is often inefficient for the federal government to mandate one-size-fits-all regulations.

There is no single best way to ensure employee involvement in approving the alternative plans. At the same time, the approval process must meet minimum standards concerning adequate information, adequate training, and a fair selection process for employee representatives.

In small workplaces, direct employee vote is often appropriate. (Regulations should contain exemptions or simplified procedures to accommodate the high cost of regulations per employee in very small workplaces.) In unionized settings, the union is a natural representative of the organized workforce.

In larger, nonunion workplaces, one possibility is to permit companies voluntarily to create employee representation committees (similar to European works councils). Such employee committees would then be able to approve programs to achieve the goals of any or all of a list of regulations. This proposal is consistent with public policy in many European nations, where works councils often have oversight over areas such as workplace safety.

To ensure lack of employer domination, these committees would need to meet minimum standards (Kochan and Osterman [1994] present a similar list). Participants would be guaranteed against loss of pay or benefits and against any retribution for their participation (or for choosing not to participate) in any element of the employee oversight system. The selection of members in the representative council would be chosen freely and fairly; they would not be chosen by management. In addition, any mechanism would need to ensure proportional representation of hourly and salaried employees. Mechanisms ranging from random choice among volunteers to elections with secret ballots would be permissible. The initial establishment of such a representative committee would need to be approved by a majority of the workforce, as would the disestablishment of the committee. Finally, employers would not be permitted to set up a committee when it knows a union organizing campaign is taking place. Such a standard would minimize employers' establishing committees solely to defuse employee dissatisfaction during union organizing campaigns (Morris 1996).

Even with employee-approved waivers, each regulatory arena would remain subject to minimum standards. For example, the employees or their representatives could approve the enterprise's safety program and opt out of many detailed safety regulations. Nevertheless, the safety program would need to meet minimum standards (detailed below), the *goals* of each regulation would still need to be met, and some Occupational Safety and Health Administration (OSHA) regulations would still be in effect. The employees or their representatives could approve the enterprise's alternative dispute resolution program and opt out of some EEOC and other antidiscrimination enforcement, but the dispute-resolution procedure would need to meet strict standards. The following sections outline such minimum standards for safety and health, for dispute resolution procedures, for employee involvement programs, and several other areas of regulation.

Each sphere of regulation, from safety to wages and hours, suffers from a common set of problems: rigid command-and-control regulations, with one set of regulations for all workplaces over a certain size, coupled with an adversarial and legalistic enforcement mechanism. Each sphere of workplace regulation also has similar problems of employer opportunism such as mismeasuring compliance or failing to meet minimum standards. In addition, each sphere has the feature that the workforce and the regulators share most objectives. Thus, it is unsurprising that a unified framework can address such different areas of regulation.

Under the proposal, companies and workers could jointly agree to modify the regulations in any one sphere or in several. This proposal provides the economy of scale of having a single representative body in place for each issue that arises. Because of the common issues that arise in each sphere of workplace regulation, proposals for reform of specific arenas will systematically miss the advantages of a unified framework for employee-monitored self-regulation.

Relation to Past Literature. Works councils are mandated in all of the continental European Union members. In most of these nations the councils have rights to information and consultation on a variety of issues. In Germany, Denmark, Luxembourg, and the Netherlands the works council must not only be informed but must also agree to changes in personnel policies such as hiring, firing, and work rules.

This proposal draws on past arguments for mandatory works councils (e.g., Weiler 1990). A key distinction is that this proposal is for voluntary creation of employee representation councils specifically to improve the quality and reduce the cost of workplace regulations.

This proposal is also related to arguments for decentralized means to achieve the goals of regulations, what John Dunlop has called an "internal responsibility system" (e.g., Bok and Dunlop 1970). A number of authors have noted how employee involvement can advance the goals of regulations and other government programs in specific spheres such as safety (U.S. Department of Labor, OSHA 1995b) or training (Lynch 1994).

The U.S. Commission on the Future of Worker Management Relations also endorsed employee involvement to help decentralize regulatory enforcement (1994). Commission member Thomas Kochan noted that the commission's approach to improving workplace regulation emphasized separating those "employment relationships with effective workplace institutions that can take on some of the regulatory functions from those without such institutions." While the former can be largely deregulated, the latter still "need to remain subject to the standard approach to regulation and enforcement." (Kochan 1995, 357). The commission's proposal endorsed separate mechanisms of employee involvement in each sphere, such as safety and dispute resolution (U.S. Commision on the Future of Worker-Management Relations 1994), while this proposal emphasizes that the common problem of workplace regulation leads to a common solution.

This proposal is closest to those of Kochan and Osterman (1994) and Freeman and Rogers (1993, 63–64), who also propose voluntarily established employee committees that can further the goals of multiple spheres of workplace regulation while enhancing flexibility and employee involvement. Their proposals emphasize the role of the committees in enhancing employee voice. The system proposed here emphasizes the converse proposal, employee involvement is necessary for improving workplace regulation.

The proposal also draws on the long tradition among economists advocating performance-based regulations. Under this proposal, employers would be able (with their workforce) to design alternative means to achieve the goals of any regulation. Furthermore, those with good track records of success would be treated differently from those with poor records of success. For environmental regulations, preliminary evidence indicates that performance-based regulations can achieve similar performance as command-and-control regulations but cost about one third less. (Moving to performance-based regulations is already a priority of the Clinton administration's proposals for reinventing regulations [Gore 1995].) It is plausible that similar cost savings can be achieved in other spheres of workplace regulation.

Employee involvement is an important complement to performance-based regulations because measuring performance is so often problematic. For example, rewarding low rates of reported injuries gives managers incentives both to reduce injuries and to penalize employees who report their injuries. Empowering employees to approve the safety plan and to monitor its results reduces the difficulties with managers gaming the performance measurement system.

Safety and Health

The Problem

Every year more than 6,000 Americans die of workplace injuries, an estimated 50,000 people die of illnesses caused by workplace chemical exposures, and 6 million people suffer nonfatal workplace injuries. Injuries alone cost the economy more than $110 billion a year (U.S. Department of Labor, OSHA 1995a). These numbers are high in absolute terms and are high compared with other nations, such as Sweden and Japan (even acknowledging difficulties in international comparisons [Freeman and Rogers 1993, 23]). Moreover, OSHA had not inspected three-fourths of work sites that suffered serious accidents in 1994 and early 1995 during the preceding five years (Port and Solomon 1995).

Some economists dispute the need for any safety regulations. They assume that workers have good information before taking jobs or that workers fairly quickly find out about hazards and find it easy to move between jobs. In this setting, employers will face market incentives to provide the efficient amount of safety because unsafe employers will need to pay higher wages that compensate workers for hazards.

Unfortunately, the empirical support for this theory is mixed (Brown 1980). In addition, a number of market failures suggest government intervention is called for. For example, information on safety and (especially) health risks that may take decades to materialize is often far from perfect. Moreover, the presence of social insurance implies that injured workers do not pay the full cost of their injuries; thus, the free market will lead to inefficiently little safety. Finally, even if markets work well, we should still favor proposals such as this one that reduce the costs of the politically chosen level of safety regulation.

More regulation does not seem to be the answer: after the IRS, OSHA may be the most hated part of the federal government (see, for example, Potter and Youngman 1995, 319). The reasons for this hatred are easy to understand. As OSHA describes the problem:

> In the public's view, OSHA has been driven too often by numbers and rules, not by smart enforcement and results. Business complains about overzealous enforcement and burdensome rules. . . . Too often, a "one-size-fits-all" regulatory approach has treated conscientious employers no differently from those who put workers needlessly at risk. (U.S. Department of Labor 1995a).

The Role of Employee Involvement in Improving Safety

Improving safety and health requires that managers and employees actively participate in identifying and eliminating hazards. A number of enterprises have already established mechanisms for such employee involvement. For example, in one survey about 75 percent of establishments with more than fifty employees reported having safety and health committees, as did 31 percent of smaller ones (U.S. Commission on the Future of Worker-Management Relations 1994).

Mandatory Programs

About ten states currently require employers in some or all sectors to sponsor safety committees (U.S. Commission on the Future of Worker-Management Relations 1994). A majority of state workers' compensation systems are beginning to require workplaces to establish a safety and health program, at least in hazardous sectors (U.S. Department of Labor 1995b). Most of these required programs contain minimum standards similar to those listed below.

Although no careful evaluation exists, preliminary evidence on the effectiveness of such committees is favorable. For example, both state and business officials agree that mandated safety and health committees have contributed to the $1.5 billion decrease in injury costs experienced by Oregon employers between 1990 and 1993 ("Oregon Safety Committees Touted" 1993).

Voluntary Programs

OSHA's Voluntary Protection Program is a small well-respected program that recognizes companies with excellent safety programs. VPP employers have injury rates about 40 percent lower than the average of their industries, although it is unclear how much of the decrease reflects actions measured by the VPP program (U.S. General Accounting Office [GAO] 1992b, 10). More generally, employers that voluntarily adopt safety and health programs have lower injury and illness rates than do other employers, and their managers often attribute the difference largely to the existence of the program (U.S. GAO 1992a).

Unfortunately, current federal law discourages, instead of encourages, such safety and health programs. The discouragement arises because the National Labor Relations Act's definition of "company unions" is broad enough to forbid many safety committees. The missing encouragement is because OSHA does not systematically provide incentives for proactive safety and health programs. (OSHA does provide a small incentive in that good-faith efforts can lower fines slightly.) Even if a safety and health program identifies a better and cheaper way to achieve a safety goal, OSHA does not grant a waiver from its detailed regulations.

Box 8.1. **What Works: Maine 200**

In a pilot program called Maine 200, OSHA targeted the 203 companies in Maine with the worst injury records over the preceding years.
Each company in this group was allowed to choose either to undergo
an immediate and detailed safety inspection or to create a safety and
health program meeting certain minimum standards. All but two of the
companies opted to create a safety program.

Results thus far have been impressive. Participating companies
have identified and eliminated 55,000 hazards in the program's first
year—as many hazards as OSHA identified in the entire state during
the previous eight years. In addition, the injury rate declined at 59
percent of these companies, sometimes dramatically (Clinton 1995,
Appendix 1). OSHA is currently expanding this program to any state
that will help it identify the companies with the worst safety records.

Examples of the New Model.

Fortunately, the situation is changing, and OSHA is moving to encourage
proactive safety and health programs (box 8.1).

Similarly, in construction, OSHA has begun rewarding work sites with
an adequate safety program, defined as having a written safety program and
a trained safety person. OSHA rewards such sites by promising that any
OSHA inspections will focus only on the four main deadly hazards, not on
minor violations such as paperwork violations or poor communication
about possible hazards (Clinton 1995, Appendix 2).

Ensuring Minimum Standards

Within the writings of safety professionals such as industrial hygienists,
ergonomists, union safety representatives, and regulators, a consensus is
arising about the elements of adequate safety programs. Such programs
must ensure both managers and employees have the training to understand
safety, incentives to improve safety, and the authority to make safety-en-
hancing changes. To be more specific, the following elements are common
to most proposals for an adequate safety and health program. (See, for
example, Clinton 1995, Appendix 3.)

- Managers and employees receive training and education about identifying and controlling hazards. They (or outside experts they choose)
  perform periodic joint workplace inspections to identify hazards.

- Managers and employees have incentives to participate fully in the safety and health program. Employees or their representatives have the authority to develop recommendations to the employer with assurance that the employer will respond to recommendations in a timely manner. Employees are protected against retribution due to their contributions to the safety program.
- When accidents occur, an emergency response plan is implemented and first-aid services are available. An investigation to eliminate root causes follows each accident.
- The employer provides appropriate medical surveillance for all health hazards.
- Written records include a description of the safety and health program, records of injuries and illnesses, and plans to abate hazards. These abatement plans have timetables and procedures to track progress.

Good process matters, but so do results. Under this proposal, employers with very high accident and illness rates (compared with their industry) or with fairly high accident rates and no pattern of improvement would lose the presumptions otherwise due to employers with good safety programs. (Employers requesting exemptions would be required to submit their OSHA safety and health logs and workers' compensation records to OSHA so that OSHA can compare its safety record with its industry.) For employers with poor safety records, or those in particularly dangerous industries, additional certification of the safety program by a third party such as the workers' compensation insurer may be required. (Workers' compensation insurers are appropriate certifiers because they also save money from reducing injury rates. Several states require these companies to certify safety plans as adequate [U.S. Department of Labor 1995a].)

Finally, not all regulations will be automatically waived if the workers approve. In situations with hard-to-detect hazards that may lead to rare or long-to-develop harms, even trained employees will have trouble dealing with the scientific complexities involved. In these situations, OSHA should continue to promulgate regulations.

OSHA has already proposed some incentives for excellent safety programs and records: OSHA inspections focused on major hazards, not every hazard; lower fines; and lower priority for random inspections (Clinton 1995, Appendix 3). Unfortunately, these incentives alone will not be very effective, because fines are almost always trivially small, and random inspections are very rare.

OSHA can provide more effective incentives by giving automatic waivers from detailed command-and-control regulations to safety programs that achieve the goals of each rule. In addition, OSHA could agree that for approved safety programs, all complaints except imminent danger would have to satisfy the internal safety procedures before OSHA would inspect the workplace. For example, a worker would first have to submit a suggestion or complaint to the in-house safety committee. Only if this committee then found no need for action (or did not act in a timely fashion) could the worker call in an outside regulator. OSHA does not have time to inspect every complaint and still engage in sufficient random inspections of the most dangerous workplaces; giving deference to excellent in-house systems will permit OSHA to focus their scarce resources on the most dangerous and worst-run workplaces.

The Role of Employee Oversight in Ensuring the Programs Are Not a Sham

Permitting companies to exempt themselves from OSHA regulations if they have a safety program runs the risk of companies establishing sham programs that reduce safety. Fortunately, employees have an interest in a safe workplace and are ideally placed to oversee the workplace safety plan. In addition, under this proposal, employees have the threat to revert to detailed regulations coupled with an OSHA inspection if the employer does not follow through on important safety and health improvements. Both case study (Adler, Goldoftas, and Levine 1997) and statistical evidence (Weil 1991b) suggest that the combination of employee involvement in health and safety and the ability to call in safety regulators when disputes arise can lead to better outcomes than either alone.

Dispute Resolution

The United States is unique among the industrialized nations in permitting companies to fire employees without the need to show cause. Ironically, the United States is also unique in having the most expensive and conflict-laden legal system, one that frustrates both employees and managers. Alternative dispute-resolution programs such as mediation, arbitration, and ombudsmen have the potential to increase fairness in dismissals, promotions, and other management actions, while reducing costs. The key is to ensure these alternative dispute-resolution programs are not mere shams but actually provide due process under the law.

The Problem

Employees have statutory rights to a workplace free of discrimination and sexual harassment. Unfortunately, as noted earlier, surveys suggest that several million employees each year feel they have been sexually harassed or discriminated against. Evidence of continued discrimination is not just from self-reports. When matched pairs of employees (black and white, Anglo and Hispanic, or male and female) are sent for job interviews, employers are more likely to offer white men employment, especially for better jobs (Bendick et al. 1993; Glaster et al. 1994; Neumark et al. 1995; Fix and Struyk 1993).

Workers also have a statutory right to appeal to the EEOC and eventually the court system for redress. Unfortunately, many workers cannot enforce their statutory rights. As noted earlier, when employees bring charges before the EEOC, they find themselves at the back of a line almost 100,000 people long (Duffy 1995). When the EEOC does find the employer guilty of malfeasance, most claims do not result in meaningful monetary damages. Lawsuits, although occasionally leading to enormous awards, are largely the preserve of those in high-wage and high-status occupations, almost irrelevant to most of the workforce (Donahue and Siegelman 1991)

Even without the backlog, many victims of discrimination do not find EEOC enforcement well suited to their problems. Some find the EEOC process too adversarial. Many do not want to bring formal charges but want low-cost, low-intensity dispute-resolution procedures. Sometimes the employee wants nothing more than a formal apology or for the behavior to stop (Rowe 1990). Other employees find the EEOC process too costly, particularly if they need a lawyer at some stage. A third group of employees finds the EEOC process too public. For example, the EEOC process does not permit anonymous complaints, as would operate through many companies' in-house ombudsman (Rowe 1990).

In short, many employees find themselves with no workable recourse to discrimination: some quit and suffer unemployment or wage declines; others continue to work after what may have been largely a misunderstanding, with no simple means for clearing up the misunderstanding; and others endure work with bosses who persist in violating their rights (Rowe 1990).

At the same time, nonunion employees in the private sector are employed at will, meaning the firm is allowed to dismiss the employee "for good cause, for bad cause, or even for cause morally wrong" (cited in Steiber 1984, 2). Many states have carved out several exemptions to pure employment at will, most importantly based on employers' handbooks or other promises that imply an employment contract (Potter and Youngman 1995, 141). Unfortunately, these protections, like those against discrimination, apply in fact primarily to high-wage employers who can afford a lawyer (U.S. Commission on the Future of Worker-Management Relations 1994, 30).

While many employees feel their rights are not protected, many employers resent the cost of litigation and regulation and what they perceive as EEOC's combative and antiemployer stance (Potter and Youngman 1995, 141). Two bad effects can result if employers find it expensive to dismiss people from protected groups. First, fear of lawsuits may stop them from dismissing unsatisfactory employees from these protected groups, reducing efficiency and incentives. In addition, employers may resist hiring the disabled, blacks, or females because they fear future lawsuits. (In fact, almost all EEOC and antidiscrimination cases are about unjust dismissal, not unjust failure to hire [Donahue and Siegelman 1991].) When the courts do find a contract was implied, many employers resent the high costs of lawsuits and the uncertainty and risk relating to the (small) chance of very high damages (Goldstein 1995).

Companies already have some incentives to have good in-house processes for avoiding and resolving cases of discrimination because both discriminating against good workers and becoming involved in the EEOC process are costly. Nevertheless, current employment law does not provide direct incentives for good in-house dispute resolution processes.

The Role of Employee Oversight in Creating
Credible Alternative Dispute-Resolution Procedures

While no legal system alone can end all discrimination, this proposal should both reduce discrimination and lower the costs of fighting discrimination. Alternative dispute-resolution procedures can reduce costs, increase the speed in which problems are resolved, and increase both employees' and employers' satisfaction. A key element of alternative dispute-resolution procedures is that they can be flexible and tailored to the needs of the organization and its members (U.S. Commission on the Future of Worker-Management Relations 1994, 28). For example, in-house dispute resolution procedures often provide employees with the choice of either confidential or public means of addressing complaints (Rowe 1990; U.S. Commission on the Future of Worker-Management Relations 1994, 28). In another setting, an employer that has many employees who are not native English speakers might ensure that any appeals board of workers and managers had at least one native speaker of the accused worker's language. Because so many complaints require primarily better communication, in-house procedures can begin with mediation, not the more legalistic EEOC procedures.

Ensuring High Standards

A serious problem with alternative dispute-resolution procedures is that an employer may establish procedures rigged in its favor. For example, one law firm proposed that employees give up their legal rights in return for the right to use a company-designed dispute-resolution program. This program's highest level of appeal was a partner from another large law firm (U.S. Commission on the Future of Worker-Management Relations 1994, 27). It is likely that a young woman working in a law firm who accuses her older male boss of sexual harassment will feel that an (older, male) partner in a nearby large law firm is not a neutral decision maker. Other alternative dispute-resolution procedures companies have established have had maximum penalties far below those permitted by law, and others have taken years to resolve disputes. Because of these risks, the EEOC has argued that employers should not be able to require employees to sign away their rights to EEOC hearings just because an employer has an in-house dispute-resolution procedure (Bompey and Stempel 1995).

To avoid these problems, any in-house dispute-resolution program would need to meet high standards. The first standard is approval by the employees' representation body described above. Employees will be loath to approve a procedure that gives employers the ability to act with no disregard for the facts. At the same time, minority employees cannot have their rights suspended because their colleagues feel a given dispute-resolution procedure is adequate. The majority of current employees may themselves discriminate, or may just care less about the concerns of the minority than the law does.

Fortunately, a recent high-level commission found that both employers and employees agree on a set of standards alternative dispute-resolution procedures must meet if they are to serve as a legitimate form of private enforcement of public employment law. Specifically, these systems must provide a neutral arbitrator who knows the laws in question and understands the concerns of the parties; a fair method by which the employee can secure the necessary information to present his or her claim; a fair method of cost sharing that ensures all employees can afford access; the option for employees to have independent representation; a range of remedies equal to those available through litigation; a written opinion by the arbitrator explaining the rationale for the result; and sufficient judicial review to ensure that the result is consistent with the governing laws. The standards might also require a timely decision. In addition, in cases where due process is in doubt, the worker retains recourse to appeal to the standard court system.

The proposed system would not preclude court cases when management practices systematically discriminate against a group or potential group of employees. Particularly in such a setting, a majority of the existing workforce may favor discrimination that favors incumbent workers; thus, reliance on outside enforcement is called for.

In unionized settings, unions might retain their current right to stop certain grievances from being appealed all the way to outside arbitration. As under current law, in discrimination cases a worker should not need the union's permission to appeal a grievance.

At the same time, when management has practices in place that have been approved by the workforce and that appear effective (such as education on sexual harassment and prompt and effective investigations of complaints), then the employer should not be held liable for the misdeeds of a single manager (Potter and Youngman 1995, 352).

The new system has several possible drawbacks. Unlike court cases, arbitration does not provide clear precedents. In addition, arbitration can lead to different arbitrators imposing different settlements for identical facts without judicial review of the settlement. (Judges would only review whether due process was followed.) These problems will probably not be too serious because arbitrators try to be consistent with each other both as a measure of professional competence and to ensure repeat employment—employees and employers will not jointly agree on arbitrators with records far from the norm.

While the concern about repeat business reduces the odds of arbitrary and capricious awards, it also implies arbitrators will rarely provide the very large awards that some juries provide. If fear of large (but unpredictable and rare) awards is a major deterrent to employer discrimination, then the new system will not reduce discrimination (Kochan 1995, 358). It is likely that reducing the costs of protesting unfair treatment and increasing the probability of sanctions in cases of unfair treatment will protect more workers than the risk of a few large but arbitrary awards.

Problems can also arise when most of the workforce would prefer a discriminatory dispute-resolution procedure. As noted earlier, this proposal requires outside neutral arbitration and permits judicial review of due process, precluding the worst abuses. To enhance the rights of minorities further, this proposal expands the right of individuals to bring class action lawsuits outside the in-house dispute resolution mechanism when employment practices are systematically biased against a group. (This right is broader than the right under current law because it permits a class action suit even if only a single employee is in the discriminated-against group at this time, if the practice has reduced the number of employees in the group.)

Employee Involvement

The Problem

The National Labor Relations Act (NLRA) makes it illegal for employers to discuss "conditions of employment" with company-sponsored committees of employees. Under Section 8(a)(2) of the act, such a committee is an illegal "company union." Thus, committees of workers that influence training, work schedules, and promotions are typically not legal. Even a safety committee can easily run afoul of labor law (Kamer et al. 1994; Sockell 1984).

The situation is no better at unionized establishments. In high-involvement workplaces such as the Saturn auto factory, workers make many decisions that were once the province of management. Unfortunately, U.S. labor law defines workers performing such "managerial" tasks as managers and does not permit managers all the rights of traditional union members.

These legal barriers are important because, as cited above, new forms of work organization with higher levels of employee involvement are desired by most of the workforce (Freeman and Rogers 1995). In addition, recent research shows that such innovations typically have positive effects on outcomes ranging from product quality to stock market value. (See the evidence reviewed in Levine 1995, which also describes several market imperfections that impede the spread of employee involvement.)

One possible solution is legalizing all forms of employee involvement. For example, in 1997 Congress passed and President Clinton vetoed) the TEAM Act that attempts to permit all employee involvement groups that do not negotiate or enter into collective bargaining agreements with the employer.

Unfortunately, this approach is not a good solution because company unions can be a threat, even if they do not sign a collective bargaining agreement. As Senator Wagner stated in pushing for the National Labor Relations Act sixty years ago, company unions posed "one of the great obstacles to genuine freedom of self-organization" (cited in AFL-CIO 1994). Most Americans support the right of employees to form their own organizations free of management domination to bargain with management and to protect employees' rights (Freeman and Rogers 1993, 30–32).

If employers can establish company unions of any sort, they can impede workers' right to self-determination. For example, employers that perceive themselves at risk of a union organizing campaign can set up a sham employee representation program that alleviates some employees' perceived need for a union. Employers that already have unions can establish alternative problem-solving mechanisms that bypass the elected representatives of the workforce. Moreover, the strong opposition of the American labor movement to the new law makes it likely its passage will do little to increase cooperation and involvement at work (Kochan 1995).

The role of employee oversight can ensure teamwork is not just a facade. Under this proposal, employees will need collectively to approve any employee involvement mechanisms that would otherwise run afoul of the NLRA. In organized workplaces, the union would need to approve the plan. In other workplaces, either the democratically chosen employee council or a direct vote would need to approve each exemption. If a high-quality employee representative body approved an employee involvement program, such a program would be exempt from the NLRA ban.

This oversight would make it much less likely that employers would propose sham involvement mechanisms or that they would set up an employee involvement program primarily to weaken a union organizing campaign. If the employees ever felt the group was a sham, they could rescind their approval and the plan would no longer be legal.

At the same time, this oversight would increase employees' confidence that the proposed involvement program was in their best interest. Some evidence exists that employee involvement programs are more long-lived in unionized establishments (Drago 1988); presumably, part of the advantage reflects the union's role in discouraging employers from setting up exploitative and short-run programs.

Ensuring Minimum Standards for the Involvement Groups

Even with employee oversight, several standards would be required of all involvement plans. For example, all participants would be guaranteed against loss of pay or benefits and against any retribution for their participation (or for choosing not to participate) in any employee involvement group. Once an employee involvement group begins, the company could not disband the group without the approval of the employees or their representatives.

Other Spheres of Regulation

The basic insight that workers have an interest in both effective and efficient workplace regulation implies that the same framework of employee oversight can be applied to other spheres of workplace regulation. This section outlines how employee oversight can improve overtime rules, employee stock-ownership plans, and government-subsidized training programs.

Wage-and-Hour Regulations

Wage-and-hour rules also do not always make it easy for a company to implement flexible schedules. Few companies permit someone to choose to work six days one week and four days the next because the company must pay overtime for the sixth day. Also, employers may not offer partial vacation days to salaried employees for fear they will become eligible for overtime (Potter and Youngman 1995, 293). Even worse, people who work too few hours or days in a row sometimes run the risk of losing eligibility for unemployment insurance or other benefits. In addition, some employees would prefer time off to higher pay, but companies are not always permitted to offer compensatory time instead of overtime wages (Potter and Youngman 1995, 295).

At the same time, several million workers work longer shifts than they desire (Kahn and Lang 1992). Any move that simply relaxed overtime rules would worsen this problem.

Employee oversight can help provide flexibility. One possibility is to permit the employees or their representatives to authorize limited forms of flexibility in hours. For example, an employee council might be permitted to approve replacing the 40-hour week with the 160-hour month (or the 80-hour two weeks) to allow for flexible schedules. Employees would have some bargaining power in this process. Thus, the council might modify the rules to allow flexible time schedules and compensatory time instead of overtime wages, in exchange for the company ending mandatory overtime.

Employee Stock-Ownership Plans

For over a generation, the federal government has given tax subsidies to employee stock-ownership plans (ESOPs). When the U.S. Congress created the ESOP program, an important motive was to increase worker commitment and productivity. Over the life of this program, the cost in reduced tax collections due to subsidizing employee stock ownership has been more than $20 billion. (The current set of ESOP tax subsidies is quite complicated. See Joseph Blasi and Douglas Kruse for a short presentation [1991, 23–24].)

In spite of the continued tax expenditures on this program, "there is no evidence whatsoever that employee ownership itself automatically causes improved productivity or profitability except when combined with employee involvement" (Blasi and Kruse 1991).

Despite this evidence, under current law ESOP trustees are chosen solely by management. They can be company officers or outsiders such as banks. These outsiders often receive large fees, however, and can be replaced at will by management. The potential conflicts of interests are clear, and ESOP trustees often act more for the benefit of managers than for either shareholders or employee-owners.

For both reasons, tying the ESOP subsidy to policies indicative of worker participation is appropriate. Such a change in ESOP legislation can potentially reduce the federal deficit, better meet Congress's original intent, and increase national productivity.

One solution is to restrict the ESOP tax subsidy to employers that permit employees to have oversight over their ESOP shares. For companies with an employee representation council, for example, the council could vote the ESOP shares or could appoint or approve the trustee. Furthermore, employees or their representatives should be able to vote shares held by other retirement plans such as 401-K defined-contribution pensions, stock bonus plans, savings plans, defined-benefit pension plans that own company shares, and deferred profit-sharing plans. Workers should be able to vote both allocated and unallocated shares of the ESOP. (Unallocated shares are owned by a leveraged ESOP but are not yet purchased by workers.)

Following similar logic, the employee representative might also be useful in helping appoint trustees for employees' pension funds.

Training Programs

Currently, the federal government and forty-four states have created programs to work with employers to provide training (Potter and Youngman 1995, 195). A problem with public funding of training is that employers may take public funds and either not provide training or only provide training they would have given even without the government assistance.

Kirsten Wever (1995) and Lisa Lynch (1994) note that in Europe, employee oversight via works councils helps ensure training programs are well run. The same logic applies in the United States, implying that public subsidies should be given preferentially to employers whose training programs have been approved by employees or their representatives.

Promoting Government Responsibility

The counterpart of the move to internal responsibility by employers and employees is government taking responsibility for improving its regulatory actions. These improvements have a number of related elements.

Regulatory Culture Change

Regulators must move from a culture of policing to a culture of compliance assistance: changing inspection agencies' internal rules, standard operating procedures, and inspector general policies to encourage providing more training and assistance; focusing inspections on dangerous hazards while giving fix-it tickets for minor violations; precertifying changes in the workplace; and having inspectors give immediate waivers to companies whose policies achieve the goal of a regulation. The ultimate goal is for companies to invite in inspectors to help solve problems.

One-Stop Compliance Assistance and Enforcement

The vice president has emphasized the advantages of creating a virtual Department of Cleveland to integrate the economic, social, and environmental programs run by the federal government that affect Cleveland. Following the same intuition, there should be (from the customer's point of view) a Department of Dry Cleaners in southern Maryland that answers their questions and helps them maintain a safe, environmentally sound business. A dry cleaner has no desire to have employee safety regulations for a chemical run by a different agency than environmental regulations for that chemical; they do not want OSHA whistle-blower regulations different from other whistle-blower protection regulations; they do not want the definition of "independent contractor" to differ for over-time rules (Fair Labor Standards Act), safety (OSHA), pension rules (ERISA), and tax rules (the Internal Revenue Service).

At least for smaller enterprises, compliance efforts (both training and enforcement) would be carried out from a one-stop Workplace Improvement Agency. One-stop inspectors would specialize in a set of industries or technologies, and would be able to call in specialists for complicated situations. This one-stop Workplace Agency would not only cover Department of Labor regulations, and include state regulations, environmental regulations, and so on. In a given industry such as education or health, that industry's workplace officer could also manage many Department of Education and Department of Health and Human Services (which oversees Medicaid) programs, simplifying life even further.

This reform would simplify life for businesspeople, who could call a single source for information, and could deal with a single agency for solving regulatory problems. If the workplace improvement officer dealing with a company was unable to answer a manager's questions, he or she would be clearly responsible for finding out the relevant information. The proposal is unlike the current situation, where multiple phone calls are often required to find out about break times or paint fumes.

One critique of such a proposal is that no single inspector could learn all the rules that apply to a dry cleaner. In fact, if rules are too complicated for a full-time inspector to learn, then they are too complicated for a small business to deal with. Thus, a workplace improvement officer should receive training in those regulations that most affect safety and employee well-being, and other regulations should be waived for small businesses.

Information System

Underlying this compliance agency would be an excellent information system. Regulations, information and applications for funding, information on best practice, and other sources of information should all be online. The goal is not "DOL On Line" but "Workplace Information On Line." For example, a manager does not care if the regulating agency is state government, the Fair Labor Standards Act (overtime), ERISA (pensions and ESOPs), or the IRS. Most managers just want to know: "What is the rule, why is it there, and how do I comply?"

In addition, we must make it easy for workers to know their rights so that they can put pressure for compliance. Right now, for example, finding out rules on work hours for each state is difficult. When individuals know their own rights, some self-regulation will occur automatically.

Consistent Enforcement

Replace the complicated system of National Labor Relations Board, Office of Administrative Law (OAL), state and/or federal OSHA citations and appeals, rights to private action under common law as defined separately in each state, workers' compensation insurance appeals, and so forth, into a single system of workplace law administration, with a single trained set of mediators, arbitrators, and workplace-oriented appeals judges. Accompanying such a reform would be a rationalization of penalties, with an emphasis on matching penalties to the severity of the crime. Furthermore, the system should increase the consistency of punishment and the confidence employees have that they will receive reimbursement (as opposed to unpredictable lotteries with some big winners and many losers).

Recordkeeping should also be rationalized. Several million very small employers should submit quarterly photocopies of pay stubs, not seventeen different forms for state unemployment insurance, federal unemployment insurance, Social Security, and IRS W-2 and W-4—merely because they have a single employee. Multistate employers should not need separate unemployment insurance forms for each of fifty states (and a few territories). All forms should be accessible online, with a standard format for the data describing the company name and employer identification number. (The Small Business Administration has already proposed a standard Federal Form 1 to reduce paperwork burden for small businesses.)

Critiques

The main critique of in-house systems, even those approved by the workforce and meeting high standards, is that some workers will lose compared with the status quo. For example, some safety programs will not listen to valid complaints that an OSHA inspector would have caught, and some in-house dispute-resolution procedures will be manipulated by management, endorsed by a discriminatory workforce, or poorly run.

These problems are serious because each of these problems will surely arise. At the same time, this critique is unconvincing because many workers now work in unsafe conditions and are not treated fairly. This proposal must be judged by whether it improves safety, lessens discrimination, and improves the situation for most workers; not whether it achieves perfection. Given the inadequacies of the current system and the likelihood of continuing funding cuts for regulatory agencies, the current system is unlikely to become more effective at protecting workers without dramatic reforms.

Some unions have opposed past proposals for various forms of employee representation committees in the United States because they are too close to company unions. At the same time, some managers have resented proposals for works councils as thinly disguised entry points for unions. The evidence supports neither view strongly—for example, no evidence exists that union organizing has increased or decreased in states that begin requiring safety committees.

An additional argument against permitting workers to renegotiate regulations in areas such as safety is that they may agree with management (perhaps under the threat of job loss) to reduce safety or other protections below the socially optimal level. (Recall that because of workers' compensation and Social Security disability insurance, often neither workers nor employers pay the full cost of injuries.) It is likely that workers and managers at some workplaces will agree to reduce safety below the level that OSHA now requires on paper. Unfortunately, given OSHA's resources for enforcement, under the status quo OSHA has almost no ability to enforce safety rules in workplaces where workers and managers do not want to obey them. Thus, it is unlikely that many workplaces will reduce their level of safety, although it may remain below the socially optimal level.

One obstacle to the new system is the required change in the priorities of regulators. Currently, as noted earlier, regulators are often required to inspect after every complaint, and to write up all violations, no matter how minor. Under the new regime, many regulations would be waived for workplaces with effective internal systems. Regulators would need to redirect resources from nit-picking inspections to providing training materials and other resources for in-house systems. (Inspections at companies without effective in-house systems would remain an important part of regulators' jobs.) Congress would need to provide sufficient resources for regulators to assist compliance, particularly in the early years when participants in in-house systems will need the most training.

Politically, this proposal has many hurdles. The current system has relatively strong workers' rights on paper, but often not in practice. The proposed system weakens some of these formal rights, while it intends to enlarge rights in practice. Politically, few proponents of workers' rights are willing to accept this weakening de jure, even if it strengthens rights de facto. After a generation of increased de jure rights for employees, many advocates of employees' rights look to the law, not to employees and employers, to protect workers' rights. These advocates must be willing to trade off some rights on paper to strengthen rights in practice, if effective reform is to succeed.

At the same time, many critics of employment protections feel that complete deregulation is the answer. Everyone agrees the current regulatory system has many shortcomings. Unfortunately, continued discrimination coupled with the many imperfections in labor markets make it unlikely that complete deregulation will enhance the workforce's well-being. Similarly, although savings are possible, budget cuts to destroy the limited regulatory capacities of the enforcement agencies are also unlikely to improve things. It is in the long-run interests of both managers and employees to improve regulation, even if not along the lines of this proposal.

Finally, many proponents of reinventing regulation focus on the importance of measuring outcomes, not inputs. This proposal, in contrast, promotes a focus on both outcomes and a metaprocess (that is, an employee-led process for approving the process). The reason to involve employees is simple—because outcomes are always difficult to measure, employers will face incentives to game any outcome measurement system. In many cases we can achieve better results with a combination of outcome measurement and employee-led monitoring of internal processes.

Conclusion

Almost all observers of American workplaces would like regulations to be more flexible and employees' to have more involvement on the job. The government has substantial control over the first, but must be concerned that any flexibility will be used by employers to defeat the goals of the regulations. In contrast, the government has few mechanisms for encouraging employee participation. Fortunately, the proposed system both promotes flexibility in regulation and, by using employees to monitor management, increases employees' voice in how their workplace runs. The government thus moves from discouraging to encouraging employee involvement in decisions at the workplace at the same time it reduces direct government regulation.

Importantly, the proposed new system is voluntary. Each employer has the option of establishing an alternative system with high standards and employee oversight, or the option to remain subject to the current regulatory scheme. The government provides incentives to those employers with good records of success and good programs to work with their employees to ensure continued progress. Often, an important incentive is conditional deregulation from detailed command-and-control regulations.

In short, the status quo provides poor incentives to workers and managers—they have incentives to hit the letter of the regulation but not the goal of the law. The reinvented system provides incentives for workers and managers to achieve and exceed the standards of today. The status quo provides poor incentives for regulators; for example, OSHA inspectors forced to play "gotcha" instead of increasing safety. The reinvented system permits many employees of regulatory agencies to focus on compliance assistance, while others focus on the truly bad apples. Finally, the status quo relies on top-down regulations, while the reinvented process encourages workers and managers to improve compliance with flexibility to meet local conditions.

Under this proposal, an employer can establish an alternative regulatory system in any single area of workplace regulations such as safety, dispute resolution, or wage-and-hour rules. But the new system can be fruitfully applied to all these areas of regulation. Moreover, creating a single employee committee to provide oversight for all spheres costs less than creating separate oversight mechanisms. This approach to reinventing regulation, by providing employers incentives to work with their employees, has the potential both to improve workers' lives and to improve companies' bottom lines.

* * *

Bringing the Excluded into the New Economy

The previous chapters have dealt with creating a life cycle of policies to create skilled workers and jobs that build on these skills. A key has been adapting our economic policies to the new economy and creating flexible, customer-focused government programs.

The following chapters emphasize groups often left out of the new economy: the poor and disabled. Reinventing urban housing policy and policies focused on ghettos can improve the lives of our most disadvantaged citizens. Our disability policy currently condemns millions of working-age Americans to poverty-level pensions.

As before, the tools of reinvention will involve focusing on incentives and creating flexible, customer-oriented policies. At the same time, the new policies must be in touch with the realities and needs of the citizens they try to help—unlike some recent proposals for reform.

9

ENDING PUBLIC HOUSING AS WE KNOW IT

Sixty years ago the federal government began subsidizing public housing projects. We now know these well-intentioned efforts often create the worst neighborhoods in America. Housing assistance should be delivered with flexible housing vouchers that permit recipients to move from bad neighborhoods and toward jobs and good schools.

Franklin D. Roosevelt launched the federal government into the business of funding public housing with the remark, "Within a very short time people who never before could get a decent roof over their heads will live here in reasonable comfort and healthful, worthwhile surroundings" (cited in Lick 1996). Sixty years later, those under the roofs of public housing all too often lack the comfort or healthfulness. Then Secretary of Housing and Urban Development (HUD) Henry Cisneros acknowledged to Congress in June 1993 that "HUD has in many cases exacerbated the declining quality of life in America." In Cisneros's words, much of public housing, "which began 30 years ago as transitional housing for working people who had come upon hard times, has become a trap for the poorest of the poor rather than a launching pad for families trying to improve their lives" (cited in "Look Out, Landlords . . ." 1995).

HUD-assisted housing programs are not small. At a cost of $24 billion in 1995, they cost about as much as each of the two other large welfare programs, AFDC and food stamps (although still dwarfed by the cost of Medicaid, running over $100 billion). HUD-assisted housing helps roughly 4.5 million people. Of these, roughly one-third receive housing vouchers that help them afford low-rent apartments; one-third are in privately owned low-income housing projects, and one-third are in large public housing projects.

These large public housing projects, in turn, are managed by public housing authorities. The managers of public housing authorities are usually appointed by combinations of state and city governments, but the authorities are primarily funded by HUD. These large public housing projects are also the ones that often deserve the moniker of "the worst neighborhoods in America," with extremely high rates of crime, drug abuse, nonemployment, and single-parent families. (That is, the vast majority of HUD projects are well run and do not contribute to urban problems; nevertheless, the troubled ones tend to be very large and to hold a substantial share of HUD-assisted residents.)

Problems with Public and Assisted Housing

Like many other social insurance programs, work disincentives are a problem with HUD public and assisted housing. HUD sets occupants' rents at 30 percent of (adjusted) income. The 30 percent benefit reduction rates reduce incentives to work, particularly when combined with implicit marginal tax rates from other programs. For example, according to HUD calculations, a mother of two children in California who works full time for $10 per hour brings home only $1,000 more per year (after taxes, child care, and work expenses) than a woman who works zero hours. It is possible that HUD assistance also leads to disincentives for marriage and to intergenerational scarring that raises future durations on public assistance, although no evidence exists on these effects.

Additional problems are specific to HUD public and assisted housing. HUD benefits also create inefficiencies and inequities due to their limited supply. Unlike AFDC or food stamps, HUD housing assistance is not an entitlement. Thus, only half of the low-income families eligible for housing assistance receive it. The others who apply are put on waiting lists, some of them many years long. This rationing implies similar families receive very different levels of assistance, violating norms of fairness as equal treatment. The rationing can lead to corruption as prospective recipients try to leap the waiting list.

Some eligible applicants do not apply because they do not want to live in public housing, even if heavily subsidized. HUD has created many of America's worst neighborhoods. It appears that parents and especially children do better when they leave the ghetto for mixed-income neighborhoods (box 9.1).

Some of the problems of HUD projects are caused by the poor incentives project managers face because they do not have market incentives to maintain quality. In a HUD survey, residents in public housing reported living in worse neighborhoods and with no better housing quality than did those eligible for housing assistance but who received no HUD assistance. Furthermore, residents in public housing reported worse conditions than those with housing vouchers. (Voucher holders and residents in the small private projects reported similar neighborhoods and housing conditions.)

Some of the poor incentives for project managers are the result of one-size-fits-all command-and-control regulations. Regions of the country differ vastly in their real estate markets, and landlords differ vastly in the quality of their management and the quality of their housing stock. Nevertheless,

Box 9.1. **What Works: Gatreaux and Housing Deconcentration***

In 1965 Dorothy Gatreaux successfully sued the Chicago Housing Authority for exhibiting discrimination in its location of new public housing in largely black neighborhoods. The courts ordered the housing authority to fund what became known as the Gatreaux experiment—providing rent vouchers that moved a number of central-city Chicago public housing residents into the suburbs or elsewhere in the central city. Because the assignment of families to suburban or city apartments was almost completely random, the Gatreaux experience provides a natural experiment for understanding the gains from housing desegregation.

Parents who moved their families to the suburbs exhibited at least as good employment success as those who stayed in the central city, in spite of often having to give up their jobs when they initally moved. More important, children who moved to the suburbs had much better school success than those staying in the cities. In a follow-up study when the children who moved were approximately eighteen years old, those who moved to the suburbs had one-fourth the high school dropout rate of their counterparts who moved within the poor neighborhoods of Chicago (5 percent vs. 20 percent). Moreover, children who grew up in the suburbs were more than twice as likely to attend college

These results suggest that providing housing vouchers, particularly if coupled with policies that encourage a deconcentration of the poor, can help the children of the poor break the cycle of poverty.

*This box draws on Rosenbaum 1995, 231–269.

many HUD rules for projects are uniform nationwide. Although these sometimes provide an effective minimum on housing quality, they also impose burdensome reporting requirements and limit flexibility and innovation.

Finally, when a resident in a public or privately owned project finds a job, the resident cannot move to be near the job. Furthermore, if the employer moves, the employee cannot also move without losing the housing subsidy. Even tenants with housing vouchers have some disincentives because if they take a high-wage job that does not pan out, the voucher is lost and the family goes to the end of the waiting list. AFDC and other means-tested welfare programs usually provide poor incentives but provide valuable insurance; HUD assistance is bad at both functions.

Housing Vouchers

One possibility is to give housing vouchers for the current value of rent to current residents of public and privately owned assisted housing. The value of these vouchers should be adjusted according to the current formula for rent as a function of income.

Rents should remain controlled for current residents but should be decontrolled when they move out. (The 1995 House of Representative bill 2406 would decontrol rents immediately, with the possibility that many of the poorest residents would be unable to find alternative housing. The Senate version S1260 would decontrol rents only for tenants making more than half of the area's median income.)

The housing voucher plan would not necessarily apply to residents in projects that primarily serve the elderly or disabled (where work disincentives and crime problems are less severe). Landlords would be able to rent vacant units to other voucher holders or to middle-income tenants at rates set by the landlord.

As housing vouchers expire, new and smaller vouchers should be issued. For example, if 50 percent of the eligible population receives vouchers (approximately the national average), all new vouchers should be set at 50 percent of the current level. In this case, the entire eligible population can eventually receive smaller vouchers. The transition can be accelerated by decreasing the real value of current housing vouchers a few percentage points per year and using the savings to fund new and smaller vouchers.

The housing assistance application process, verification of income, and administrative definitions (family, income, assets) should be integrated with cash welfare, food stamps, and other programs to cut administrative costs and simplify the lives of applicants. States should be encouraged to use their low-income-housing tax credit funds for housing vouchers, if they so choose.

This plan solves most of the problems specific to housing assistance using the basic tools of reinvention: decentralization, market forces, and empowering individuals.

- Project managers will face market incentives to improve. Decision-making authority will be decentralized to the unit of government or to the private landlords closest to the citizens and housing customers.
- Tenants with housing vouchers are empowered to move to jobs and will be able to move to better neighborhoods if they find a good job, increasing incentives for work.
- Concentrations of poverty and segregation will be lessened as more poor people choose economically diverse neighborhoods and as landlords are permitted to rent to higher income tenants. (This effect is amplified as more people receive housing vouchers and counteracted by any reconcentration due to the reduction in maximum size of the vouchers.)

For private project-based assistance, we can merely fail to renew contracts when they come up for renewal and instead grant housing vouchers to tenants. An educated guess is that within five years, at least three-fourths of the project-based assistance would be converted to housing vouchers.

Making Work Pay

Any reform of HUD must improve incentives for work. Moving to smaller housing vouchers makes it easy to reduce the marginal tax on additional income. (Working in the other direction, if more people have vouchers, then more people face some work disincentive.)

In addition, recipients should face time limits and have all or most of the work-related services provided to recipients of Temporary Aid to Needy Families (TANF) under welfare reform (child care and government-provided jobs as a last resort). Unfortunately, these services all cost money. Time limits without assistance are a possibility, although there is bad press (as well as ethical problems) associated with evicting families from public housing. Time limits coupled with work-search requirements similar to those for unemployment insurance are a low-cost alternative.

Under current law, each dollar a public housing resident receives leads to thirty cents in higher rent. For residents in public housing, some portion of any income should be able to escape the 30 percent rent increase if it is put into an account to pay for education, a down payment on a house, or for the first and last months' rent in a private apartment. Furthermore, housing vouchers should be usable for home purchase, as well as for rental.

Critiques of Housing Vouchers

Although appealing on many grounds, housing vouchers face a number of important criticisms.

Substandard Housing Will Increase

Critics claim that with housing vouchers such as those described above, some people who move out will use their vouchers to pay for substandard housing. Low-value vouchers will lead to the concentration of the poor into very poor neighborhoods and into substandard housing.

In fact, raising tenants' purchasing power appears to raise housing quality as much as building units. In one study, raising the housing grant portion of AFDC to the value of a HUD housing voucher raised housing quality as much as did living in HUD public and assisted housing. (The exception to this result is in New York City, where low-quality housing is abundant [Newman and Schnare 1992, 64].)

To fight concentration into ghettos, HUD should expanded the Choice in Residency program that counsels and assists families to move to less concentratedly poor neighborhoods. Importantly, evidence from matched pairs of white and minority testers applying for rental housing routinely finds that minority tenants are discriminated against (see box 9.2). Anecdotal evidence suggests additional discrimination against those holding housing vouchers. As is usual when lawbreaking is common, increased fair housing enforcement is the key, especially enforcement relying on matched pairs of testing applicants.

Homelessness Will Increase

Some critics fear that housing vouchers will increase homelessness because with smaller vouchers, fewer people will be able to find housing of any sort.

In fact, homelessness will almost surely decrease under this plan, not increase. Almost every family on the housing assistance waiting list finds *some* housing. Giving them all a small voucher will raise the probability of their finding housing, and this effect is almost surely larger than the decrease in the probability of housing for those who would have received large housing vouchers.

After Decontrol, Some Rents Will Rise or Fall Dramatically

Several analysts have (correctly) noted that in a free market rents will differ from the HUD-set rents of the past—some will rise, and some will fall (Henderson 1995). In cases where rents rise, units will be lost to the low-income housing stock. Because rents are frozen for current tenants, this effect will be delayed until the current tenants move out. Thus, landlords may pressure some residents to move out to speed-up decontrol.

In other cases, the units are in such disrepair that decontrol may lead rents to fall and tenants to move out. As vacancies rise, gangs and the homeless may move in, making life even worse for those who stay. Eventually, high vacancy rates and falling rents will lead to foreclosures or to bankrupt public housing authorities. Units will be lost to the low-income housing stock, and some long-time residents will be forced to move out.

These critiques have more validity than those mentioned earlier. That is how markets operate—well-run projects (and some lucky ones located in pretty good neighborhoods) will have prices go up, poorly run projects (and some that just are not economically viable) will see rents go down. Residents will retain their housing vouchers, so few will be badly harmed. While some projects will gain and others will lose, states should be able to average out good and bad projects to mitigate the costs of some bankruptcies.

More important, the provision of market incentives to housing authorities will improve incentives to maintain the quality of the housing stock; thus, far fewer bankruptcies are likely than would be projected with current cost structures.

Political Issues

Most economists who examine welfare policy find little justification for specific housing policies that involve building special poor-people's housing. Poor people need a safety net, but if given sufficient purchasing power, they will house themselves. Moreover, markets work pretty well, even in housing, so if consumers have purchasing power for low-rent units, low-cost units will be built (or more realistically, they will be converted from larger units, or they will remain in existence when otherwise they would be torn down).

Given this background, this proposal moves to meld housing assistance into a smaller entitlement for all poor people, not a housing voucher or unit that is given to only half or so of those eligible. The proposal retains the housing-specific nature of the voucher (instead of just providing an equivalent amount of cash) for several reasons. First, housing is particularly valuable for children, and housing vouchers cannot be easily turned into alcohol or other drugs for the small proportion of the poor who would mistreat their children to feed their addiction. Perhaps for this reason, politically, voters appear to prefer assistance in kind. Real estate interests such as builders and building trades unions also prefer housing assistance, presumably because they feel it increases poor people's demand for housing and, thus, their own incomes.

Housing vouchers are politically often less popular than hard units for several reasons. Some liberals like the semi-irreversibility of hard units; they commit future funding to maintain the projects.

Some motives are particularly selfish and sometimes reprehensible. In many cases, representatives of middle-class suburbs prefer public housing projects to housing vouchers so that the poor stay away. Given the high proportion of nonwhite residents of public housing, this last motive can involve racism.

Will Vouchers Weaken Neighborhoods?

Like schools, public housing projects "create" neighborhoods. Thus, some proponents on public housing oppose housing vouchers because they will facilitate exit when voice (i.e., resident organizations) is more socially desirable. Several important cases of residents in public housing projects creating resident organizations to improve their living conditions exist. For example, the residents of Kenilworth-Parkside in Washington, D.C., organized themselves to create a remarkable turnaround in their drug- and crime-ridden development (Osborne and Gaebler 1992, 60–64). At the same time, on average, the large public housing projects are not very good neighborhoods. Moreover (and ironically) by strengthening exit we can improve the neighborhoods in two fashions.

First, exit creates much better incentives for the managers of public housing projects to create desirable living spaces. As Albert Hirschman (1970) pointed out when he made the exit/voice dichotomy, the threat of exit can increase the effectiveness of voice. Second, the worst housing projects are so bad that it is unlikely that resident organizations (voice) can effectively improve them. At the same, time creating a system (described in more detail below) where youth know that if they play by the rules they can leave the ghetto, may induce a substantial number not to join gangs and engage in other undesirable behaviors. With some decline in these activities, the neighborhoods may improve enough to make residents' organizations worthwhile.

In general, public policies should work to strengthen neighborhoods. At the same time, trapping Americans in the worst neighborhoods is unlikely to be effective at doing so.

Promoting Housing Desegregation

Ultimately, housing desegregation is the best long-term solution to the problem of concentrated poverty and to the disadvantages faced by many minority-group members. As long as most blacks have a majority of neighbors who are also minority-group members, equality of access to jobs, information networks, and social services will be difficult.

The current status of housing segregation is not grounds for optimism. Analyses of the 1990 Census indicate that 65 percent of urban blacks or 65 percent of urban whites would need to change neighborhoods in order to integrate our cities completely (Farley and Frey 1996, 13).

Much of current residential segregation is the legacy of generations of local and federal government policy. These policies ranged from restrictive covenants on housing developments that prohibited sales to blacks and other groups, to federally subsidized mortgages that were primarily available for whites in white neighborhoods, to siting public housing in largely minority areas (Farley and Frey 1996). Unfortunately, although public policies no longer explicitly promote segregation, measures of residential segregation have shown only slow declines since peaking around 1970.

Box 9.2. What Works: Fair Housing Testers

For decades, debate has raged concerning the importance of discrimination in employment and housing. Chapter 2 summarized the evidence that blacks, Hispanics, and women fare poorly compared to matched pairs of white male applicants for employment. Housing testers can be even more effective than employment testers. Employment testers can demonstrate patterns of discrimination but can rarely demonstrate that a particular instance was discriminatory or just randomness. Housing testers, in contrast, can often provide evidence of a specific landlord illegally discriminating.

In these tests, matched pairs of applicants for an apartment apply for a rental unit, with the minority applicant applying first. Frequently, the minority applicant is told the advertised unit has been filled, or no vacancies are available; the white applicant is then offered a unit. Overall, roughly half of all blacks faced discrimination by rental agents and real estate agents in one widely emulated set of studies (Kingsley and Turner 1993, 16). A more recent study examined a hundred attempts to find rental housing in predominantly white neighborhoods of New Orleans. Blacks faced discrimination 77 percent of the time (Treadway 1996).

The preferences of law-abiding Americans are one factor in promoting housing segregation. The good news is that the proportion of whites who agree in a survey that it is acceptable to exclude blacks from their neighborhood declined from 60 percent in the 1960s to 20 percent in 1990 (Farley and Frey 1996, 7).

The bad news is that most whites who would like to live in an integrated neighborhood consider 80 percent white and 20 percent black to be a comfortable level, while most blacks who would like to live in an integrated neighborhood consider 50 percent white and 50 percent black to be a comfortable level (Kingsley and Turner 1993, 14). This combination implies that few neighborhoods will remain integrated for long—as the proportion black rises to near 20 percent, more blacks will be attracted, and fewer whites will be.

Unfortunately, much housing segregation involves breaking the law (box 9.2). Discrimination in housing pervades almost every step of the housing process. For example, landlords often discriminate in choosing tenants for their apartments. Furthermore, realtors show black potential homeowners different homes than similar whites a substantial fraction of the time (Yinger 1996).

Discrimination also appears to affect which loans a bank approves for lending (Munnell et al. 1996). Controlling for virtually every piece of information a bank lending officer has about an applicant, black loan applicants were turned down approximately 80 percent more often than similar white applicants. This evidence is less conclusive than that provided by housing testers because the bank loan officer may have observed subtle differences between black and white applicants that predicted loan default rates. Nevertheless, the completeness of the information measured by the researchers suggests discrimination probably played a role.

No single policy can address all sources of housing discrimination and segregation. Some federal funds can be tied to local efforts to end discrimination and segregation, particularly funds to support the two efforts that appear to work: fair housing testers, and dispersed suburban housing of recipients of housing vouchers (boxes 9.1 and 9.2).

Zoning laws that essentially prohibit the construction of low- and moderate-income housing and apartments also lead to concentrations of poverty and disadvantage, as well as perpetuating racial segregation (Downs 1992). Such restrictive laws are often rational for suburbs because they keep out potential residents who would utilize social services and pay below-average taxes. Thus, such suburbs impose externalities on neighboring towns and cities. To the extent suburbs create such laws, they should face penalties from various state and federal funding agencies. Conversely, suburbs without such laws should receive extra funds to help reward cities that take on the burden of meeting social services. In addition, inner-city residents need better information on housing and employment availability in the suburbs. As is often the case, the Internet can help (see box 9.3).

Conclusion

For sixty years America's policy toward our poorest neighborhoods have been based on providing housing and bribing businesses to relocate. Public provision of housing was noble in intention, but it is basically a failure. It has led to poor incentives for public housing authorities, to rigid command-and-control rules, and to some of America's worst neighborhoods. To add insult to injury, the housing assistance did not help those who received it as much as it should, often trapping them in neighborhoods with few employed role models while limiting families' ability to move to be near a job.

This chapter explains how housing vouchers can achieve the goals of housing assistance without most of the current problems. Replacing detailed command-and-control regulations with market incentives should also improve the lives of employees at housing authorities, as well as their projects.

Box 9.3. **What Could Work: Promoting Housing Desegregation Using the Internet**

The labor market information system described in chapter 6 can promote good matches between workers and employers. Similarly, a housing market information system can promote good matches between renters and apartments. Importantly, a well-designed system should promote integration of historically segregated neighborhoods and communities. To do so, the system would need to be easy to use and would need to provide information to inner-city residents on available housing in nearby communities.

Rent Net, an easy-to-use interactive database of more than 1.1 million apartment units in the United States and Canada provides a nationwide model of such a search tool (http://www.rent.net/web-rent.html). Local fair housing groups should work with local landlords to create metropolitanwide versions. If these search tools help fill vacancies, they should be appealing to both renters and landlords. To the extent they help inner-city residents of color find appropriate housing in traditionally white suburbs, the search tools should also promote desegregation.

Empowering the recipients to move to the best housing they can find can only expand their opportunities. Housing allowances (a policy closely related to housing vouchers) have been widely implemented in Europe, with largely beneficial results (Howenstine 1986). The analysis and evidence presented in this chapter suggests that vouchers would be useful in the United States as well.

The following chapter examines the other large set of place-based policies, grants to cities and businesses that are supposed to induce businesses to locate within poor neighborhoods. As with other chapters, a focus on investment and learning leads to quite different proposals than the federal government has implemented in the past.

10

GILDING THE GHETTO, NOT!

Many of the most important problems of poor regions are problems of youth. This chapter describes a new youth-oriented strategy for poor regions, Education Empowerment Zones. In these zones, schools form partnerships with parents, businesses, teachers' unions, local communities, nonprofit organizations, and local colleges. Education Empowerment Zones create a seamless system to help youths stay in school and avoid life on the street. Federal and state funds are delivered in a flexible form, but with accountability for results. Youths in these zones are assured that if they avoid dropping out of high school, crime, and pregnancy, then a job or a place in college is waiting for them. This direct approach, with appropriate accountability, is more effective than previous federal policies to help specific regions. These policies have emphasized expensive subsidies to businesses and have met with little success.

So far, the policies addressed in this book have focused on helping individuals and families, especially children. Complementing these policies, the United States has a long history of place-based policies to help poor rural regions such as Appalachia, and poor urban areas especially inner cities. This section reviews policies for inner cities and other poor urban areas and then notes some important differences for rural place-based policies. While most past policies have emphasized subsidies to business, this chapter outlines a policy focused on changing the lives of youths.

Why Urban Youths Need a New Policy

The problems of the inner city are largely the problems of youth: low high school completion rates and employment rates coupled with high rates of crime, teen pregnancy, and welfare dependency. This section describes why these problems are unsurprising: because ghetto youths face such poor incentives to play by the rules. At the same time, the many social service agencies, both public and private, that try to help ghetto youths do not make

---

This section was written with Maya Federman. An independently designed but conceptually related proposal is being put into effect in several communities by Public/Private Ventures (1996). Fortunately, that effort contains a research component, so evaluation of these ideas should be forthcoming within a few years.

up a coherent system. In short, this nation's urban policy is ripe for the reinvention similar to that outlined elsewhere in this volume.

Poor Incentives for Youth

Fewer than 10 percent of poor children live in big-city ghetto neighborhoods (Bane and Ellwood 1994, 144). In spite of their modest numbers, many of these 2 million or so disadvantaged children are growing up in America's worst neighborhoods, surrounded by high rates of crime, high school dropouts, teen fertility, unemployment, and single-parent households. These are the youths most likely to enter crime or welfare. Thus, both fairness considerations and the search for high social payoffs emphasize the importance of changing this group's current life patterns.

In the nation's worst neighborhoods, young men are more likely to find gangs, not school, as the dominant institution. In these settings, "playing by the rules" by working hard in school and staying out of trouble with the law often does not pay: schools are often quite bad, and employment prospects even after graduating from high school are poor. As low-end wages decline relative to the rest of society, the perceived rewards of joining the very bottom of the mainstream continue to decline. Moreover, youths are more likely to be punished by their peers than rewarded for academic success.*

Unfortunately, for many poor youths, crime, teen pregnancy, and other socially costly behaviors may not be irrational. When the payoffs to playing by the rules appear small and uncertain, it often makes more sense to enjoy the more sure pleasures of the moment. Youths who perceive that they will not share in the rewards of good behavior or achieve success through traditional means in the society at large may be unwilling to make the short-term investments in good behavior. Furthermore, it may be difficult for youths with little positive reinforcement from peers, parents, or other adults to overcome short-run temptations even if they have chosen to play by the rules.

Poor Coordination among Service Providers

Employees at schools, public social service providers, and private volunteers often make valiant efforts to improve the lives of inner-city and other poor youths. Yet, most programs address only a single facet of a youth's problems: health problems at one agency, problems within the family at

---

*Robert I. Lerman and Hillard Pouncy (1990) make this claim. Philip J. Cook and Jens Ludwig review the fairly large body of evidence that ghetto youths who try to play by the rules are sanctioned by their peers although their own study (1997) finds no such sanctioning.

another, or violence at school in a third. Unfortunately, youths and their families who suffer difficulties in one sphere often have other difficulties and need multiple services. Thus, the myriad of current programs, though well intentioned, do not create a coherent system to assist youths and families in need. Youths often have no idea where to access needed services, and their families have difficulty navigating the maze of available services. Further, service providers often have no idea of the related problems a youth and family might have, or the other services the youth or family are receiving.

For social service agencies, whether government, nonprofit, or for profit, the multitude of funding sources further complicates matters. Many agencies spend a substantial portion of their limited resources raising funds. Each funding source makes its own grants, often targeted to a specific arena: teen pregnancy prevention, drug education, or cops on the street. Each funding source has its own accountability mechanism. To ensure targeting, many government programs have rules limiting who can receive services financed by each funding stream. Finally, once programs are established and serving the community, additional time and resources must be spent applying for new grants just to keep the projects going. Although usually well intentioned, such rules limit the community's ability to spend resources flexibly. Just as youths need coordinated services, service providers need a coordinated set of means for acquiring resources. Similarly, service providers must face incentives to work together to achieve common goals and avoid conflicts over "turf."

Some of these lessons about the importance of coordination have been learned, but more is needed. For example, one medium-sized city, Oakland, California, has at least ten different coordinating bodies focused on youth issues. The mantra of accountability has spread along with the mantra of coordination, but (again) additional refinement is needed. An agency receiving funding from multiple sources often has to file multiple reports with different measures of success. We need to coordinate not just our programs but also our data-collection efforts, accountability mechanisms, and efforts at coordination. Moreover, in spite of the recurring mantra of performance measurement, few programs face clear rewards for good performance.

Poor Incentives for Potential Partners

Local businesses and nearby inner-ring suburbs could benefit by solving inner-city problems and are important potential partners in addressing them. Residents in nearby suburbs suffer some of the ill effects of living near gangs and less comfortable access to the amenities of the city for fear of crime. Local businesses and companies could benefit from lower neighborhood crime and from access to a better-educated local workforce. For example, most large corporations headquartered in a city do very little hiring from the worst neighborhoods. Unfortunately, these potential partners have only weak incentives to participate in the improvement of nearby poor areas, especially of the worst neighborhoods of the inner cities. Each of these groups has an incentive to "free ride" on assisting neighborhoods and youths in need, hoping other interested parties will solve the problems. Further, local businesses and organizations in nearby suburbs may want to participate but may be reluctant to pour resources into neighborhoods with overly bureaucratic or poorly functioning institutions.

Poor Results

The results are familiar to anyone who reads the daily paper. Although the evidence on the rising importance of "the underclass" is mixed (Jencks and Peterson 1991), few dispute the difficulties inherent in the interlocking set of problems that face youths in our poorest neighborhoods.

These costs spread far beyond the wasted lives of many of our nation's youths. The costs of poor neighborhoods, including those in the inner cities, are shared more broadly, as all citizens pay taxes for prisons and welfare, and most are adversely affected by higher crime rates and gangs and a less productive workforce. For example, our worst neighborhoods suffer from dropout rates of over 50 percent. The evidence presented in chapter 2 suggests that $40,000 direct gains in lower prison and welfare costs are possible if the typical dropout behaved instead like the typical high school graduate, in addition to the increased productivity, taxes, and neighborhood safety.

Education Empowerment Zones (EEZs)

One sensible means to improve the lifetime chances of the underclass is to target assistance to disadvantaged youths. This proposal would create "education empowerment zones" focused on the place-based items that matter most: schools and other services that affect the lives of youths.

The proposal described here follows the principles for reinvention: flexibility, coordination, accountability, and continuous improvement. The proposal would be appropriate at either the federal or the state level. Congress has recently been moving toward consolidation of federal programs with the money given to states as block grants. This proposal could serve as a model for states spending their block grants or other state spending to help poor neighborhoods by focusing on improving outcomes for youths. We also propose that some of the federal money remain at the federal level to address the special needs of inner-city neighborhoods with many of the nation's worst schools and youths at highest risk. The following develops the proposal in the context of a federal program and grant-giving process for inner-city neighborhoods. It can easily be extended to a state program for at-risk youths. In fact, many states have begun to develop programs following similar principles (for example, Healthy Start in California).

Improve Incentives for Youths and Coordination among Service Providers

The theory of EEZs is to create a path to success for any youth who is willing to play by the rules. Students will see that attending school while avoiding drugs, crime, and pregnancy will very likely lead to attainable success. In addition, students receive continual support in pursuing and reaching their goals. In the ideal case, students would have alternatives 24 hours a day and 365 days a year to life on the street. When a sufficient number of youths begin to follow this path, they can create a social network that further lowers the costs of additional youths "playing by the rules" (see box 10.1).

In addition, EEZs would support greater coordination and information sharing among service providers. Finally, EEZs are about more than just giving federal money to neighborhoods, but should also encourage the larger surrounding community to provide greater assistance and participate in the reinvention progress by sending a signal that the neighborhood organizations are moving on the right path to effectively and efficiently addressing the problems of youths. EEZs can serve as a catalyst for other groups providing support of funding to come together and coordinate their programs, data collection, and evaluation efforts.

Flexibility

To promote flexibility and experimentation, the funding would be accompanied by a waiver of federal rules and regulations resulting from other federal programs in that region. (Most environmental and antidiscrimination laws would not be waived.) State and local government agreements on waivers from burdensome state and local rules and regulations would be considered as favorable elements of the application process.

Coordination

The key to education empowerment zones is coordination of service delivery, along with coordination of funding streams and improvements in

Box 10.1. **What Works: "I Have a Dream" Foundation**

In 1981 Eugene Lang, founder of Refac Technology Development Corporation, was speaking to the graduating sixth-grade class at the East Harlem grammar school he once attended. He knew that roughly half this class was expected not to graduate from high school. Not coincidentally, he noticed that many children appeared to be sleeping. On an impulse, he shook them awake with an offer to pay tuition for everyone who got into college.

Specifically, he promised the young people that, if they stayed in school and then worked for five years, he would see to it that they could go to college. The money for the program was accompanied by personal involvement channeled through a Youth Action Program Center in Harlem. In addition to his personal involvement and the promise of scholarships, Lang also hired a counselor to work with the youths through their teen years (Libman 1991). According to Lang, the personal relationship he built up with the class was also crucial in the program.

It worked. Ninety-five percent of the class graduated from high school, compared with the school's usual 50 percent rate, and half of those who graduated went on to college (Libman 1991).

In 1986 Lang formed the "I Have a Dream" Foundation to promote similar efforts; it invests the scholarship funds that sponsors put up (roughly $400,000 per project). Each project operates independently—rather like a franchisee—but it can get training and advice from the foundation. The idea has spread rapidly. By 1992, 159 programs in 47 cities worked with over 10,000 students (Nulty 1992).

The model appears to be replicable, although not all programs succeed as well as Lang's initial effort. For example, one well-financed program chose to work with students who had behavioral problems severe enough to have them kicked out of other "I Have a Dream" programs. In spite of extensive counseling and tutoring, as well as the intense involvement of a top executive, fewer than half of the twenty-three participants graduated from high school. (Even this graduation rate was probably substantially above what these youths would have experienced without the interventions [Nulty 1992].)

The success of Lang's initial efforts, although hardly a controlled experiment, suggests that the model for Education Empowerment Zones can succeed. First, a critical mass of students sees that playing by the rules is likely to lead to work and/or college. Then the students receive the help they need to overcome the many obstacles to educational attainment present in disadvantaged neighborhoods.

individual programs. The schools in the EEZ together with their partners will create a seamless delivery system responsive to youths' needs. Because small-scale interventions typically have only small and short-lived results, we should focus on integrated and long-term programs to increase rates of high school completion rates, employment rates, and college attendance, and to reduce rates of crime, welfare dependency, and teen pregnancy. Thus, the EEZ application must demonstrate coordination across programs, cities, the private and nonprofit sectors, and levels of government (box 10.2).

Accountability

Accountability can be created in two complementary fashions, from above (the federal government), and from below (parents and other EEZ partners). First, the federal government should measure and reward good results. Applicants would need to present a plan to improve performance on a variety of measures, including high school completion, employment or college attendance after high school, and low rates of pregnancy and crime. Evaluation measures should be somewhat flexible to reward progress in those areas identified as the most important problems in the neighborhood.

In most cases, the federal government does not know the right way to achieve any of these goals. Fortunately, if the government rewards EEZs for good outcomes, the zones themselves can experiment. For example, to increase employment rates for zone graduates (or dropouts), is it best to emphasize job placement assistance, job-related training, skill certifications, wage subsidies, or some combination?

Great care must be taken in choosing and agreeing upon evaluation criteria at the federal level. For example, focusing on short-term measures of increased employment rates for target youths give EEZs incentives to emphasize wage subsidies to increase short-term employment even if training and certification programs may have more lasting effects. In addition, performance measures must be designed so that communities are not penalized for short-term regional or national economic shocks. For example, paying EEZs for job placement rates puts the zones' funding at risk for macroeconomic shocks that raise the region's unemployment. For example, if oil prices decline, employment in Houston is likely to decline. It is likely that youth employment rates will also decline, regardless of how well its schools are functioning. It is neither fair nor sensible to deprive schools and antipoverty programs in Houston funding just when the need is increasing. (See chapter 3 for additional discussion of the problems of pay for performance.)

Because many important dimensions of performance are difficult to measure and, for others, attempts at evaluation may distort incentives, this

Box 10.2. What Is Starting to Work: Using the Internet to Promote Service Integration

Consider a fictitious sixteen-year-old woman who is about to have a baby, is thinking of dropping out of high school, and who has been beaten recently by her drug-abusing boyfriend. In most cities, such a woman would be eligible for services from literally dozens of social service agencies. Unfortunately, even experienced practitioners within the social service system might not know how to identify all the assistance she needs or could access. Moreover, each time she starts interacting with a new agency, she will need to fill out more forms with her name, address, and relevant portions of her life story. Finally, each service provider will deal with only a piece of her problem—the bruises from the beating, or her poor performance in school, or her need for help being a new parent. They are unlikely to be aware of other problems, or of other services the young woman is receiving.

Fortunately, information technology can help create an integrated system that can help this young woman find the services she needs, reduce the hassles of receiving services, and improve the quality of services received—and even improve her privacy protections.

Social service agencies are just beginning to use the Internet to promote service integration. Fuller integration will require that agencies have an Internet presence and increasing access for those who need services. (See chapter 5 for policies to increase Internet access.)

The most basic level of integration involves helping users identify relevant services. For example, the Berkeley Public Library maintains a Community Info database that briefly describes the purpose of and services provided by 2,400 organizations in and around Berkeley, California (http://demo.iii.com:103/search). The database also provides the phone number, address, hours, and information on eligibility and cost. Some agencies are beginning to post important information that clients can use directly to their home pages, ranging from job openings to health information (Law and Keltner 1996). As a complementary facilitator of integration, many social service agencies are putting links to related agencies on their own home pages.

A more extensive level of integration requires that social service agencies begin to share data—subject to stringent privacy protections. It makes no sense for this young woman to have to write her address, age, Social Security number, and so forth each time she interacts with a different agency. (For the more privileged audience of this book, recall how often you had to fill out nearly identical forms when applying for college.) The client should have the option of sharing portions of her personal database with other social service providers. This will require

Box 10.2 *(continued)*

establishing protocols to describe the most basic information (name and address), as well as more detailed information such as descriptions of services rendered that clients can optionally disclose to other service providers. For example, the Playing to Win network of social service providers in Boston has begun this integration. "When a client is moved from a hospital to a residential facility, he or she can contact the large number of social workers and social service agencies attached to the case via one network message" (Law and Keltner 1996).

More generally, the Internet can promote communications among social service agencies. For social service agencies, "the ability to communicate rapidly and reliably with key stakeholders, e.g., potential collaborators, regulators, and clients, as well as being able to gain access to and advertise information, is of substantial benefit" (Law and Keltner 1996).

proposal emphasizes improving the channels for accountability at the local level. The process of designing and implementing the EEZ should improve governance of local schools and government programs. Additionally, the involvement of businesses, parents, colleges, and nonprofits will require youth service providers to convince partners they can deliver high-quality school graduates. Thus, this involvement can create monitors who ensure good performance. Parents are also an important resource. When parents participate, they become more involved with the school, feel more ownership over the programs, and acquire a sense of confidence in their ability to contribute.

Ensuring Continuous Improvement

The EEZs must evaluate which of their activities are effective. The grant application should describe evaluation processes at the programmatic process level (e.g., satisfaction of students with a training program; number of parents attending a school activity) and at the outcome level (employment, out-of-wedlock births, etc.) The EEZ evaluation procedure should not be simply another level of evaluation on top of the evaluation requirements of programs administered at the local level. Ideally, the EEZ should be encouraging the coordination of existing evaluation requirements with the EEZ evaluation piggybacking on existing processes. Over time, as experience grows, the lessons of the early successes and failures will provide greater information about effective efforts to improve outcomes for youths from the project itself and for other neighborhoods creating an EEZ.

The Application Process for Creating EEZs

The basis for EEZs is a competitive bid for federal grants. The bidding entity would be the extended neighborhood with the focal point being the neighborhood schools. The target population would be those twelve to eighteen years old, with the understanding that communities can spend the funds for younger or older youths if they so choose. The bidding entity should be a coalition with input from the schools, service providers, local government, business, parents, teacher, and so on. The winners of this competition would receive federal funding proportional to the number of disadvantaged youths in their zone. The plan would revolve around a competition for a modest number of large EEZ grants in the first year, with future competitions awarding more EEZs as more communities develop quality plans. After a few years, much of this funding would be based on success in meeting agreed-on goals. All communities would be eligible for small planning grants, with funds proportional to the youth population. These grants would permit applicants to hold planning meetings, conduct community needs assessments, and prepare the EEZ proposal.

Not every poor neighborhood in America can rapidly make the transition to EEZ. Furthermore, no single city has the knowledge and resources, even with additional federal aid, to make the transition work seamlessly. Thus, the proposal here begins with those neighborhoods that are able to create a strategic plan to achieve the EEZ goals, in partnership with businesses, parents, nonprofits, and others.

A strong application should begin with a statement of broad goals (e.g., improve health, education, and employment while reducing crime, drugs, and teen pregnancy), as well as detailed measures of success on these goals (e.g., proportion of children immunized; test scores and high school graduation rates; employment rates of high school leavers; youth arrest rates).

The application should also describe the planning and coordinating mechanisms. These should begin with identification and measurement of specific problems hindering the achievement of these broad goals. Complementing the descriptions of needs should be an assessment of the strengths and resources in the broader community that can be mobilized. Program applications should give evidence of significant participation by teachers, parents, and students in the needs assessment and grant-writing process.

The heart of the EEZ proposal would be a description of how service delivery to youths would be coordinated, including periodic community needs assessment, youth outreach, strategic planning, and interaction with local stakeholders including business (e.g., job development), government, community-based organizations, and unions. The plan will describe how service delivery will be coordinated, for example, with common youth intake, and sharing of resources and information systems. The plan will also describe private and nonprofit resources to be contributed from the immediate community and from the broader metropolitan area; how those resources will be coordinated; links between programs for youths of different ages and for the transition from school to work; and how the components of the plan will be evaluated in an integrated fashion. Programs could include dropout prevention (truant officer, tutoring, and parental involvement), pregnancy avoidance, and after-school and summer programs. Applications could be by all schools in a neighborhood, starting as early as funding and neighborhood initiative allowed.

Past experience shows that the preliminary communitywide assessment and planning itself can have great benefits for the community. For example, the application procedure in the Empowerment Zone/Enterprise Community program of the Clinton administration required disparate community groups to come together and create a common plan. Even communities that did not win substantial funding found the community planning process extremely beneficial—for the first time, often warring groups of citizens, government officials, and employers sat down and began to work together (Birnbaum 1995).

An Example

What might life look like for a youth in an Empowerment Zone? Because the initiatives would be designed by communities, there would be no single answer. Nevertheless, drawing on the experience of successful existing models, we can construct a possible scenario.

Schools in Educational Empowerment Zones are clean and well run. Parents and local businesses provide resources such as tutoring and mentoring. Importantly, their presence and involvement also improve oversight. The governance structures of the schools are better than those of most inner-city schools because the school consortium has created a strategic plan that involves partnering with parent organizations, local businesses, and nonprofit community-based organizations.

In addition to an academic counselor, each student has an individual case worker who moves with a class cohort as they advance within their school. Additional case workers are assigned to youths who are no longer in school. The case worker is the access point for students and their families to all available programs and services. He or she connects students with safe full-day, year-round activities appropriate to their interests and needs.

Young students might be involved with an after-school study hall run by a community-based organization, or in volunteer activities. Older students might be connected with a computer-oriented study hall run at a National Guard Armory or a part-time job. While in school, students receive extensive academic assistance, adult mentoring, and career and college planning. (A careful study found that the Big Brothers/Big Sisters mentoring program can have beneficial effects on outcomes such as drug use and school performance [Public/Private Ventures 1996].) For many students, graduating from high school leads to a guaranteed college scholarship or a job with a participating local business. All students receive counseling about avoiding pregnancy and gangs. Students with children have access to child care and parenting instruction.

Case workers address the needs of families as well. Case workers serve as the primary connection between families and both the public social welfare system and private charitable organizations, making sure that basic needs of the families and youths are met: food, clothing, housing, medical and dental care, transportation, and child care. Parents who receive services are expected to volunteer some time to help with programs, perhaps providing child care, helping with filing, or staffing study hall centers a few hours a week.

The evidence suggests that many students at risk of dropping out are helped by guidance, academic assistance, career information, and general support in order to stay in school and succeed. After-school and summer programs and linkages to postgraduation jobs and schooling can be effective in keeping children in school and in improving academic achievement and other outcomes (box 10.3).

The local business community can provide summer jobs; give preferences for hiring to Empowerment Zone graduates; provide mentors and tutors, career days, and guest speakers to discuss future career paths; donate class materials; and participate in the School-to-Work program. Local unions can provide preapprenticeship positions (as in current programs such as Youthbuild and Step-Up) and apprenticeship slots, as well as mentors, tutors, and career exposure. Organizations of teachers and of parents can be effective monitors for the interests of children. Health providers can provide immunization, dental care, preventive care, nutrition education, and child-abuse detection, prevention, and counseling. Local communities, nongovernmental organizations such as social service nonprofit organizations, and national organizations such as National Service Corps and the National Guard can provide mentoring, run after-school programs, and provide in-

Box 10.3. **What Works: The QUOP Experiment**

The Quantum Opportunities Program (QUOP) was an experiment in the use of community-based organizations to improve the academic and social competencies of disadvantaged students by providing continuing adult support throughout their high school years. In each of several cities, QUOP programs offered tutoring, adult mentoring, career and college planning, and other services and activities to children from families receiving welfare, starting in the ninth grade. There is also a financial incentive: participating students receive small stipends and bonuses for completing segments of program activities, as well as payments into a trust fund for their eventual postsecondary education. Because participants were randomly chosen, the program provided a test of whether the combination of a rich array of services and tangible financial rewards for success, sustained over the whole of a high school career, can induce students to stay in school and out of trouble, and go on to college.

Over four years, the average QUOP student participated in 1,286 hours of educational activities beyond regular school hours and accumulated $2,300 in his or her postsecondary account. Overall four-year costs of the program were $10,600 per enrollee. At the end of the program's demonstration period an evaluation comparing randomly selected participants and nonparticipants (controls) found that 53 percent of QUOP students, but only 42 percent of controls, had graduated from high school. Only 23 percent of QUOP students had dropped out, versus 50 percent of the controls. (Numbers total less than 100 percent because some students were still in high school.) And 42 percent of QUOP students, compared with 16 percent of controls, were enrolled in postsecondary education. Participants were also half as likely to report engaging in criminal activity and one-third less likely to have had children. The experiment was small, following only 100 students at four of the sites, and results varied widely across sites, yet for the experiment as a whole all these differences in outcomes were statistically significant (U.S. Department of Labor 1995c).

The results of integrated programs such as QUOP defy the common presupposition that disadvantaged youth will not take advantage of, or cannot benefit from, enhanced educational offerings. Rather, they support the notion that many students need both academic help such as tutoring and the incentive of being assured that academic success has a payoff, in the form of better prospects for employment or college.

kind services. They can also provide slots for student volunteers to work and gain experience. Local community and four-year colleges can provide their students as volunteer mentors and tutors, particularly to provide assistance in setting up college preparation courses. Guaranteed scholarship funding is particularly important so that EEZ students know that hard work leads to further education.

An Example in Addressing Incentive Problems: Links to Employment

Successful Education Empowerment Zones will need to create an integrated approach to reducing crime, drug use, and pregnancy. This section highlights how EEZs are likely to go about the final step in the process: restoring connections between ghetto youth and the job market. As noted in chapter 2, lack of connections to employers appears to be a major handicap for ghetto youths. It is appropriate for government policy to perform some of the functions of intact labor market networks because linkages to the job market can enhance the working of the labor market and improve incentives for young people in poor neighborhoods (Matthes 1991; Blake 1997).

Fortunately, several program appear to be effective in restoring these connections. What these various programs share is a focus on employment and short-term training to prepare people to work (as opposed to lengthy training in skills that employers may not need). These agencies provide many of the functions that social networks containing many jobholders provide to youths in more advantaged neighborhoods.

For example, these agencies often teach the basic skills of holding a job, such as the importance of showing up on time; some also provide assistance for the first few weeks. The mere requirement to show up promptly for these job-readiness classes can provide this important training.

These programs' repeated contact with employers permits them to establish reputations for the quality of their applicants. By learning about the characteristics of employers and jobs, as well as about the skills and desires of the applicants, the agencies can also improve job matching. Improved matches, in turn, benefit both employers and employees.

One important role that these labor market intermediaries play is certifying the quality of the young people they place. This certification has several implications, both good and bad.

On the downside, when certification is a function of the placement agencies, they have an incentive to work with the best youths. This cream-skimming, in turn, can lead agencies to appear quite successful even when their value added is low. (That is, the agencies help place youths who would probably find jobs anyway.) It also implies that extending the enrollment of job placement agencies can be ineffective, even if their enrollees have high placement rates. For example, consider a program that works only with students whose high school teachers recommend them. Graduates of the program may have a high placement record compared to the neighborhood, but these students might do well even without the program.

More positively, this screening is socially useful to the extent it permits at-risk youths to find jobs for which they would otherwise not be considered. For example, a program that required youths to show up for job-readiness classes five days in a row on time might not teach much, but it at least can certify that the youths can accomplish that basic task. If employers assume that ghetto youths never show up on time, this certification can be useful. At the same time, to the extent the agencies primarily screen, they are not helping those at-risk youths most in need of help.

Finally, the cream-skimming and selection effects provide positive incentives to youths to work hard before entering the labor market so they can pass the screens. These incentives will be most effective when they are teamed with the mentoring and other assistance described earlier to ensure all youths have the capabilities to pass the screens.

The EEZ proposal does not resolve the conflict that local employment agencies have to limit other agencies' access to "their" employers. At the same time, the federal payment for results is to the zone as a whole. Thus, the EEZ proposal rewards those communities that find ways to induce their agencies to cooperate.

A number of unknowns remain about how best to move at-risk youths not in the labor market. Are there ways to make wage subsidies work without stigmatizing youths? Should job placement agencies be public or private sector? Can it work to get up-front commitments from employers to hire a certain number of workers? The advantage of the EEZ proposal is that it encourages experimentation and learning so that all communities can learn from the zones' experiences.

Why a Federal Role in the Inner Cities?

A federal role is appropriate because fighting poverty and improving equality of opportunity are both national goals. Many citizens care about high poverty or low opportunity for children in other states; it is the role of the federal government to address such cross-state concerns. Similarly, the costs of welfare, crime, and gangs span state boundaries, both because disadvantaged youths move and because federal taxes go to pay many of the costs of supporting everything from federal prisons to education for poor children. In addition, the learning that is built into the EEZ process will benefit neighborhoods in many states. Similarly, many of the nation's largest metropolitan areas (New York, Washington, D.C., Philadelphia, Chicago), as well as many medium-sized cities, have suburbs in more than one state. Thus, solutions found in one part of the urban area benefit residents of neighboring states. Finally, the federal government has spent billions in trying to assist poor urban areas; at a minimum, those funds should be redirected to helping youths and schools, the highest payoff use of these funds.

Critiques

In spite of its promise, the EEZ proposal is subject to several critiques. One problem is that while some schools and neighborhoods will be winners, others will be left out of the process. It is not fair to young people growing up in our nation's worst neighborhoods to abandon them because their elders could not agree on a plan to improve their schools and access to a career. Even worse, those neighborhoods that are most troubled and those in regions suffering bad macroeconomic shocks are likely to be those that are least capable of designing a strategic plan that will convincingly improve youths' lives. Nevertheless, these are precisely the neighborhoods most in need of help.

This is a serious problem, but it is not one that the federal government can solve. If a community's government, schools, neighboring communities, businesses, unions, and nonprofits cannot agree on how to solve its problems, the federal government cannot step in to save the day. Improvements in assistance to individuals through reinvented housing vouchers (described in chapter 9) have a role to play; at the same time, it is unlikely that place-based programs will succeed. As a partial compensation, the lessons learned from successful EEZs should help inform policymakers in other troubled communities.

A second critique of large-scale competitions of the form proposed here is that they favor cities that hire high-priced consultants to help prepare proposals. Moreover, many "partners" may sign on to the agreement to make it look good, but will not contribute resources such as mentoring or jobs. Thus, the process of creating the proposal may consume, not add, value.

The response here is that such consultants can add value if they bring interested parties together to create integrative solutions. Furthermore, if the signatories do not follow through with the projects in the proposals, the funding will decline over time. EEZs are intended to pay for performance, so low effort in some cities should not lead to high levels in wasteful funding.

EEZ versus Alternatives

EEZs should be more cost effective than other place-based economic development strategies. Unfortunately, the history of American place-based strategies has relatively few successes, given the tens of billions of dollars that have been spent on them (box 10.4). Instead, we should focus on youth. To the extent we want place-based strategies, they should focus on schools, the major place-based institutions that are not mobile.

Economic development grants such as those granted by the Departments of Agriculture, Commerce, HUD, and both the Reagan and Clinton versions of enterprise zones often subsidize zero-sum economic development activities that merely redistribute businesses between states. Government policies should attract business with high-skilled workers, but not by granting tax breaks or pure transfers to businesses.

Unless we can make youths growing up in the ghetto into good workers, no job-moving scheme will help much. Conversely, if youths growing up in the ghetto become good workers, no job moving will be needed because so many jobs are already so close.

Block grants to cities, as HUD has proposed under the Clinton administration, remove the inflexibility of command-and-control regulations. HUD's proposal also adds some accountability, improving on unconditional block grants. At the same time, EEZs combine accountability with a focus on those with biggest needs and a focus on youths, where the economic payoffs to investment are largest.

Individual-oriented welfare cannot solve the problems of entire neighborhoods. We need our poorest neighborhoods to have a culture of success, where playing by the rules implies youths can grow up and leave the ghetto.

Finally, some solutions rely on increased entrepreneurship. The relatively high rates of business ownership of some immigrant groups (e.g., Koreans) shows that starting a new business can sometimes help move people from poverty into the middle class. Thus, it is quite important that all levels of government remove barriers to business formation by ensuring that regulations and tax policies have the lowest possible paperwork burdens on small businesses. At the same time, few government policies appear successful at changing the rate of business ownership in a cost-effective fashion. Some of the most popular proposals, such as cutting the capital gains tax rate, appear particularly unlikely to help poor neighborhoods (box 10.5). (Programs that provide very small loans to groups of small-scale entrepreneurs are the only policy that appears to promote new businesses cost effectively, in part because the small size of the loans keeps costs low [Microcredit Summit 1997].)

Republicans and Democrats agree on the need for change and the importance of equality of opportunity. Education Empowerment Zones can change the lives of our poorest citizens, helping them and helping all of us.

Box 10.4. **What Doesn't Work: Tax Incentives to Bribe Businesses to Relocate to the Ghetto**

Since the 1980s tax incentives to promote business relocation into poor regions has been the most popular form of place-based assistance. Tax incentives have played an important roll in antipoverty efforts proposed by both major parties. The "enterprise zones" established by the Reagan administration relied heavily on tax incentives and "empowerment zones and enterprise communities" created by the Clinton administration also included many tax incentives, in addition to significant direct funding to community coalitions. Although different in many important details, both plans involve giving tax breaks that provide incentives for businesses to locate in distressed (mainly urban) neighborhoods.

It is ironic that this rare political consensus flies in the face of another rare consensus: both the theory and evidence of business relocation incentives suggest they are extremely cost ineffective at improving the lives of citizens in poor areas (Bates 1995; Wilder and Rubin 1996).

The reasoning behind the failure of enterprise zones can be observed within three miles of the nation's Capitol building, where so many of these tax breaks are passed. The impoverished ghettos of southeast Washington, D.C., are all within easy commuting distance by bicycle, bus, or subway to thousands of entry-level job openings every month. The problem is that most of the restaurants, stores, banks, and offices in downtown and suburban Washington do not want to hire bussers, retail clerks, tellers, or receptionists who grew up in these impoverished neighborhoods and attended the often disastrous local ghetto schools. Although just one example, in most of America's ghettos job relocation for businesses is not as important as job readiness for ghetto youths.

The result is that tax incentives to move a few hundred jobs into the high-crime ghetto are extremely costly. Moreover, even when jobs *do* locate in ghettos, employers often prefer to hire employees from outside the neighborhood. This bleak reasoning is supported by the available evaluation evidence, which routinely finds enormous costs per job created in the ghetto, and even higher cost per job created for a ghetto resident.

Even these high costs per job are actually overstatements of the true benefits of enterprise and empowerment zones because they largely reflect jobs that would have been located somewhere; they just moved to a poorer neighborhood. To the extent the jobs hire low-wage workers, low-wage workers elsewhere in the city or nation lose their jobs. In short, the strategy of "gilding the ghetto" is doomed to fail, as it has.

Box 10.5. **What Doesn't Work: Cutting Capital Gains Taxes***

Along with enterprise zones, cutting taxes on capital gains is one of the rare cases where members of both parties often agree. Proponents claim lower rates will spur investment and create jobs for all people (including the disadvantaged).

Unfortunately, this cheerful scenario is unlikely to occur. A capital gains tax cut provides no direct incentives to boost investment. No manager deciding whether to build a factory, buy a computer, or engage in research and development changes his or her calculation of expected profit because of a reduction in capital gains taxes.

Capital gains tax cuts are rewards for people who save, not businesses that invest. Thus, some proponents believe the tax cut will boost investment and growth indirectly by increasing savings. They note that the tax cut raises the after-tax returns on savings placed in risky assets such as shares of stock. They then claim higher returns on these assets will, in turn, induce higher savings. Higher savings will drive down interest rates, which, in turn, will raise business investment and growth.

But this roundabout chain of cause and effect falls apart at the first touch. Both the capital gains tax rate and the after-tax return to savings have wandered all over the place in the past generation. Private savings have barely shifted in response. All serious analyses have concluded that each dollar of tax cuts increases private savings by less than a dollar. The net effect of the tax cut is to *lower* the pool of national savings available to fund investment. Continued hope that lowering tax rates will boost American savings and investment is the triumph of faith over experience.

The problem is that this tax cut provides an enormous windfall gain to those who have unrealized capital gains on assets they acquired in the past. The top 1 percent of American families with unrealized capital gains hold about half of these unrealized gains. While many people realize a small amount of capital gains in any given year, these few families hold trillions of dollars of unrealized gains. Good tax policies provide incentives for people to work, save, and invest. Bad tax policies reward a wealthy few for decisions they made in the past.

A capital gains tax cut may well raise revenues in its first year or two, as people liquidate their unrealized gains before the next increase in capital gains rates. But once the first wave of selling is over, a standard guess is that the capital gains tax cut will cost about $20 billion a year. When the government decides to spend $20 billion a year on a tax incentive, it should choose one likely to boost economic growth, not one whose primary effect will be increasing inequality.

---

*This box draws on DeLong and Levine (1995b).

Rural Policy

The focus of EEZ is on making youths ready to work, not on moving jobs to the ghetto, for the simple reasons that most poor urban youths can easily commute to thousands of entry-level jobs. Unfortunately, this reasoning usually does not apply to impoverished rural regions. Unlike most major cities, job openings are not common near most residents in much of Appalachia, Mississippi, or southern Texas.

Nevertheless, the reasoning that business relocation incentives are not cost effective remains. For hundreds of years, the goal of finding a better life has led millions of Americans to migrate from farms to cities. The primary goal of our rural policy must be to ensure that children grow up able to succeed in the world twenty and fifty years from now. For the vast majority of these children, much of the next half century will be spent away from the rural region where they now live. Thus, just as for poor urban children, investing in poor rural children makes more sense than spending money moving businesses around.

In general, no compelling reason exists to favor the preservation of employment in rural regions. On the one hand, some arguments imply policies should encourage rural residents (at the margin) to stay put because of the externalities they cause by moving. For example, people moving to an urban area do not take into account the increased congestion they impose on people already there. In addition, when people leave an established community, they do not fully take into account the disruption they cause in the lives of those they leave behind.

On the other hand, some arguments imply policies should increase geographic mobility. For example, liquidity constraints may impede some people from moving even when moving would raise their expected productivity and happiness. In addition, people thinking of moving to an urban area do not take into account the positive agglomeration economies (that is, economies of scale) they may create when concentrations of a given industry are created. For example, an engineer or technician moving to Silicon Valley is likely to create knowledge that will "leak out" to benefit multiple employers in the region. Also, as people leave rural regions, more land becomes unspoiled, which can create positive externalities for ecosystems and society. Given the lack of empirical information on the magnitude of these effects, it appears sensible to invest in children's capabilities to make informed choices about where to locate and to give them the skills to compete in the nationwide labor market.

(Native American reservations are an exception to this principle that place-based strategies are inefficient. In this setting, preservation of the culture and the preferences of many individuals involve providing attractive choices for youths to remain employed on the reservation as adults.)

Conclusion

After decades of well-meaning subsidies to urban areas, theory and evidence both suggest that current strategies are failing. Strategies to gild the ghetto do not work. Instead of categorical grants for business development, block grants for business development, or enterprise zones for business development, we have to invest in ghetto youths. These youths are the source of many of the ghetto's problems. More important, they are the victims of the ghetto. An integrated strategy that makes playing by the rules a high-payoff approach holds the promise to accomplish what no amount of simple business subsidies can ever do.

11

REINVENTING DISABILITY POLICY

The disability system in the United States spends approximately $120 billion a year to keep millions of working-age people on poverty-level stipends while essentially banning them from working. A reinvented system would focus on moving people from dependence to independence with flexible vocational rehabilitation vouchers, work-oriented assessments, and simple rules that guarantee that nobody would ever be made worse off by working. A problem with creating a system that combines work and partial disability benefits is that it may attract new entrants onto the disability rolls. A key insight of this proposal is that these generous work incentives can be tested on the current 6 million working-age recipients without inducing entry that raises costs.

The disability system in the United States spends over $120 billion a year, yet most people who receive benefits from it consider it a failure. This attitude is understandable because the system typically pays stipends near the poverty level, but it makes work not only not pay but just short of illegal.

Every American, including the able-bodied, has a large stake in the disability system. Most directly, everyone who lives long enough will eventually have numerous physical impairments.

In addition, the disability system in the United States is exploding in costs and reducing work incentives for millions of Americans. Social Security Disability Insurance (SSDI) and Supplemental Security Income (SSI) for the low-income disabled now have more than 6 million working-age claimants, double the number in the early 1980s. The Social Security Administration predicts that with current trends the rolls will more than double again in the next decade, largely due to an aging workforce and rising retirement age for Social Security retirement pensions. To put these figures in perspective, the disability system costs more than the welfare system in the United States, even though the latter is much more controversial. (This statement counts the means-tested programs for disabled people as both disability and welfare programs.)

Understanding the Disability System

To understand the disability system, consider the programs an injured worker encounters after a work-related injury leads to long-term disability.

A newly injured person will need to prove his or her disability a number of times. Many of these "proofs" will use a different one of the forty-three definitions of disability that appear in federal regulations, as well as different standards for workers' compensation and perhaps private disability insurance. Many of these definitions are needed: for example, temporary disabilities have different consequences than permanent ones, and perceptions of disability suffice for someone to be discriminated against under the Americans with Disability Act. Nevertheless, forty-three definitions reflect a lack of coordination of services.

Workers' Compensation

After a waiting period of a week or so (varying by state), an injured worker can receive benefits from the state-run workers' compensation insurance. These benefits typically cover medical expenses and about two-thirds of lost wages.

Workers' compensation insurance programs have several desirable incentive properties. For larger companies, insurers typically reduce insurance rates when injury rates decline. This experience rating provides employers with incentives to reduce injuries. Some insurers give assistance to employers (often with some implicit coercion) to improve safety. In states that permit it, many large companies self-insure, providing them with even stronger incentives to increase workplace safety.

The workers' compensation system also has several severe problems. Rising medical costs, a large increase in claims related to stress and other hard-to-measure injuries, and rising time lost from work per injury are increasing costs in many states. In a 1991 survey, small employers reported that workers' compensation is their second largest problem, second only to the cost of health insurance (and ahead of low sales, high taxes, or burdensome regulations [National Federation of Independent Businesses 1992]). Many workers must jump through many expensive hoops to receive benefits, and some are denied benefits when they are actually disabled. Conversely, some workers who are not disabled claim workers' compensation and then enjoy vacation or work another job, adding to the system's cost.

Applying for SSDI

After six months, if the disability is severe, the worker is eligible to apply for Social Security Disability Insurance (SSDI). This social insurance program covers only workers who have worked roughly five of the last ten years and who appear to be totally disabled. The principle underlying SSDI is to permit disabled workers to take their standard old-age Social Security retirement pension at whatever age they are when they become disabled, instead of waiting until age sixty-five.

Applicants without a sufficient work history for SSDI are eligible to apply for the lower benefits of SSI. Applicants with a long work history but low wages can receive benefits from both SSDI and SSI. After a two-year waiting period, SSDI recipients receive medical insurance under Medicare, the same insurance program that covers recipients of old-age Social Security. SSI recipients receive health insurance under Medicaid, the means-tested insurance program that primarily covers people on welfare.

The process of applying for SSDI has several problems. Staying off the job for six months and appearing sick enough to win SSDI benefits depreciates work skills, while the gap between the end of workers' compensation and the start of SSDI can lead many workers to poverty. importantly, people may not be able to pay for rehabilitation services until they have Medicare or Medicaid, but in many cases early interventions will be the most cost-effective means of returning to work.

Delays in the application process can also often be substantial. In California, a disabled worker typically faces an eighteen- to twenty-four-month delay after applying before receiving his or her first check. (States differ by a 3:1 ratio in average speed of processing a claim.)

The application process often works much like a lottery. On average, about half of all denials are appealed, and administrative law judges reverse almost half of the Social Security Administration's denials of SSDI benefits. (Administrative law judges do not follow the 40,000 pages of Social Security Administration rules on how to determine benefits.) Furthermore, some administrative law judges reverse 25 percent of the denials of SSDI benefits; other judges reverse 75 percent (Parsons 1991). While not conclusive, such divergences (which also occur for other gatekeepers in the disability system) suggest both a lack of equity across people with similar disabilities and a lack of accuracy.

Many of the truly disabled are denied benefits, and others who could work are given benefits. For example, the rate of returning to work of those denied benefits is quite low (Parsons and Bound 1991), implying that many truly disabled are denied benefits. Conversely, Jonathan Leonard (1986) provides evidence that some beneficiaries could work because the increase in SSDI rolls has been paralleled by a decrease in labor force participation. If applicants to the SSDI rolls were truly unable to work, expanded rolls should consist of people who were not working; it appears some of those entering the rolls would have been working if the SSDI system were less generous. Moreover, a number of studies (many carried out by the Social Security Administration) find that reexamination of SSDI determinations would reverse the initial findings, with reversals in typically one in four or five cases of both acceptances and denials. (Donald O. Parsons [1991] reviews this evidence.) Such studies do not show whether the initial findings are too lax or not sufficiently severe, but do indicate that one of those two cases (or both) must frequently obtain.

The rules for admission are quite outdated. Some diagnoses lead to automatic approval, even if new computer and other technologies make the impairment irrelevant for many jobs. Currently, about half of the U.S. workforce uses a computer at work (Krueger 1993), and it no longer makes sense that physical impairments that preclude some forms of construction or industrial work are considered automatically disabling from employment. In fact, people with spinal cord injuries (these typically lead to use of a wheelchair) who had computer skills had earnings equivalent to those in the general population, while those without computer skills had a significant earnings gap. (Unfortunately, computer use and training are lower among those with spinal cord injuries than in the general population [Kruse et al. 1996]).

The lifetime nature of the benefits also often makes no sense. If someone is clearly disabled enough to need benefits for the next year, for example, but is then expected to recover, the SSDI benefits are still granted as a lifetime benefit, although the file may be marked for early review. At that review, the Social Security Administration must attempt the disruptive and difficult process of taking away a lifetime benefit previously granted.

Some disabilities, such as certain forms of depression, are debilitating in the short run, but the work-related impairment can be controlled or eliminated with proper medication. Other conditions, such as AIDS and some psychiatric disorders, often become more and then less severe over time. Many people cannot afford the medications unless they are classed as disabled and given Medicare or Medicaid, but these are lifetime programs poorly suited to the potentially temporary or recurring nature of the work-related impairments. Even worse, SSDI recipients must wait two years to receive Medicare benefits. (Medicaid benefits for SSI recipients have no waiting period. Although there are arguments for and against waiting periods, no policy reason exists for *different* periods in these two programs.)

Other disabilities will never go away *medically* but can stop being impediments *vocationally* with appropriate training or technology. Nevertheless, the standard for ending SSDI benefits requires medical improvement, not cessation of barriers to work.

Vocational Rehabilitation

After admission to the SSDI or SSI program as incapable of working, a Social Security Administration employee may determine that the individual is potentially capable of working (using definitions that differ by state). The new enrollee's name is then sent to the state Vocational Rehabilitation Agency, and the individual is informed that he or she is eligible for services such as physical therapy, equipment such as wheelchairs, and retraining. About one in twelve entering files is sent to Vocational Rehabilitation each year, yet Vocational Rehabilitation Agencies place only a tiny fraction of that number, often not even because of the referral (Berkowitz and Dean 1996).

Vocational Rehabilitation is funded by over $2 billion in grants each year from the federal Department of Education to the states. Although this assistance is statutorily targeted on the severely disabled, almost none of those served are SSDI or SSI recipients, presumably because less severely disabled populations are easier to serve. Yet those on the SSI and SSDI rolls are precisely the ones with the largest social product and savings to the government from returning to work. (At the same time, their substantial disabilities may make it not cost effective to try to return some on the disability rolls to work.)

Although the Vocational Rehabilitation program is over seventy-five years old, no formal evaluation of its effectiveness exists. The existing evidence is scarce, but it suggests that most vocational rehabilitation programs are of limited effectiveness. Only about one out of each thousand SSDI and SSI recipients become employed and leave the rolls each year with the assistance of state Vocational Rehabilitation Agencies.

Work Disincentives

According to a recent Louis Harris poll, 79 percent of people with disabilities who were not working claimed they wanted to work. At the same time, SSDI defines a disabled worker as an oxymoron: if you can work, even part-time, you are not disabled enough to receive *any* SSDI. Anyone earning $300 to $500 per month for much of the preceding three years is at risk of losing SSDI. The result of this system is that fewer than 3 percent of disability insurance beneficiaries ever terminate from the program because of work (Hennessy 1996).

SSDI typically provides an income below the poverty line. Nevertheless, individuals who work even a few hours a week are likely to lose SSDI, Medicare, eligibility for housing subsidies from the Department of Housing and Urban Development, and other benefits. If they take a job for a few years and then lose it, they will have lost their eligibility for all these benefits and must show their condition has worsened substantially since they first applied to reestablish eligibility.

Supplemental Security Income

Supplemental Security Income (SSI) is available to disabled individuals who do not have sufficient work history to receive SSDI, or whose SSDI leaves them with a very low income. The number of disabled SSI recipients increased 49 percent between 1975 and 1991. This increase far exceeded the increase in disability rates in the population.

Unlike SSDI, SSI has some meaningful work incentives. Most importantly, SSI stipends decline by only fifty cents for each dollar recipients earn above a minimum level, in contrast to the over 100 percent benefit reduction rate for SSDI. In fact, there is an entire book describing the numerous SSI work incentives (Social Security Administration 1995). Unfortunately, although I have a Ph.D. in economics, I was unable to follow much of the material in this book. (Box 11.1 provides an overview of the disability system.)

A Vision for Change

Several recent proposals focused on shifting the disability system from one that provides lifetime poverty-level stipends to one that helps people return to the workforce (Mashaw and Reno 1996; Batavia and Parker 1995; U.S. General Accounting Office 1996; World Institute on Disability 1996). All these proposals are consistent with a common set of goals for the disability system. First, nobody should ever become worse off by working. Second, the disability system should be both integrated and comprehensible. Integration requires coordination among gatekeepers and service providers in schools, rehabilitation services, and health care, as well as integration among work incentives. Third, disabled people must have choices concerning how to acquire needed assistance for employment. Fourth, service providers must be freed from detailed regulations but must be accountable for results. Finally, the system must focus on people's capabilities and what help they need to function fully, not just on medical impairments. This list of goals is widely agreed on; the challenge is to find cost-effective proposals that satisfy most of them.

In spite of these common goals, the recent proposals differed along a number of dimensions. This proposal draws heavily on these ideas but makes extensions to improve work incentives without induced entry; to create integrated work incentives, to improve the application procedure; and to improve incentives for reducing long-term disability in the first place.

A key problem with effective work incentives is that they are likely to raise the costs of the disability program, as new entrants are induced to apply for benefits. Millions of Americans have some partial disability.

Box 11.1. **The Complex Web of the Disability System**
(An Incomplete Summary)

Program	Agencies
Workers' Compensation: Partial wage replacement for the initial months after a disabling work-related injury	Varies by state. Typically the state, private insurers, and employers are involved, with use of the courts for some appeals
Temporary wage replacement after partial disability	Some state workers' compensation systems; some private insurers and employers
Wage replacement after complete disability (if with a work history): SSDI	Social Security Administration and state-run Social Security gate-keepers Disability Determination Services. Independent administrative law judges and federal courts handle appeals. Some employers and private insurers provide supplements
Wage replacement after complete disability (if low-income or short work history): SSI	Social Security Administration and states, as with SSDI
Medicare provides some health insurance for SSDI recipients	Department of Health and Human Services Health Care Financing Authority and states fund the state-run Medicare systems. Claims processing by 80 HCFA contractors
Medicaid provides health insurance for SSI recipients	State-federal partnership, with a core set of benefits and others that states can agree to cover (or not)
Vocational Rehabilitation	Department of Education funds state Vocational Rehabilitation Agencies. Social Security Administration funds can go to private providers
Job placement	Department of Labor funds state employment service. Also Vocational Rehabilitation providers
Job training	Department of Labor funds states that fund local Private Industry Councils that fund education providers; Department of Education funds state agencies that fund local Vocational Rehabilitation providers

---

Box 11.1 *(continued)*

Subsidized Housing	Department of Housing and Urban Development and states fund local Public Housing Authorities that own housing set aside for the disabled. Some recipients receive housing vouchers
Holistic social service providers such as a local Center for Independent Living	Multiple federal and state agencies as well as private funds from foundations and other sources

Note: Most veterans, Native Americans, railroad employees, federal employees, and many state and public employees have distinct systems that provide some combination of disability stipends, medical care, and vocational rehabilitation services. Many employees also have private insurance to provide many of these benefits, often supplementing those provided by the public sector.

Many who are already working part-time would become eligible for a partial stipend. Others might reduce their work hours to become eligible. (This induced entry is sometimes referred to as the "woodwork effect," as people come out of the woodwork to apply for benefits [Hoynes and Moffitt 1995].) Actuaries at the Social Security Administration are very concerned that reform proposals may lead to costly induced entry, potentially bankrupting the Social Security System. No policy for reforming the disability system is likely to be politically palatable unless it addresses the problem of induced entry (at least to the satisfaction of these important policy gatekeepers.)

People already on the rolls cannot, by definition, be induced to enter the disability rolls. This proposal differs from its predecessors by exploiting this simple fact. Thus, work incentives can be focused on current enrollees with little concern for induced entry. The experience of helping move a substantial fraction of the current population into employment (at least part-time) should provide important lessons for creating a work-oriented system for new entrants as well.

Past proposals have also focused solely on the work incentives within the Social Security System. They have ignored that many disabled people receive subsidies and face work disincentives from multiple programs. This chapter proposes a simple integrated work incentive that ensures that disabled people always find that working leaves them better off than not working.

This proposal also differs from its predecessors by reinventing the disability application procedure to minimize delays while maximizing accuracy. The insight here is that unusually low rates of employment by applicants after they are rejected for a disability pension is an indicator of overly severe gatekeeping. Using postdenial earnings and employment rates as a benchmark, the Social Security Administration can determine combinations of gatekeepers and diagnoses that have low error rates and permit these gatekeepers to approve applications with low levels of oversight. SSA staff would be reserved for the more difficult cases to decide and as back-ups for gatekeepers without successful track records.

Finally, this proposal differs from its predecessors by its more comprehensive view of the disability system. Past reform proposals typically have focused on a single element, such as Social Security work incentives. In fact, disabled people face complicated work incentives, assistance, and disincentives from up to a dozen separate agency. A coherent plan must create an integrated work incentive system. Moreover, an integrated system must create incentives to reduce rates of injuries and illnesses, especially those that lead to job loss, not just systems to repair the damage at minimal cost.

For Six Million Current Enrollees: Make Work Pay

The work and disability systems described below provide incentives and the ability for the 6 million current SSDI and SSI working-age enrollees to return to work and for new enrollees to get a first job, a new job, or (best of all) to stay on their current job. Because current enrollees already have entitlements to lifetime cash stipends and medical care, almost any work incentives will save the government money. At the same time, generous work incentives can increase costs by motivating some people who want to mix part-time work with a partial stipend to join the SSDI rolls. Thus, for new enrollees it is important to alter the system dramatically to ensure that all disabled people have the ability to work without providing disincentives for work.

The system described in this section encourages those currently on the rolls to return to work. Because so few SSDI recipients currently return to work, these changes will save money as well as increase the standard of living of those currently on the SSDI rolls.

Improving Work Incentives

SSDI and SSI could offer three forms of incentives to work that ensure nobody is worse off working than not working. The basic goal is to ensure that the cash stipend and the value of the health insurance subsidy decline by less than a dollar each time a disabled person earns a dollar; conversely, benefits should rise back up if the disabled person loses his or her job.

The starting point is to provide a 50 to 60 percent benefit reduction rate for pay above impairment-related work expenses plus a minimum earnings threshold. (This is similar to the SSI work incentives [known as section 1619] and unlike the current abrupt cutoff for SSDI.) This benefit reduction rate should include *all* income and payroll taxes and the loss of other welfare benefits (food stamps, housing subsidies, Temporary Assistance for Needy Families [TANF, formerly AFDC], state and workers' compensation disability payments, and so forth). Current research shows some, but not enormous, work disincentives for total tax rates under 60 percent (e.g., Moffitt 1992). For example, the current top combined rate of payroll taxes plus state and federal income taxes is roughly 50 percent (varying by state), and medical doctors and most other high-wage professionals facing these tax rates typically work long hours. We should strive to keep the overall benefit reduction rate from rising much above 50 or 60 percent; eventually it causes more serious disincentives.

Maintain SSDI Status for Workers

Full-time work is risky for SSDI recipients because after a period of employment, reestablishing eligibility for SSDI is difficult. We could permit SSDI recipients to retain the right to return to the SSDI rolls automatically after employment ends, to promote reemployment without fear of losing a benefit stream. (An Extended Period of Eligibility exists for some SSDI enrollees, but is complicated, time limited, and ineffective.)

Continue Medical Coverage

SSI currently continues Medicaid coverage with a sliding-scale subsidy for two years; this benefit should be made permanent and a similar incentive provided for SSDI workers. After workers "earn off" their disability stipend, they should begin to pay for their medical insurance subsidy. (Because of the smooth nature of the phaseout, only those who earn very high incomes or who have employer-provided health insurance will ever lose the subsidy completely, and even they will automatically regain it after any job loss.)

Ending the restriction of coverage for preexisting conditions is key to providing effective health insurance for disabled individuals.

In addition to maintaining the option of retaining Medicaid or Medicare, people can have more choice concerning their health-care provider. If a person has a disability that typically costs $5,000 a year for government-subsidized care, the person should be able to apply that sum to purchase private-sector insurance or to subsidize the employer's medical self-insurance, and so forth. (Alternatively, some portion of the funds could be used to purchase private-sector insurance, with the remainder retained for employing personal assistance.)

For example, in one pilot study the government gave disabled people who were members of the Kaiser Health Maintenance Organization before the onset of their disability the option of remaining Kaiser members. Patients must use Kaiser services, and the government covers medical costs that Kaiser does not pay. Results so far have been very positive, and very few people opt for Medicare alone. This pilot could be expanded to other regions.

More generally, SSDI and SSI recipients who begin working should be able to apply any full or partial company-provided health insurance toward buying their Medicare or Medicaid. Conversely, they should be able to mix the cash value of the subsidy they receive for Medicare or Medicaid to help pay for company-provided health insurance. Any system should be designed so that if the employer of a half-time employee will pay half of a medical insurance policy, the health insurance voucher will pay the other half of the cost of the company's health benefits.

Vouchers for Vocational Rehabilitation

We should replace the states' monopolies on Vocational Rehabilitation Services with a system of vouchers for the disabled to use to buy employment-related services. These vouchers would be flexible because people's needs are so varied. For example, some workers need therapy, others need adaptive equipment, others need specialized training, others need help at home, and many need combinations of these forms of assistance.

One possibility is to make the value of the vocational rehabilitation vouchers depend on the results, such as job placement, wages, and job tenure—most easily summed up by rewarding service providers with a portion of clients' earnings over several years. The value of the voucher to the service provider should be keyed to clients' earnings as well as employment, to reward services that assist clients in finding higher-paying jobs. Monroe Berkowitz (1996) has proposed a performance-related voucher in which the value depends on the savings the SSDI system realizes when a disabled person becomes employed. Given that under this proposal the SSDI system's savings would also be proportional to earnings, the two forms of performance-related vouchers are quite similar.

The goal of moving to a voucher system for vocational rehabilitation is to provide more choice for the disabled. The needs of the disabled vary widely, and the means for helping them are often not well understood. We need a flexible system that rewards success both to experiment and to evaluate those experiments in order to determine what works.

Importantly, the vocational rehabilitation voucher can be used by an employer or service provider to purchase adaptive equipment such as ramps or special computer interfaces. As an added incentive for those employers who provide health coverage, the value of the Medicare of Medicaid coverage an employee is eligible for can be applied to the cost of the employers' health-care plan. Additionally, the voucher can be given directly to employers, acting as a wage subsidy to employers who hire the disabled. Such a subsidy could then be used by employers to defray any extra costs of health insurance for the disabled.

One problem with vouchers is often cherry-picking, where the easiest to serve are served first. Given the negligible movements from SSDI to employment, the program would at least initially have little problem with cherry-picking—any movement off SSDI will save the government substantially and will increase opportunity and living standards for SSDI recipients.

Even the most generous work incentives will not move the majority of current recipients off the disability rolls. Many are too near retirement; others are too disabled; still others will fear that any work experience will lead to future rule changes that will eliminate their benefits. Nevertheless, moving to a work-oriented system for those already on the rolls should induce a substantial number of the current 6 million recipients to work. Importantly, these work incentives for existing recipients will not induce new entry—a problem that plagues most reforms of the disability system.

For New Applicants: Work First

SSDI is designed to give lifetime income support to those with permanent and total disability. Changes in the workplace, technology, and society imply that a diminishing share of medical impairments actually lead to permanent and total inability to work. Thus, we should create a system in which demand for cash benefits due to permanent and total disability is minimal—instead, most people with medical impairments should receive the help they need to return to work.

Because it is unclear how many people can return to work, it may make sense to phase in this new system for younger applicants. For example, the first version could apply to applicants under age twenty-five. (importantly, these applicants have the longest expected stay on the disability rolls.) Evaluations should be built in to determine the effectiveness of the new program for different age groups and disabilities.The goal should be to extend the work-oriented system over time to whatever groups are cost effective.

Reinventing Assessments

The medically based disability assessments used by the Social Security Administration should be replaced by a vocational assessment. This assessment should determine what impairments inhibit employment and what assistance will lead to employment.

The assessment should not be solely to determine benefits; instead, it should be joint between Vocational Rehabilitation Agencies, school systems (when needed to establish benefits under the Individuals with Disabilities Education Act), and the Social Security Administration. SSDI should drop its five-month waiting period to permit assessments soon after the onset of disability if the condition is stable.

Gatekeeping and assessments can be greatly improved, simplified, and made more accurate using two tools: conditional deregulation and ongoing analysis of Social Security Administration data on work histories of those accepted and those denied benefits.

Conditional deregulation involves reducing the number of assessments for many cases where it is likely that reassessment would not change the result. Specifically, the Social Security Administration should examine its records of millions of applications and identify diagnoses that are relatively simple to determine and rarely appealed or reversed. In these cases, a doctor's diagnosis and description of vocational impairments should suffice to determine eligibility (subject to random quality-control audits). Some diagnoses may require a board certified specialist's opinion. Similarly, any private-sector gatekeeper such as a doctor, clinic, or vocational rehabilitation service provider with a record of assessments that are repeatedly found to be in accordance with what Social Security determines should also move to a system of random quality-control audits. In this fashion, the Social Security Administration can focus its limited resources on difficult cases. At least as important, disabled people will have fewer appointments reperforming the same tests.

Analysis of data on work histories of those accepted and denied benefits can also improve the gatekeeping function. Some gatekeepers deny benefits to a high proportion of applicants who then fail to return to work; such gatekeepers are probably too harsh. (This proportion should be standardized for the age, sex, and occupation of those turned down, as well as institutional factors such as whether the applicant had hired a lawyer.) Conversely, some gatekeepers deny an average proportion of applicants (controlling for characteristics of the applicants) and have an above-average proportion of those denied benefits return to work. These gatekeepers appear to have especially accurate decision-making rules. Computerized expert systems should be developed that help all gatekeepers learn from these, especially accurate gatekeepers. Similarly, all gatekeepers should benchmark their procedures on those who process claims rapidly as well as accurately. Recall that some disability offices make disability determinations in only one-third the time of others, indicating substantial room for improvement.

Deeming

The grants for employment and training services for young adults (ages 18–25) should be decreasing in family income using a formula similar to that for other forms of education and training (Pell) grants. It is reasonable to expect family members to contribute financially to a young adult's vocational rehabilitation, just as it is the practice to expect family members to contribute for a college education. (Such a financial contribution is referred to as "deeming." Of course, many family members contribute both their time and money regardless of government practices.)

A political problem with a work-first disability system is that the start-up costs of the system and the initial assessments can appear as increases in costs, even if lifetime costs decline. An advantage of phasing in a work-first disability system first with young adults is that the ability to deem a small portion of parents' incomes can make the proposal budget-neutral even in its first years.

Time-Limited Benefits

Those judged currently unable to work should create a plan with a counselor to alleviate the vocational impairments. (Lifetime stipends would still be provided for those who have very serious disabilities or who are near retirement age and do not want to work.) For those judged permanently and totally disabled unless they receive help, SSDI, SSI, and Medicare should pay for needed services. For less severely disabled, Vocational Rehabilitation should pay for the services needed to return the person to work. SSI and SSDI should provide income support during the limited time of medical recovery, classes, and so forth. The income support should run out when the vocational disabilities have been alleviated, either due to medical improvement, therapy, equipment purchases, or training. Thus, this proposal replaces the current medical improvement standard with one based on removal of barriers to work.

One alternative is for the Social Security Administration to give performance-based vocational rehabilitation vouchers (as described earlier) to recipients of its time-limited stipends. These vouchers can pay for longer than the period of stipend to motivate rehabilitation providers to help people stay at work.

All cash and medical care benefits during the time limit would have the positive work incentives described in the first section.

Health Insurance

As noted above, any work-oriented disability system must ban denials of health insurance coverage for preexisting conditions. Only then will disabled people have true choice of health-care provider.

Furthermore, we should provide SSI and SSDI recipients the lifetime option to buy Medicare or Medicaid at a cost related to their income, with the flexibility described above concerning the forms of medical assistance.

A Simpler Possibility

As noted earlier, a program that enhances incentives to work also enhances incentives to enter the SSDI rolls to receive benefits and return part-time to work. Given the long application process for SSDI benefits, it is unclear how many extra people would apply. If the work incentives in the first proposal are effective, it may be worthwhile extending them for new enrollees, at least as a pilot in a few states and perhaps after a waiting period.

Reward Successful Prevention and Early Intervention

Employers and workers' compensation insurance companies pay some of the costs of work-related injuries. While they do not internalize all safety costs, their incentives are pointing in the right direction.

Unfortunately, they can shed some of these costs by shifting people onto the Social Security Disability Insurance rolls. We should incorporate more of the incentives companies face to minimize short-term disability into the long-term disability system.

To improve incentives to reduce long-term disability, the federal government should create performance partnerships with any organization that can help prevent disabilities or that can intervene early to keep people on the job. At least three sets of organizations are relevant: schools and youth-oriented programs, adult-oriented programs, and employers.

Schools

The federal government's total expenditures on the disabled will be lower if states have low levels of entry onto SSI for youths, and high graduation rates from high school for disabled students (controlling for characteristics of the youth population). Thus, federal education funding should increase for states where many disabled students graduate high school, while few children and youths enter SSI.

Adults

Additional federal funding for state vocational rehabilitation agencies, employment and training, and state mental health and mental retardation programs should be granted to states with low levels of entry of adults onto SSDI and SSI, few people reapplying after the initial assistance period on time-limited SSDI and SSI, and high employment rates for working-age adults who report themselves as disabled. (One possible data source would be national surveys such as the Bureau of Labor Statistics' March Current Population Survey, which contains several questions on disability.)

Incentives for schools and states to reduce entry onto SSI and SSDI can lead them to discourage eligible people from applying for benefits and provide incentives for gatekeepers in the disability system to be unduly harsh. Thus, increased incentives will need to be coupled with quality control measures, such as sending out testers to ensure that state systems for determining disability treat people fairly.

Employers

Employers have some discretion in how safe or dangerous the workplaces are. Employers also have some discretion concerning how much they will assist employees to remain in the workforce after accidents or illnesses. This latter discretion applies even to accidents and illnesses that have nothing to do with work. Employer behavior is particularly important because evidence indicates that early interventions that maintain links between an injured or ill person and his or her employer can be the most effective in returning the person to work.

Thus, the federal government should reward those companies that are proactive at keeping employees healthy and that are proactive at keeping employees with health problems on the job. For large employers, the Social Security Administration can calculate an expected entry rate onto SSDI given the age and other characteristics of the workforce. To provide incentives to avoid injuries and return injured workers to work, SSDI tax rates should decline if the rate of entry onto SSDI at a company is low. Conversely, the rate should rise if the entry onto SSDI is unusually high. (This experience rating is similar to the practice in some European countries of charging companies when employees become disabled.) The penalties should not apply to employers who hire workers previously certified as disabled by the schools, Social Security Administration, Vocational Rehabilitation providers, or the Veterans Administration. Entry due to work-related injuries should have a larger effect on the tax rate than entry due to non-work-related injuries.

To ensure workers' compensation insurers face incentives to return people to work, not unload them onto the Social Security system, insurers should also face penalties when workers enter the SSDI system, and be given rewards when few covered employees become disabled.

Critiques

This set of proposals holds the promise of helping millions of Americans who want to work be able to work. At the same time, it faces several difficulties. For example, time-limiting benefits will increase the costs of initial evaluations and of continuing evaluations for the Social Security Administration; moreover, cancellations of benefits will be painful for some recipients. The SSDI and SSI programs have historically granted lifetime benefits to people. In the past, when the Social Security Administration reviewed a file and tried to cancel these benefits, recipients were often quite upset.

This problem will be reduced when grants are provided explicitly for a limited time; thus, nobody will be canceling a lifetime benefit. The pain of cancellation will also be reduced when the cancellation is tied explicitly to improvement in capability to work. Cancellation of benefits for those unable to work will be further reduced if vocational rehabilitation service providers are permitted to certify which of their clients require further assistance (subject to random quality audits, as described above). At the same time, it will be important to evaluate the effectiveness of time-limited benefits and to roll out the new procedures only with appropriate training for those who will administer them.

Permitting current SSDI and SSI recipients to work while receiving benefits but not extending that option to new enrollees can lead to two problems. First, some people may apply for benefits hoping that the rules will someday be relaxed to permit them to work while receiving full benefits. The high cost of applying for benefits implies that this inflow will probably be small. A second critique is that it is unfair to treat the pool of current recipients differently from the inflow of new ones. This critique will lose some of its force if both new and existing enrollees receive adequate work assistance. At the same time, some inequity may be the price of reform that leaves both groups on average better off than they are in the current system.

Conclusion

No nation can afford to pay millions of people who want to work, not to work. Even worse, no nation should punish millions of people who want to work if they choose to work.

This chapter has outlined a disability policy that makes work pay.

First, each dollar of earnings would lower the total grant (combining SSDI, SSI, food stamps, housing assistance, subsidies for medical care, and so forth) by far less than a dollar. Furthermore, increased earnings could only expand choice of medical care provider, never lose current health insurance.

The current complex system of assistance for vocational rehabilitation would be replaced by a simpler system of vouchers. Disabled people would enjoy choice of service provider. Conversely, service providers would be freed from many detailed regulations and would face market incentives to help disabled people hold good jobs.

An important obstacle to providing work incentives is the fear that additional people with some impairments will be drawn onto the disability rolls, increasing costs. A key insight of this chapter is that a return-to-work system can be established for those already on the rolls and not be expanded to new entrants until (and unless) the system proves itself to be effective at helping disabled people hold good jobs. Thus, while many components of this proposal are familiar within the disability policy community, this proposal takes advantage of the fact that work incentives can be particularly generous to those already on the SSDI and SSI rolls because for them there is no fear of induced entry.

Ultimately, keeping people from needing long-term disability pensions is the key to improving the lives of disabled people, and in holding down costs. Thus, the incentives described above encourage schools, employers, and the public sector to help avoid disabilities and keep people with impairments attached to the labor market.

In short, the work-based systems described here hold the promise of moving a significant number of disabled Americans off of the disability rolls and keeping many from ever joining the rolls of the permanently disabled.

12

POLITICS

Politics in the United States is often characterized by Washington gridlock, misuse of social science, and a press focused on horse races, not substance. The result is often an apathetic citizenry. This chapter proposes a normative model of policy-making that integrates the (limited) knowledge of social sciences with the political process and the preferences of citizens. The chapter also outlines the numerous obstacles to this normative model of decision making and makes recommendations for addressing some of these obstacles.

Consider the following scenario, drawn from the recent history of the United States. A new regime is elected on a platform of massive change. The new regime promises that it is a new generation of political leadership that will radically alter the role of government. Its election convinces the newly elected officials and their staffs that the public shares their priorities for radically changing government.

Although elected with great fanfare and media accounts of a once-in-a-generation political shift, the new regime quickly finds that it is unable to pass most of the core elements of its political program. Some of the barriers reflect due to the convoluted process of lawmaking in Washington, but much of the opposition (even within the party of the new regime) comes from legitimate suspicion that some of the budget numbers of the main policy proposals do not add up. Moreover, the early political support for the new regime's plans appears to have been more broad than deep. As citizens learn more about the proposals, they like them less. A year or two into power, Washington's traditional gridlock is the rule, massive change has not yet occurred, and many voters are (if possible) even more cynical than they had been a year before.

This sad scenario has played out twice in recent years in Washington. First, the new Clinton administration arrived. Its "signature" policy was to revamp how 14 percent of GDP is spent in the health-care sector. Initially the administration was convinced it was addressing Americans' primary concern. Two years later we had a political debacle with no legislation passed. Much of the problem had to do with implausible budget numbers that promised to cut the pace of health-care cost increases at the same time as tens of millions of additional Americans received insurance. Even if the budget savings had been plausible, the unwieldy plan had few admirers.

Two years later, the Gingrich-led Republican Congress swept to power. Elected partly as a result of the proposals in the party's Contract with America, the new congressional majority felt that most Americans were committed to its program of a vastly smaller government with fewer regulations on workplaces and the environment. As with the Clinton health plan, the budget numbers behind the simultaneous military buildup, massive tax cut, and balanced budget did not add up. Even more serious, while the majority of Americans appear to want *better* environmental and other regulations, few were committed to massively *less* regulation.

Washington's lack of contact with budgetary reality is understandable (if not excusable): politicians enjoy passing new programs and tax cuts more than they enjoy passing program cuts or tax increases to pay for them. Moreover, politically apt folk constantly explain that American voters want both new programs and lower taxes; thus, they explain, to pass anything some budgetary sleight-of-hand is necessary. It is, perhaps, less easy to understand why these political professionals misjudge what American voters (or even congresspersons) want, whether in terms of health care, regulation, or other programs.

A Normative Model of Problem Solving

This chapter traces these failures to the systematic problems the top level of our government has in following a good decision-making process. Interestingly, both President Bill Clinton (1992) and Speaker of the House Newt Gingrich (1994) have endorsed a model of fact-based decision-making and continuous improvement, originally associated with such people as the quality guru Edward E. Deming and with companies such as Toyota. The normative decision-making model starts by creating an understanding of the problem and then creating a shared vision with widely agreed-on goals. The next steps are more difficult: prioritize the goals and make sensible tradeoffs. Finally, the process includes continuous improvement so that programs automatically check whether they are achieving their goals and modify themselves to work better over time.

Each of these steps is problematic in today's politics. Somewhat artificially, I have associated each step with one major obstacle. The social sciences (particularly as practiced within the Beltway) are not well suited to creating a shared understanding. The media focus on dissension, which impedes discussion on which goals are widely held. While the rational model requires citizen input to help prioritize the goals, rational citizens are typically too apathetic to become informed; instead, interested stakeholders push for their priorities. Ideally, even with a largely apathetic citizenry, political representatives listen to their constituents and make sensible tradeoffs. Unfortunately, our political process ensures that most politicians find it rational to listen to the powerful few more than the majority of the nation.

For each of these problems, I outline several partial solutions. It would be naive to expect all the powerful interests who gain under the status quo to embrace this alternative problem-solving model. The obstacles are profound, and the solutions suggested here contain their own problems. Nevertheless, our best schools and workplaces teach and use this problem-solving model. It is not too much to ask that our government leaders draw on these insights as well.

Understand the Problem

Careful policy analysis requires laying out the facts that underlie the problem. These facts should be widely agreed on. Citizens and politicians can give different priorities to different aspects of the problem, but citizens, analysts, and the press should work together to understand each problem's characteristics. Careful case studies are important to understanding the problem. Furthermore, almost everyone enjoys a good story with vivid characters and touching human interest. At the same time, this analysis of the problem must go beyond the anecdote. As part of his campaign against welfare, President Ronald Reagan recounted the story of a "welfare queen" buying vodka with change from her food stamps. Opponents of his military buildup told tales of $500 toilet seats. More recently, House Republican leader Archer told of a hard-working but mentally retarded janitor who lost his job when the minimum wage rose (Carville 1996, 35). While each of these anecdotes is fairly famous, each is also either wrong or misleading.

Even worse, even if these stories were factually correct, they would still not be representative of the overall effects of the welfare system, government procurement, or the minimum wage. Each of those policies has unintended harmful effects, but these effects must be measured carefully, not described with a single story (no matter how vivid).

Even well-informed citizens, politicians, and analysts will not agree on all aspects of the problem. Where disagreements remain, the source of the disagreements should be clear. For example, it is difficult to measure the problems of growing up in a single-parent family because we do not see what would have happened to the children if the parents had stayed together.

Nevertheless, careful analysis will often greatly reduce the magnitude of disagreement. For example, conservative analyst Charles Murray (1994, 19) has stated that "moderate differences in welfare benefits produce some differences in childbearing behavior, but only small ones." At the same time, Clinton's former senior policy adviser William Galston has claimed that welfare may be responsible for 15 to 20 percent of the increase in births out of wedlock (cited in Tanner 1994). That is, both analysts claim that the welfare system has led to a measurable but fairly small share of the rise in births out of wedlock.

The debate on the employment effects of the minimum wage provides a second example of how social science methods sometimes yield a consensus around a narrow range of uncertainty. For example, every economist who has looked at the data agrees that (1) the minimum wage almost surely causes some employment loss for low-wage workers; (2) the employment loss is almost surely on an order of magnitude less than the wage increase; and (3) thus the minimum wage definitely raises incomes of low-wage workers. Economists argue over whether a 10 percent increase in the minimum wage reduces employment of affected workers by 2.5 percent or .8 percent (that is, whether minimum-wage earners' incomes rise by 7.5 percent or 9.2 percent)—not a very wide range of uncertainty. From the heated rhetoric one hears, few nonexperts would guess that the range of uncertainty on both the fertility effects of welfare and the employment effects of the minimum wage is so limited.

Obstacles to a Shared Understanding: Social Scientists

Social science research is a crucial component of successful policy. Fortunately, most social scientists are honest and hard working and are trying to understand the world. Their research provides the knowledge that underlies the normative model.

At the same time, a number of obstacles impede the creation of a shared understanding. For example, the very definitions social scientists use affect what we measure and see. An apparently technical decision that only output that is sold on markets will be included in measuring GDP automatically gives zero weight to unpaid labor within the household. Unfortunately, this decision has influenced how policymakers view the value of what women produce at home (Waring 1988).

Politics also affects how we understand what we measure. For example, many conservative neoclassical economists reason that since in the frictionless supply-and-demand model there is no involuntary unemployment, then in actual labor markets all unemployment must be voluntary.

Finally, politics also influences the incentives of researchers. Within economics, several large, wealthy foundations support research that favors an unregulated market. Thus, many researchers find it easier to receive support for research on the large efficiency costs of taxation than on the small efficiency costs. The influential business media such as *Forbes, Fortune,* and the editorial page of the *Wall Street Journal* are quick to promote research favoring lower taxes on the wealthy and lower transfers to the poor, but slower to publicize results the editors do not agree with. In other social sciences, funding sources sometimes exhibit a different bias. For example, in sociology it is easier to find funding for studies on whether policies are needed, rather than whether they work.

Furthermore, within mainstream economics, research failing to find a behavioral response to a tax or subsidy is often not publishable. Instead, such results are considered "null results" and are treated under the assumption that a lack of behavioral effect reflects poor data or misspecification of the model.

The most insidious source impeding shared understanding is what my colleague Jonathan Leonard labeled "censorship at the source." During the 1980s, the U.S. government discontinued a number of statistical series. Although budget pressures played a role, so did the ideology of conservative policymakers that data bring analysis, analysis points out social problems, and an understanding of social problems leads to calls for more government programs. Lack of data is a preventable source of poor government policies, and it is especially unfortunate when a political agenda precludes collecting data needed to improve social policy.

The clearest impediment to shared understanding from within the social sciences is the tradition of advocacy research, particularly found around the nation's capital. Researchers are hired or given grants by lobbying organizations to say the most absurd things. In 1996, presidential candidate Robert Dole claimed he was unsure whether nicotine was addictive because he was not a scientist. The intellectual defense of this position comes from a small number of scientists hired by the tobacco companies to claim that tobacco is not addictive, even when all other scholars have come to the opposite conclusion.

Unfortunately, a sufficient number of social science researchers also respond to the forces of the market. The importance of political decisions ensures a steady supply of "experts" drawing funding from the sector they study. These experts are often rewarded because they are "skilled in histrionics and the uses of the media" (Wilensky 1983, 64), not because they are skilled seekers of truth.

An additional problem results from our system of multiple agencies and narrow congressional committees that each address only a single aspect of a problem. Thus, narrow experts who do not see the larger context of a problem gain power from their expertise in the arcane details of programs.

There is no simple solution to the incentives scholars face for advocacy research because such research is so likely to lead to power, fame, and funding. Nevertheless, the disciplines can appoint high-level panels to describe both the consensus positions within the discipline and the areas of reasonable disagreement. (The American Psychological Association presents such consensus findings for a number of important policy debates. A selection of their recent legislative briefings and testimony can be found on the Internet at http://www.apa.org:80/ppo/pippo.html.) The disciplines must also create mechanisms that publicize egregious cases of "junk science" that is propounded solely to further a political agenda. Finally, the disciplines must encourage the work of reasonably impartial portions of government such as the Office of Management and Budget and the Congressional Budget Office whose staffs frequently attempt to use the best knowledge of the social sciences to inform policymakers of the effects of potential policies.

Create Shared Goals

Once the problem is well described, citizens, politicians, and analysts from across the political spectrum should come together to create a common statement of goals. This process should be a democratic one, involving national discussions concerning how much we as a nation value equality of opportunity, democracy, and economic prosperity. At a minimum, each party should have a democratic conversation that includes the majority of potential voters to create a common statement of goals. In addition, any party that wants to pass legislation should widen this conversation to include the views of the vast majority of citizens.

In writing the Contract with America, the Republican Party used focus groups to find out how citizens responded to different policies. This market research was intended partly to prioritize the agenda of one bloc of the Republican Party. As such, the research was democratic, in that it identified the goals of voters. The market research also helped the politicians to package the agenda and phrase the policy proposals to be popular—an inevitable but much less democratic procedure.

It is important for citizens to discuss goals that underlie their stated preferences on issues or their voting patterns so that policymakers can search for solutions that achieve as many of these goals as possible. We need many opportunities for discussion that go deeper than national polling ("Are many welfare recipients cheats?" "Do corporations pay enough taxes?") to help determine the shared underlying values of citizens.

A Sample Vision Statement

By definition, this consensus vision statement cannot be dictated by a single person. Nevertheless, this volume has been based around several principles that will plausibly underlie any consensus policy vision.

First, policies must provide good incentives for citizens in their many roles: taxpayers, workers, employers, welfare recipients, and so forth. For example, we want policies that "make work pay" for recipients of government income support such as welfare or disability insurance.

Second, we must remember that incentives do not matter only for welfare recipients. The federal government must also provide good incentives for partners such as states, schools, suppliers, and direct service providers. Often concern about incentives leads to recommendations based on increased discretion for citizens to choose their service provider and for government agencies to face market incentives to be responsive to citizens' needs.

Third, the programs should focus on satisfying citizens' needs, even if the government has to reorganize to do so. We must create customer-focused solutions, not a myriad of programs each with its own rules.

Fourth, each program must be designed to guarantee continuous improvement. Every task the government undertakes should be designed to ensure that it is more cost effective five years from today. Thus, we must rely on facts to decide what works, not on clever ideas that do not match the data. Conversely, even if a program has some negative consequences, it should not be judged a failure until the costs are measured against benefits.

Finally, we must attempt to save money in the long term, even if we must invest this year. For example, most voters find it morally dubious, and most analysts find it economically irrational to have a large number of children who are so seriously disadvantaged they are more likely to go to prison than to college. Fortunately, some cost-effective interventions appear to increase both national productivity and equity—even if they are costly in the short run.

While these vision statements are vague, they do have some content. For example, under the current system, some recipients of welfare and disability assistance will reduce their living standard when they work. Once all parties have endorsed the goal to "Make work pay," they have agreed to change these policies (subject to needing to trade this goal off with the other goals). Even when the two parties cannot agree completely on a common vision, as in the abortion debate, they should be able to find partially shared goals, such as "Reduce the number of accidental pregnancies."

Obstacles to a Shared Vision: The Media

Creating a common vision is antithetical to news reporting and analysis in the United States. Too often, the American press treats all pages of the newspapers like the sports pages: each Democratic win or loss is matched by a Republican loss or win, and each Democratic or Republican attempt at compromise is a victory for the other side.

In fact, politics is not a zero-sum sport. Some rules and policies are better for society than others. Because each American cannot take the time to become totally informed on important policy issues, it is the responsibility of the press to be knowledgeable. Reporting must go beyond the tactics of the moment to explain the implications of policy proposals.

Thus, when the Contract with America was proposed, the reporting focused on whether it was politically wise for the Republicans to run with a platform. Few reporters asked whether the budget numbers added up, whether the tax cuts would have the promised effect on investment and labor supply, or what the good and bad effects would result from of the proposed reductions in regulation.

A year later, a candidate for the Republican nomination, Malcolm Forbes Jr., proposed a flat income tax. The reporting emphasized how it would have benefited him personally and how wooden he was in describing it. Few and far between were discussions of whether his budget numbers added up or whether the flat tax would increase savings, investment, and living standards.

Few voters care much about whether the Republican politicians have a clever ad campaign or about whether one policy will reduce taxes for a man who already has more money than he can ever spend. Most voters want to know if the politicians are honest (Do the numbers add up?) and whether they have good ideas (Will these policies raise living standards and create a healthier society?). Nevertheless, the "win or lose" and human interest stories dominate our political coverage.

When experts are called in to comment, the reporters look for "balance." Political reporting sometimes resembles a discussion on the shape of the Earth, where a "flat-earther" must be found to match each "round-worlder." This system promotes analysts who tenaciously defend their turf and who promise cures for budget deficits, moral decay, lower wages, obesity, and baldness, all from one simple tonic. Life has tradeoffs, and the press must encourage people who can explain these tradeoffs.

Economic policy is full of both hard and easy questions. "How many welfare recipients will leave the rolls for work before a two-year time limit is up?" is a difficult question. "Can we cut taxes; protect defense, Social Security, and Medicare; and still balance the budget?" is an easy question. Reagan could not do it, and Gingrich could not do it. Nevertheless, on those infrequent occasions when the press examined whether the budget numbers in the Republican Contract with America added up, they gave approximately equal time to experts who did and those who did not believe $2 + 2 = 4$.

Similarly, in the minimum-wage debate the press reports a ferocious debate about whether *any* jobs will be lost. Nobody points out that this is the wrong question—we should care about the costs and benefits of raising the average living standards for the poor. The question should be phrased in terms of whether the small gains to the several million winners are socially more valuable than the larger losses to a few tens of thousands of low-income workers plus those who pay the wage increase.

Reporters are busy people, but they need to spend time learning the answers to the easy questions and reporting those with some confidence. They must learn to save their pairs of experts for the difficult questions, where careful researchers and thoughtful analysts disagree.

The converse of the press's emphasis on conflict is that when the major political parties agree, then the press does not bother investigating whether the consensus position makes sense. For example, in the United States in 1996, both the Democrats and the Republicans agreed on the importance of balancing the budget in seven years. Few voices in the press noted that the budget numbers used to measure the deficit implied this policy made no sense: they treated government investments the same as government consumption, ignored inflation's effects on the real value of the national debt, and made no attempt to address the true long-term budget problems surrounding Social Security and an aging population. Instead of noting how meaningless the numbers were, the press reported who "won" each round of compromises on which nondefense programs would be cut more quickly.

Prioritize Goals and Make Tradeoffs

Inevitably, goals conflict. At this juncture the democratic process must again play the decisive role. Citizens and their representatives must inform themselves on the issues and make tough decisions.

For example, many reformers of welfare endorse the two goals of helping poor children while not providing incentives for unmarried people to have children. These goals are often in conflict because strong incentives to avoid out-of-wedlock fertility may involve low incomes for unmarried parents, thus harming children. Educated citizens and representatives must become aware of the evidence on the magnitudes of the tradeoffs (one with a fair degree of consensus, as noted above), and decide how much misery of poor children should be tolerated to motivate one less birth out of wedlock.

An example of this prioritization occurred in Oregon in their redesign of the Medicaid program that provides health insurance for the poor. The goal was to expand coverage to more uninsured citizens, at the cost of reducing the number of conditions covered. The state convened a group of citizens to hear from experts on the costs and benefits for a variety of medical treatments. Costs were largely financial, while benefits included the expected additional years of life and the expected quality of that life. The panel then prioritized the treatments in terms of cost effectiveness. The decisions were difficult and controversial. For example, the courts overturned the decision to treat cirrhosis of the liver differently depending on whether or not it was induced by alcoholism. Nevertheless, the eventual list was sensible and achieved in a democratic fashion by well-informed decisionmakers—the best process one can hope for.

This prioritization is difficult for political representatives to undertake because the information they receive is rarely in terms of tradeoffs. In many polls, citizens want more programs, lower taxes, and a balanced budget. Few polls measure the tradeoffs citizens are willing to make (Heclo 1994, 372).

The Problem with Prioritizing Goals: Citizen Apathy

Oscar Wilde once quipped, "The problem with socialism is that it takes up too many free evenings." In fact, the problem he identified is a problem of political involvement more generally (Barber 1992). A self-interested and rational citizen wants *other* citizens with similar priorities to be involved in politics, but to free ride on their efforts to determine good policies. Fortunately, the economists' model of rational self-interest is not completely correct on this point, and many citizens are involved in politics. Nevertheless, an important problem with democratically setting priorities is that the social returns to citizen participation are greater than the private returns.*

Improving Schools

Improving schools can help improve the incentives for citizens to cooperate, by making such cooperation more productive. Current curricular reforms usually intend to help students satisfy the needs of business. Businesses, in turn, need students who understand the rational problem-solving model outlined in this volume; that is, the skills of critical thinking, systematic problem solving, and working together in a group. For example, schools should teach everyone how to run a meeting effectively. Even with

---

*In many cases some participation is rational because people gain benefits from the social interactions (for example, at PTA meetings). In other cases, some participation is rational because some benefits will accrue to participants. For example, the PTA president may have a meaningful effect on his or her children's education by improving the school, or because the child will receive a disproportionate share of privileges. In the latter case, political participation involves zero-sum rent-seeking.

One of the great ironies of the discipline of political science in recent years has been the invasion of the rational model of decision making. While this model has often been useful in understanding political behavior, it is a problematic starting point because it predicts that political behavior should (almost) not exist.

this training, local control and oversight will require many meetings, just as Wilde feared, but at least they should be shorter and more productive. Thus, by lowering the costs and raising the benefits, improving our education system's teaching of the skills of good citizenship can, in turn, benefit the schools as citizens effectively work to improve them.

Villages and Politics

While the incentives to participate in politics are often low, they appear to be higher in smaller jurisdictions, particularly when there are numerous spheres of social bonds: schools, sports clubs, work, and so forth. When people have multiple social bonds, neighbors can give each other more valuable rewards for providing the public goods of civic participation. In Italy, for example, regions with multiple forms of social bonds appear to provide more regional public goods than similar regions with more social distance and fewer ties (Putnam 1993).

Many politicians have argued for local control on the grounds that local decision makers make better decisions. In addition, local control may also be important because the process of making decisions locally can make localities better; that is, centralized control may weaken local institutions, thereby worsening local problems.

In a recent best-selling book, First Lady Hilary Clinton argued that "it takes a village to raise a child." One argument in favor of neighborhood schools is that they, in turn, create "villages" within larger metropolitan areas, and the network of parents in these villages help in raising all the children and in providing additional local public goods.

The lesson to be drawn from this example is that policymakers must include the effects on the political process in evaluating policies. Policymakers should give preference to policies that increase the cohesiveness of communities, and promotes the political decision-making competence of citizens.

The Role of the Internet

Computers can empower citizens. Most simply, computers can increase the transparency of government, sharing more information with citizens.

The Internet also opens up possibilities for more direct quasi democracy, lowering the cost of citizen participation (Law and Keltner 1996). Agencies can float proposals for comments, and discussion groups among civic-minded citizens can float new ideas and create consensus around existing ones.

Again, promoting universal access is needed for these changes actually to be democratic. Even with universal access, those with high levels of technological sophistication, with high levels of interest, or just with the most free time can have disproportionate influence.

Academics (Again)

Just as self-interested rational citizens do not bother learning much social science, self-interested social scientists often do not bother learning about the reality of citizens. Currently, social scientists are rewarded largely for clever ideas that lead to articles in refereed journals. In addition, academics should increase the rewards they give colleagues for research that addresses proven needs. The process of proving that a need exists, in turn, will reward social scientists for engaging citizens in discussions about both the values they hold and the failures of the current system to satisfy those values.

As a complement to these conversations, academics must study the experience of front-line workers and of customers of the systems they study to understand the successes, the failures, and the obstacles to success. (In some cases, academics can be involved in administering policies to see how they work and how they fail.) Only when the social scientists and policy advisers have a bottom-up view of the system will their recommendations be likely to improve the lives of those the system is intended to serve.

A Missing Institution

The failure of the Clinton health-care proposals, the Republican Contract with America, and many other policies leads me to suspect that America is missing an institution. Part of the weakness of the Clinton administration's signature proposal health care was the proposal's lack of preparation. Unlike parliamentary systems, the United States has no shadow cabinet of officials thinking about specific key policy areas. We also have no "shadow policies" being vetted by academics, pollsters, and politicians. (Party platforms do not count because they are marketing documents whose budget numbers are not expected to add up.)

Clinton's welfare reform proposal was introduced after health care and was not seriously considered by Congress until too close to the 1994 election. At the same time, the welfare reform plan was vastly better conceived than the health-care proposal. A key difference is that two academics, Mary Jo Bane and David Ellwood (1994), had been (with their colleagues and students) thinking, writing, researching, and test-marketing these ideas for most of their careers. They had analyzed where research needed to be performed, and they and their colleagues had filled key knowledge gaps. They had performed market research of a fundamentally democratic type—

clarifying to themselves and others the widely held principles of work and responsibility that must underlie true reform. They had also performed some market research of a more traditional form, learning how to phrase their ideas in ways that resonated with the American people and legislators. They had worked the numbers and knew what would be cheap and what would need to be phased in to be affordable. Importantly, their research (Kane and Bane 1994) did not just involve studying the numbers and theory, but also included examining life at the front lines—what actually happens at welfare offices. Thus, when Bane and Ellwood were appointed to key policymaking posts by the Clinton administration, their ideas were well formed in terms of what made sense to do and what (might be) politically salable. Even with this background, the welfare reform proposal was not sufficiently in touch with the political attitudes toward poor women to command sufficient political support to pass (Piven and Ellwood 1996).

The missing institution should institutionalize the process these academics performed on their own. Ideally, it should operate with even more democratic participation to identify core widely held values from informed participants. A wide sample of citizen volunteers should be briefed to understand the issues and the costs and benefits of alternative policies. The goal would not be to create focus groups to sell policies but to have informed discussions about citizens' priorities in different areas.

The brief history of the Clinton administration's U.S. Commission on the Future of Worker-Management Relations (1994) (also known as the Dunlop Commission) demonstrates the pitfalls of this approach in the current political environment. This was a high-level commission of academics, union leaders, and corporate executives. The commission followed the first stage of the model presented here. Their first product was a fact-finding report based on existing social science research, a special nationwide poll to identify citizens' desires at work, and testimony from many groups around the nation. They also produced a vision statement that was intended to reflect commonly held goals (see box 12.1). Although one need not agree with all ten goals, they represented an attempt to reach a broad consensus based on the widely agreed-on problems of the American labor market. Only after these preliminaries did the commission make concrete policy proposals for improving workplace regulations (U.S. Commission on the Future of Worker-Management Relations 1995).

Unfortunately, their policy recommendations were issued just as the 1994 Congress took office, and many of the issues raised (e.g., lack of penalties for dismissal of prounion workers) were not on the new Congress's agenda. When the new Congress did address issues of workplace regulation, virtually none of these goals played a role in their

---

Box 12.1. **Goals for the 21st Century Workplace**
(From the U.S. Commission on the Future of Worker-Management Relations 1995.)

1. Expand coverage of employee participation and labor-management partnerships to more workers and more workplaces and to a broader array of decisions.
2. Provide workers an uncoerced opportunity to choose, or not to choose, a bargaining representative and to engage in collective bargaining.
3. Improve resolution of violations of workplace rights.
4. Decentralize and internalize responsibility for workplace regulations.
5. Improve workplace safety and health.
6. Enhance the growth of productivity in the economy as a whole.
7. Increase training and learning at the workplace and related institutions.
8. Reduce inequality by raising the earnings and benefits of workers in the lower part of the wage distribution.
9. Upgrade the economic position of contingent workers.
10. Increase dialogue and learning at the national and local levels.

---

deregulatory agenda. Perhaps because these goals are, in fact, fairly widely shared, after two years in power the Republican Congress has passed little new workplace regulation or deregulation. Similarly, the lack of preparation by the Clinton team implied that most of their reinvention efforts led to only modest changes (box 12.2).

Identify Possible Solutions

Only after decision makers and citizens agree on the problem does it make sense to consider solutions. Importantly, many problems are not what they appear. Thus, analysts must search for the root causes of the priority problems. For example, if crime is an important problem, we want to know the sources of crime before we search for solutions. If, as we see in the United States, crime appears to be highly correlated with dropping out of high school, it may be fruitful to focus on dropping out as a root cause of crime.

Only after identifying key goals/problems and analyzing the root causes of each problem is it worthwhile considering solutions. At this juncture the U.S. policy process works well—our democratic process permits many possible solutions to be proposed. What is less common is a careful evaluation of possible solutions other than those carried out by advocates or self-interested parties.

Box 12.2 **What Doesn't Work: Asking Agencies to Boldly Reinvent Themselves**

Because a key institution is missing in the United States, there is no place in government to think through ideas for bold reinvention. Instead, the party in power must largely depend on the government's myriad agencies to come up with ideas. At the same time, each agency has its own constituency, its own committees on Congress, and its own appropriations. Thus, agencies work with Congress and special interests, viewing the White House as enemies. For example, any ideas the White House push are at risk of being undone by the potent combination of permanent bureaucrats (who can outwait any administration), lobbyists, and Congress. The result is a dysfunctional relationship, where the White House and agencies butt heads with little actual improvement.

When the Clinton administration attempted bold reinvention, the results were predictable. Bold thinking starts with such questions as, "Are the goals of this agency sensible?" and "How could government accomplish the goals of this agency if the agency no longer existed?" No agency head can use these starting points. Instead, when Vice-President Gore asked agency heads for bold reinvention ideas, they described the modest and sensible improvements they had under way. The leaders of these agencies cannot both be effective leaders and question the agency's goal, or consider vastly different ways to achieve a goal.

In one reinvention process I worked with, an agency head proposed a bold and sensible reinvention idea to reduce regulatory burden. Unfortunately, the bold idea disappeared from the group's discussion a week later, after the agency staff had vetoed their boss's idea.

A further obstacle to agency heads being bold is that their constituencies will react. As one assistant secretary told me, "Talking about an idea in the Old Executive Office Building [next door to the White House] is a political statement." In addition, agencies feared (realistically) that Congress would take White House statements as starting points in negotiations, reducing agency flexibility to bargain with the Hill.

The rules of the game led agencies to view the reinvention process as a game against the White House, and most of the time the agencies (and status quo) won. In one reinvention group with which I shared many bold ideas, the head told the group that in the memo to the vice president he wrote: "We have an 'ideas rejected' section in honor of David Levine . . . who gave us something to come together on."

As a predictable result, the Clinton administration's reinventing government process had many sensible money-saving ideas, but very few ideas with a bold vision of helping customers by truly reinventing government.

Win-Win Bargaining: Making Rational Tradeoffs

In addition to disagreeing on the priority they give each goal, politicians may sensibly disagree on the magnitude of the tradeoffs that a policy will have for each goal. In principle, these are disagreements of fact. Thus, the politicians should be willing to change their position as new evidence arrives.

Even if we have careful consideration of the tradeoffs, politics will still involve some bargaining because of different values and different material situations. In addition, some of the disagreements will be the result of differences in the expected effects of policies.

Fortunately, differences in beliefs about what will happen in the future can lead to integrative (or "win-win") tradeoffs that can make both sides happy. Differences in preferences are both problems and opportunities, but differences in *beliefs* should always lead to win-win solutions via a "bet" on the outcome (Fisher and Ury 1991). If Adam thinks one team will win a sports contest, and Betty favors its rival, they should be able to bet and (at least before the match), both expect the bet has made them better off. (High levels of risk aversion can reduce the number of win-win tradeoffs.)

More generally, whenever groups disagree about the expected results of a policy change, they should be able to reach a win-win solution they both feel happy with. For example, many Republicans in Congress claimed the 1996 welfare reform legislation, by reducing welfare for unwed mothers, will lead to large reduction in out-of-wedlock fertility. Furthermore, proponents claim the time limits on welfare will so increase employment that poverty rates will decline for children in single-parent households. Critics of the legislation emphasize that current research finds small effects of welfare on the fertility and earnings of single mothers. (The prediction concerning small effects on earnings is due, in part, to the cuts in funding contained in the welfare bill that make government-subsidized employment unlikely.)

Largely based on their forecasts of large behavioral responses, Republicans also claimed that welfare reform can save money with no (or minimal) increases in misery. If they are correct in their predictions of much higher employment and lower fertility, the need for spending will decline. Conversely, if their critics are correct and the effects of welfare reform on behavior are only modest, the need for spending will increase. Thus, the nation's inflation-adjusted amount budgeted for welfare should increase (or not decline) if out-of-wedlock fertility and childhood poverty rates increase (or do not decline.) (Any increase in the welfare budget should be for the system as a whole. At the same time, the system can be designed so that each state still gains if its rates of unwed fertility and childhood poverty decline.)

The result of this disagreement about how much poor women's earnings and fertility with change is that both sides should be happy with an agreement that ties total spending on poor children to rates of child poverty. Conservatives should be content with such an agreement because they are confident employment will rise and fertility will fall. Thus, they will see policies they like coupled with the budget savings they forecast. Liberals should be content with this agreement because the living standards of poor children are ensured even if (as they expect) single mothers' employment does not rise much and out-of-wedlock fertility does not decline much.

This form of contingent deal is much better than a simple compromise where the same policies are enacted but only part of the conservative's expected budget savings are removed from the budget. With this integrative bargain the budget savings are realized if and only if the need for funds declines, while extra resources are provided if and only if there are more and poorer children. In a compromise, the agreement would provide more resources than conservatives want and fewer than liberals want, regardless of the need.

The minimum wage provides a second opportunity for an integrative bargain. Liberals typically claim that a modest increase in the minimum wage will have minimal effects on employment. In contrast, conservatives typically predict large declines of employment, particularly for out-of-school teen workers (a group particularly likely to work at the minimum wage). Because the economy has trends and cycles regardless of the minimum wage, this prediction is usually put in terms of relative employment rates: critics of the minimum wage expect it will reduce the rate of employment of out-of-school youths compared to the rates of adults. Thus, both groups should be willing to increase the real minimum wage when the employment rate of out-of-school youths is high compared to the rates of adults, and to cut the real value (perhaps by freezing its nominal value) when the relative employment rate of out-of-school youths declines. With such a deal, if a higher minimum wage reduces employment substantially (as conservatives expect), the real minimum wage should decline over time (as conservatives desire). Conversely, if the minimum wage has no measurable effect on employment (as liberals expect), it should be indexed to inflation (as liberals desire).

Because conservatives predict large employment losses, they should be happy with this deal because they expect it to reduce the real minimum wage. Conversely, liberals predict small employment losses. Thus, they should be happy with this deal because they expect it to protect the purchasing power of the minimum wage.

Caveats

These proposals have several difficulties. First, these "bets" introduce risk because many factors affect outcomes such as employment rates or fertility. For example, the "bet" on indexing the minimum wage to employment rates shifts the risk of exogenous changes in employment-population ratios to minimum-wage workers. Second, one party will have weaker incentives to solve problems because they receive compensation for bad outcomes. Finally, one or both sides will have incentives to renege in the future (while claiming it was an unforeseeable act of God or the other party's misbehavior that requires the renegotiation). For example, Congress finds it difficult to commit credibly to future appropriations, although creating difficult-to-modify entitlement programs often facilitates this precommitment.

One effect of these integrative solutions is to smoke out proponents of a policy who are only pretending to be interested in some group's welfare. For example, some proponents of lower welfare spending claim to be interested in the poor but are primarily interested in reducing spending on people who do not vote for them. Conversely, some opponents of cuts claim to be interested in the poor but are largely interested in maintaining a flow of funds that support their constituents. Similarly, some opponents of a minimum-wage increase argue that they are concerned about job loss, when they are actually concerned about lower profits for businesses. Conversely, some proponents argue that they are concerned about low-wage workers, when they are actually concerned about limiting labor-market competition from such workers. For such disputants, moving to a fact-based argument and offering win-win bargains will not resolve the conflict, but it will force them to quit hiding behind their apparently noble interests and make more clear their self-interest.

Obstacles to Rational Tradeoffs: The Political Process

When politicians make their bargains, they will often not attempt to maximize what is best for society. Politicians will disagree for at least five reasons: the first reason is noble, the second reason is useful, and reasons 3 through 5 are neither noble nor useful.

1. The noble reason for disagreement is when politicians or their constituents differ on values. One politician may be more concerned with reducing teen pregnancy and be willing to reduce the living standards of children born to poor parents. Another politician may be more concerned with ensur-

ing welfare recipients work and can support their children somewhere near the poverty line and be willing to endure slightly more births to welfare mothers. These are disagreements about values and are appropriate to resolve through the political means of citizens electing representatives who share their values.

2. The second reason policymakers disagree is that they have different understandings of the facts and of how policies will affect behavior. These disagreements, even if self-interested, can be useful. As noted earlier, when the disagreement concerns primarily facts, a win-win bargain should be possible where each side gambles that its view of the facts is correct.

Unfortunately, politicians often vote against programs they believe to be in the best interest of the nation for less noble reasons: selfish voters, powerful special interests, and short time horizons until the next election.

3. Politicians sometimes vote against programs they believe to be good for the nation because their voters do not benefit from the program. For example, farmers often do not care about urban problems; the reverse is also often true. There is no quick solution when self-interested citizens disagree other than logrolling within the political process.

4. In other cases, politicians vote against programs they believe to be good for the nation because powerful interest groups do not benefit from the program. These groups consist disproportionately of the very wealthy. For example, a vastly disproportionate share of campaign contributions come from the very wealthy, from business owners, and from high-level executives. All three groups typically prefer lower taxes rather than improvements in public schools (because their children attend private schools) or a stronger safety net for poor children. When donors' opinions carry many times more weight than other voters', campaign finance reform is needed.

These groups also control employment opportunities for many congresspersons, congressional staffers, and executive branch decision makers both before and after government service. The "iron triangle" of people moving between the executive branch, the legislative branch, and lobbyist for or employee of a large company further distorts politicians' decisions away from efficiency. The common school and social background of these different groups further enhances the power of the already prosperous.

Just as powerful donor groups can influence political outcomes, they can often influence political processes to reduce transparency and opportunities for democracy. In many cases, powerful groups receive a hidden subsidy. For example, in the United States imports of foreign sugar are restricted. This government-run cartel "taxes" sugar consumers by raising sugar prices far above world levels. The form of this tax leads to distortions and much more economic inefficiency than most other taxes. Thus, government actions give sugar producers several billion dollars worth of implicit subsidies at a cost to consumers that is several times as large. This costly policy is politically tenable because the tax is off-budget and the subsidy is hidden.

The sugar industry has no interest in creating a more rational, transparent, and democratic decision-making process. It is likely that a more open process would end the costly subsidy this industry receives. This logic in favor of obfuscation and against democracy, unfortunately, applies to numerous portions of the government.*

5. Finally, sometimes politicians vote against policies they believe are in the long-term interest of their constituents because the payoff to the policies will not occur until after the next elections. When voters have trouble monitoring the expected long-term benefits of programs, and elections are every two, four, or six years, politicians face incentives to give too little weight to the long-term consequences of policies. When social science research implies that cost-effective policies take years to take effect, rational politicians may ignore their advice. (Heclo [1994, 471] gives examples of this decision in the welfare policy debates.)

In short, good policies often involve being willing to invest in the long run, particularly in our children, even if it is costly in the short run. The problem is that children neither vote nor make campaign contributions. In addition, disadvantaged children's future crimes (for example) are concentrated in a modest number of jurisdictions. Even when citizens living in low-crime districts will need to pay higher taxes to build prisons for these criminals, these costs are sufficiently distant that few politicians consider them in their voting. The result was that in the 1994 debate over a large federal anticrime bill, a number of congresspersons labeled all prevention funding as "social pork" and greatly reduced its share of the funds.

Partial Solutions

No simple solution can address the short-term and narrow horizons of politicians, although three partial solutions can help: capital budgeting, reform of campaign financing, and bipartisan commissions. A fourth solution can broaden politicians' horizons, but risks increasing interest groups pursuing narrow goals instead of efficiency.

Under capital budgeting, increases in investments do not show up as budgetary costs immediately; instead, as in the private sector, the costs of

---

*In principle, one could design a system of taxes and subsidies that increases efficiency while leaving both sugar producers and consumers better off. Given that voters would vote against an explicit tax of this sort, it is likely that sugar producers are rational in supporting the current inefficient system of quotas.

the investments are charged to the budget over the expected lifetime of the investment. Capital budgeting reduces the incentive for politicians to cut investments to look good this year because the budget shows only a fraction of the lower investment as budget savings this year.

Campaign finance reform can also help. One possibility is for the government to fund most campaign costs for candidates who accept strict limits on outside funding yet show at least a modest level of support from voters. (This proposal is currently being implemented in Maine.) Any immediate cost to taxpayers should be vastly repaid by lower pork-barrel spending authorized by government officials who owe large favors to major contributors.

Unfortunately, all but a handful of congresspersons came to Washington at least in part because they were successful fund-raisers. Now that they are in the Capitol, they are often unbeatably good fund-raisers. It is difficult to motivate Congress to change the rules of the game when they have done so well playing under these rules, and the rules are so well rigged in their favor.

A third solution often used in the United States to ameliorate the political problems impeding rational tradeoffs has been bipartisan commissions. These have addressed issues as varied as closing military bases and "fixing" the problems of social security. Consistent with the normative model, bipartisan commissions often stress consensus and base their conclusions on a careful analysis of the facts. On the downside, they tend to stress policy experts and powerful politicians, with some loss of democratic accountability. Furthermore, because the resulting policies are written by policy experts and politicians, the nation has no opportunity to reach a democratic consensus on the desirability of the policy. Furthermore, when experts create policies, citizens are uninformed of the tradeoffs, costs, and delays associated with the policy (Heclo 1994, 413). When the promised benefits are slow to appear, citizens often feel betrayed and discontent.

Ultimately, reforms that break the power of those currently powerful will require bottom-up organizing of those not well represented in the status quo. Such organizing can either increase or decrease efficiency.

On the one hand, organizing those currently not well represented will create a counterweight to the power of the prosperous we see today. To the extent their interests are considered, tradeoffs will occur that better include the interests of those currently underrepresented. Hence, efficiency will increase. Importantly, if we can find better ways to represent the interests of children, then the spending on them is more likely to act as an investment, not merely a transfer to a newly powerful group.

On the other hand, if each interest group gains control over a sphere of rent-creating activities within the government, then we can end up worse off than in a situation of powerlessness (Olson 1982). For example, under the current regime, it is very difficult for the government to reduce subsidies to enormous corporate farms that wastefully use subsidized water in California, to unionized construction workers who earn high wages on federal highway projects, to sugar beet growers who enjoy a government-run cartel, to broadcasters who do not pay for the right to use scarce bandwidth, or to weapons makers who are paid billions of dollars for weapons systems that were appropriate for the Cold War but are no longer needed. These are only a few of many cases where a concentrated powerful interest group is acquiring resources for its own, not the public's, benefit. As we multiply interest groups that are represented, the outcome can be stagnation and a worsening of the use of government to achieve selfish gains.

No simple solution can resolve the tension between the inefficiency of nonrepresentation and the inefficiency of representation targeted on selfish goals. A partial answer can come from the creation of encompassing groups, large enough to take into account many of the costs that smaller groups might impose. For example, very large union federations that cover most of the workforce sometimes restrain nominal wage increases that can lead to inflation, while scattered and divided unions do not internalize the inflation externality that their industry-specific contracts can impose on the rest of the economy (Calmfors 1993).

Continuous Improvement

The final step in the normative decision-making model involves continuous improvement. Best-practice management in the private sector requires each organization and its suppliers to gather and analyze data so that quality and productivity are always rising. Similarly, government programs must be designed so that in five years they work better than they do today. We need to institutionalize mechanisms for learning and continuous improvement to ensure that the programs are always serving their customers better.

Obstacles to Continuous Improvement: The Government

Systematic continuous improvement faces a number of obstacles within government. Federal regulations can be incredibly difficult to modify, even when almost all groups agree change is needed. As mentioned before, one agency used an eighteen-foot chart with 373 boxes to describe its rulemaking process (U.S. Office of the Vice President 1993). Politicians prefer to campaign on a platform of having solutions, not merely on having a good plan for empowering and motivating decentralized agencies to search for solutions. Moreover, Congress and the executive branch have incentives to reduce budgets when agencies show efficiencies, penalizing efficient agencies.

At the same time, the media and governmental oversight bodies such as inspector generals for each department, the Office of Management and Budget in the White House, and congressional committees have incentives to find clear examples of failures. Particularly if partisans do not like a program, a few examples of failure can stigmatize an entire program. For example, a few widely cited cases of drug use and sexual relations on Job Corps premises hurt that program substantially in Congress. Ironically, this program was one of the most successful in terms of cost-benefit ratio when subject to a careful evaluation (U.S. Department of Labor 1995c).

Conclusion

This book has emphasized that systematic problem solving can be good for workplaces in both the public and private sectors. This chapter has turned this prescription onto government policymaking. The normative model we should teach in schools and reward at work begins with building an understanding of the problem and an agreement on (largely) shared goals. Then, decision makers should build on this common understanding and goals to prioritize the goals and make tradeoffs. In this process, they must always search for win-win bargains. Finally, decision makers must realize that whatever solution appears the best today, it can be improved on tomorrow. Thus, they should design new programs to monitor their own performance and to ensure continuous improvement.

This optimistic scenario rarely plays out in reality. Important obstacles include citizens' rational apathy, social scientists' pursuit of grants, the media's pursuit of readers and viewers, and politicians' pursuit of contributions.

No simple solution can fix politics, the social sciences, and policy. At each step of the process from problem identification through to implementation, powerful forces have incentives to move away from this normative model. For example, any attempt at campaign finance reform will lead to politicians and donors finding new loopholes. Strengthening the ability of social scientists to "slap down" junk science will also increase the ridicule heaped on some ideas that challenge the status quo yet later become widely accepted. No set of modest reforms can completely eliminate politicians' incentives to promise more than they can deliver. As noted earlier, those receiving benefits from the status quo do not favor a more open, democratic, and rational decision-making model.

In spite of these cautions, the incremental solutions presented here can move policymaking in the direction of the normative problem-solving model. The proposed policymaking model does not guarantee instant success. Instead, it guarantees a number of failures. The difference is that the failures should be learning experiences that lead to a government whose programs are better targeted at citizens' needs, and whose programs are always improving at meeting those needs. Importantly, as citizens use these skills at work and in their own political process, the skills of decision making and working together will be amplified further. Finally, a more substantive political process would also engage more citizens.

13

LESSONS LEARNED

Over the last quarter century, the U.S. labor market has led the industrialized world in job creation. At the same time, however, wages have stagnated for many Americans and declined markedly for those at the bottom.

Social scientists do not fully understand what has caused these trends. Some portion of the problem is due to the three-way reinforcing system of rigidity in workplaces, schools, and government programs. A vast number of workplaces rely on rigid top-down hierarchies, where front-line workers are largely expected to follow their bosses' commands. Many schools support this system: they teach obedience when doing boring and repetitive work, but do not emphasize higher-order problem-solving skills. Government programs close the cycle by typically relying on rigid top-down rules and regulations.

Regardless of the causes, we have a new economy with new challenges and new opportunities. The facts of the new economy must inform our policy decisions. To take one example, as inequality increases, it becomes increasingly difficult to protect poor children without policies to raise the productivity and wages of the bottom sector of the labor market. As a second example, with computers common at work, physical disabilities are much less likely to be obstacles to productive employment.

The solution to the problem of stagnating wages and productivity can be seen in the nation's most productive workplaces. These workplaces typically train all workers in the skills needed to work together to solve problems for customers. Moreover, they combine this training with incentives and work structures that promote such problem solving. The result is that high school graduates as well those with advanced education can be highly productive, earn decent wages, and have interesting work.

This model of the new American workplace has several implications for social policy. First, it informs schools and other training providers about the skills on which they should focus, such as working in teams and searching for and solving problems systematically. As a corollary, the certifications provided by high schools and created by industries must certify these skills. Finally, at workplaces where employees are empowered to solve problems, regulators can build on these skills and work structures to achieve the goals of their regulations.

The Keys to Improvement

The new workplace model also suggests a way of organizing the provision of government services that is very different from the traditional U.S. model. Rigid hierarchies, with their detailed command-and-control rules for workers and suppliers, no longer produce world-class quality in the private sector. Government must also move away from its reliance on similar regulations when dealing with its agencies, employees, and partners. Instead, it must create partnerships that combine fewer command-and-control regulations with greater accountability for results.

Incentives and Accountability

The formula for improved incentives that reappears throughout this book is to hold service providers accountable to their clients. For this model to work, the clients must have meaningful choices so they can switch away from unsatisfactory providers, or have meaningful levels of political power to change the quality of services they receive.

Choice is only meaningful if clients have the information to judge whether service providers are likely to provide the services clients will value. To enhance accountability to citizens, the federal government has a role in collecting and disseminating information (typically on the Internet) on the results and value added of different service providers (box 13.1).

Although no performance measurement is perfect, appropriate accountability and incentives can usually replace the bulk of existing command-and control regulations. With accountability instead of regulation, each service provider can choose the best means of achieving its customers' goal. Even when regulations retain a role, service providers with a record of success should earn deregulation from most rules. This conditional deregulation is itself an incentive to provide high-quality service.

For example, under this proposal, schools will report student achievement of standardized goals as measured by widely used and well-rounded assessments, as well as student achievement of widely recognized skill certifications. These measures will be standardized to measure schools' value added, not just the quality of their incoming students. Parents will see these data and be able to influence schools through local governance institutions such as the PTA and the local school board. When this influence is unsatisfactory, parents and students will be able to change schools through vouchers good at local public schools (public school choice).

Box 13.1 **Accountability to Customers Can Improve Incentives for Service Providers**

Service provider	Produces information on their results and capabilities	Accountable to	With meaningful choice/voice because of
Schools	Student achievement of standardized goals as measured by widely used and well-rounded assessments; achievement of widely recognized skill certifications	Parents	Public school choice, voice through PTA and local politics
Colleges and adult-oriented training providers	Skill certifications, placement rates, earnings of graduates (and comparison to pretraining wages)	Students	Skill vouchers (scholarships) and flexible loans; information system reports outcomes of previous students
Students and employees	Achievement of educational goals and of skill certifications	Employers	Information system with data on national labor market
Employers	Safety records and safety plan	Employee committee that approves safety plan	Employees can call in regulators or disapprove safety plan
Suppliers to the government	Baldrige and related evaluations of capabilities to improve quality and meet customer needs	Customers who want suppliers that meet their needs	Ability to switch suppliers

Box 13.1 *(continued)*

Companies	Baldrige and related evaluations of capabilities to improve quality and meet customer needs	Investors who want to reward long-term value creation	Ability to sell shares, vote for new board of directors
Government departments, suppliers, and partners such as states or nonprofits	Baldrige and related evaluations of capabilities to improve quality and meet customer needs	Public-sector executives, president, Congress, and voters	Voting process by citizens, funding levels, continued business
Public housing authorities	Housing quality (easily observed by residents)	Recipients of housing subsidies	Housing vouchers that can be used in private housing
Providers of vocational rehabilitation services to the disabled	Earnings of graduates (controlling for diagnosis and other factors)	Clients	Rehabilitation vouchers valuable at any service provider; information system reports on outcomes of previous clients
Providers of vocational rehabilitation services to the disabled	Earnings of graduates	Government and taxpayers	Value of the rehabilitation vouchers is based on government savings when clients' earnings increase

Colleges and other education and training providers for adults will also report student achievement of skill certifications. In addition, the national labor market information system will report placement rates and earnings of graduates (including a comparison to pretraining earnings). Students will have access to these performance measures. Even low-income students should be able to exercise choice because of skill vouchers (scholarships) and flexible loans.

Schools must motivate students, just as students and their families must provide incentives for the schools. Fortunately, this system creates appropriate incentives for students as well as for schools. Both students and employees will be able to achieve widely recognized certifications of their skills. Job applicants will be able to provide evidence of these certifications over the Internet to all employers. This certification system will provide incentives for students to work hard toward meaningful goals. (For other means in which the Internet can help reinvent policies, see box 13.2.)

In many cases, the government is trying to provide incentives to employers, usually through detailed command-and-control regulations. If employees can hold employers accountable, workplace regulations can achieve both better results and lower cost. Employers who choose to opt out of the current command-and-control regulations should be accountable to employees for their success in meeting the goals of workplace regulations. Consider the example of safety. Employees will be able to see the workplace's safety records and safety plan. An employee committee will need to approve the safety plan for the workplace to be exempt from detailed command-and-control regulations. If employers do not achieve the goals of the regulations, employees will be able to call in regulators or disapprove the safety plan.

The government also needs to create incentives for its suppliers. Just as better measurement of employees' skills can help both employees and employers, better certifications of government suppliers' capabilities can help both suppliers and the government. Suppliers will be evaluated by Baldrige award criteria and related evaluations of their capabilities to improve quality and meet customer needs. These evaluations can benefit suppliers in their relations outside the public sector, as their certifications become more widely recognized.

Identical logic holds for government departments and partners of the federal government such as states or nonprofits. All these service providers can be evaluated by the Baldrige criteria and its derivatives. However an agency or business partner is producing a good or service, it should be rewarded for implementing systems that ensure increasing effectiveness over time. Public-sector executives, the president, Congress, and voters can then use the voting process, funding levels, and the promise of continued business to reward agencies that enhance their capabilities to improve quality and meet customer needs. Many of America's most successful private companies reward divisions and suppliers that have excellent programs to improve the quality and effectiveness of their operations. The federal government should build on this best practice. For example, the move from command-and-control regulation to deregulation should be accelerated for service providers having programs that lead to continuous improvement.

Box 13.2. **What Works: The Internet**

A theme running through this volume has been the role of computers, the Internet, and other forms of information technology in creating problems and creating possible solutions. A downside of new information technology is that it remains a chief suspect for the growing inequality in earnings we have seen (chapter 4). Fortunately, information technology such as the Internet can also be part of the solution.

Computers and the Internet provide new tools for teamwork and systematic problem solving (chapter 5). In addition, the Internet provides new tools for teaching these skills. A precondition for the technology to live up to its promise is ensuring universal access at schools, libraries, and government offices.

A sophisticated labor market information system can also play a key role in matching workers and jobs (chapter 6). In addition, new group-oriented technologies open up new forms of worker empowerment (chapter 7). As the government introduces more empowered workplaces, it will need to use the Internet to combine decentralization with consistent use of best practices.

The Internet can also play a key role in reinventing workplace regulation (chapter 8). Information on how to run a safe, legal workplace should be posted for all businesses and employees to use. Disseminating information on workers' rights directly to them is a low-cost, but sometimes quite powerful, means of increasing compliance.

The Internet can also promote housing desegregation by helping inner-city residents learn about housing opportunities in the suburbs (chapter 9). In addition, social service agencies in Education Empowerment Zones will need to use the Internet to deliver information and services and to improve their coordination of services (chapter 10).

Computers and the Internet both create the need and improve the opportunity to reinvent disability policy (chapter 11); such technologies provide new opportunities to empower the disabled. Computers can make daily life easier (reading for the blind), and promote community with online discussions. Computers also create new job opportunities for people with many disabilities.

Finally, computers can empower citizens, an essential part of improving politics (chapter 12). Most simply, computers can increase the transparency of government by sharing more information with citizens. The Internet can also lower the cost of citizen participation. Again, promoting universal access is needed for these changes to actually to be democratic.

In short, information technology such as the Internet can greatly increase all citizens' access to the information they need to be productive workers and engaged citizens. A key to this possibility is widespread access to the new technologies and universal training in their use.

The formula of improved accountability applies to all the means the federal government uses to provide a good or service: direct provision by federal agencies, procurement of the good or service (perhaps by privatizing a current government function), providing vouchers or tax credits so that citizens can purchase the good or service themselves, or partnering with a state or local government. Partnering can occur with any combination of regulations, incentives for high effort, and incentives for good results.

For example, until recently much federal aid to states and localities was in the form of matching grants. The federal government's matching of state and local funding of antipoverty and other efforts provided incentives for programs that had benefits outside the states. Unfortunately, the block grants now popular with many in Congress do not include measures for accountability. Without accountability, the move from matching grants to block grants penalizes those states that try hard to help their disadvantaged citizens.

The Role of Vouchers

Choice is only meaningful if even low-income citizens have the purchasing power to choose alternative service providers. Thus, in many situations, vouchers or refundable tax credits can create such accountability to customers. With vouchers, citizens have a direct role in monitoring quality.

For example, skill vouchers (perhaps implemented as scholarships or refundable tax credits) can improve our system of adult education by providing the unemployed with choices over where to acquire skills. (School vouchers are more controversial than most other forms of vouchers because some versions may not increase choices for the poor, and because neighborhood schools can help create a true community among the nearby families.)

In addition, public housing authorities can be made accountable to residents for the quality of their housing. Recipients of housing subsidies will be able to penalize poorly run projects by using their flexible housing vouchers to move to other (often private) housing.

Similarly, providers of vocational rehabilitation services to the disabled can be held accountable for their success in providing value to their clients. First, clients should see labor-market outcomes such as changes in earnings of graduates (controlling for diagnosis). Clients should receive flexible rehabilitation vouchers that are valuable at any service provider so that they can provide market incentives for providers to give great service.

A variant of vouchers can make providers of vocational rehabilitation services accountable to the government and to taxpayers. If the value of the rehabilitation vouchers to the service provider rises when clients' earnings reduce government benefits, then the system is guaranteed to make both the government and the disabled clients better off.

Incentives for Citizens

We must improve incentives for citizens in their many roles. Federal employees must know that their ideas to improve efficiency or quality will not cost them or their colleagues a job. Disabled adults must know that taking a job will not lower their standard of living or deprive them of health insurance.

A converse to the theme of improved incentives is the importance of responsibility. Youths should stay in school. Parents have a responsibility to support their family. Disabled people who can work should work.

It is not appropriate to require "responsibility" for an outcome unless individuals are given the ability to achieve it. For example, a responsibility system implies that students should stay in school to achieve widely accepted skill certifications that employers will often require. This requirement is fair only if students have access to early childhood health care and decent child care so that they enter schools ready to learn. It is fair only if schools have adequate funding and if teachers and administrators have appropriate skills and incentives.

A responsibility system implies that teachers are accountable to parents and students for providing valuable skills and certifications; otherwise the students can exit to other schools and parents can vote a new school board. This is fair only if schools have adequate funding and teachers have appropriate training.

A responsibility system requires that many people with physical disabilities work for pay. This is fair only if they have access to the training, rehabilitation, transportation, special medical or workplace equipment, and other resources they need to work. Moreover, they must know that their income and health insurance will improve (instead of decline) as their earnings rise.

This mixture of incentives and responsibility reappears within the public sector. A true reinvention of government must ensure that every employee of the federal government has the training, incentives, and authority and responsibility to improve how their work is done. Our citizens demand no less, and our citizens deserve no less.

Reinventing a Life Cycle of Policies

The approach to reinvention outlined above applies to any area of policy, from pollution control to defense procurement. This volume has applied these lessons to labor market and social policy. In spite of its length, this volume has left out issues ranging from mandatory family and medical leaves to affirmative action. At the same time, the policies identified here describe a life-cycle approach to creating more and better jobs, with a strong focus on investing in children.

The starting point is literally before the child is born. We need to expand our prenatal and infant care programs so all children are born healthy, and all receive appropriate pre- and postnatal care. The good news here is that early interventions can greatly reduce the costs the government pays to care for premature infants.

These interventions must continue with increased access to high-quality child care so that children are ready to enter school. Universal access to child care has the additional benefit of reducing the barriers that single mothers face when they enter the labor force. No reform of welfare can succeed if poor mothers must pay for child care while they try to earn enough to support their families.

Excellent preparation up to age five does no good unless it is followed by excellent schooling. This book describes decentralized but powerful school reform so that children in all neighborhoods can attend good schools. The goal is to make schools more interesting and more useful to employers and (future) employees by stressing skills such as working in groups to solve interesting problems. The model proposed here couples decreases in command-and-control regulations with increases in account-ability—accountability to state and federal funders and (most important) accountability to parents. This accountability, coupled with parental in-volvement, appears to be the key to long-term success. We must go beyond the skills needed for productive workers and build the skills needed for engaged citizens: from the craft of running a meeting to the deepest levels of critical thinking.

In some settings accountability to parents and students can be enhanced by permitting them to choose students' schools. The term "school choice" covers a range of programs. Some "choice" programs largely lower the costs for those families that already choose private schools. Because these families are disproportionately privileged, such programs can worsen school funding for the majority of our children.

We must ensure that choice programs do not primarily enhance privi-leged children's ability to choose. For example, on the opposite extreme, a minimalist choice program would give school vouchers largely to the disad-vantaged currently attending public schools. This program ensures that choice expands while it targets incentives to areas where schools are per-forming worst. Because the nonpoor largely have effective school choice by choosing where to live, this form of choice maximizes the increment of effective choice for each dollar spent on vouchers.

A more expansive version of school choice permits students to choose among all existing public schools and encourages new charter schools to form. Finally, a version of school choice in which schools would not charge tuition above the value of the voucher, and in which schools would not cherry-pick students, would permit private schools to compete for students as well.

The United States is unique among its industrialized peers in having no means for high school students to forge the transition to good jobs. At the opposite extreme, German high school graduates typically receive a high-quality apprenticeship. They then earn roughly twice what their counterparts in the United States earn. Moreover, until the recession brought on by reunification, they had no higher unemployment. Although the German system could not translate directly to the United States, the potential for improvement is there. Thus, the proposals here include school-to-work programs so that youths are prepared for work and have jobs when they become adults. Improving these connections can both increase learning and motivation of youths in high school and improve productivity for businesses.

Programs linking high school to jobs for young adults are particularly important for youths growing up in our poorest neighborhoods. Thus, the strategy for improving ghettos stressed in this book does not involve continuing to bribe businesses to locate in the ghettos. Instead, we should create a system in which youths are confident that if they finish school, avoid crime, and avoid pregnancy, they can grow up to leave the ghetto.

To create this promise, high schools in poor neighborhoods need to partner with local governments, businesses, nonprofits, religious institutions, and others to find things for disadvantaged youths to do all day and all through the year. Moreover, these services must be integrated so that youths and disadvantaged families see a coherent system of assistance. The federal government and the states should offer the following deal to high schools in poor neighborhoods: If you can create these partnerships and provide this level of integration, then graduates of high school who avoid arrest and pregnancy will be guaranteed either a scholarship to college or an entry-level job.

Regardless of our success in moving people into the labor force, millions of workers will continue to quit or lose their job each year. This book describes a reemployment system that moves people from one job to the next with maximum transferability of job skills and without loss of health insurance or the value of pensions. A decentralized form of training loans and grants would replace the command-and-control training system of today. Flexible loans with repayment rates that are tied to future income should also increase access to education after high school for students of all ages.

When people enter the labor force, they enter workplaces subject to hundreds of command-and-control regulations from numerous levels of government. This volume presents a novel proposal for deregulation. This deregulation would not be for all employers, but only for those who voluntarily work with employees and their representatives to solve workplace problems. Each plan to replace current regulations would still need to meet strict standards and show good and continuously improving results. Moreover, employees themselves would approve alternative plans, creating a decentralized means of ensuring compliance.

If OSHA is the agency most hated by business, large public housing projects are perhaps the most hated government function. We must end public housing as we know it so that children are not trapped in some of the worst neighborhoods in the industrialized world. Housing assistance should be provided with housing vouchers that promote mobility and employment. As an important complement, the federal government should increase its efforts to search out housing discrimination; for example, by extending its use of matched black and white testers who apply for housing, rentals, or mortgage loans.

A little-realized fact in discussing labor market policy is that we are all just temporarily able-bodied. We must move to a disability system that rewards prevention of long-term work impairment. When disabilities occur, the system must remove the enormous disincentives for work that disabled people face. The proposal here suggests that total benefits for the disabled be reduced by fifty cents for each dollar they earn—ensuring that work always pays. Moreover, the disabled would be ensured of subsidized medical insurance forever, although the subsidy would decline as their earnings rose.

To couple flexibility with incentives for both the disabled and for service providers, assistance in vocational rehabilitation should be provided with vouchers that pay for results. An important insight of the analysis presented here is that it is possible to grant the 6 million working-age people already on the disability rolls very strong work incentives, because with this population there is no fear of inducing new entry onto the rolls. For many new entrants, particularly the younger and less seriously disabled, the system must move from a model of lifetime poverty-level stipends to a model of providing the assistance needed to work.

Investing in Our Future

Unfortunately, some of these policies cost money. The key to sensible social policy is to realize that it can cost less to improve the life of a child than to deal with the consequences of an impoverished and problematic childhood. Thus, investments in building a society with opportunity for all can repay themselves many times.

A second basic set of investments involve investments in learning. When a single agency, state, or city identifies a better way to serve its clients, others should benefit from this innovation. Conversely, no single agency captures all the benefits of its new ideas. Thus, the federal government has a key role in building the information infrastructure of the nation. Some of this infrastructure is literally wires, helping all citizens have access to the Internet. Much of this knowledge infrastructure is disseminating best practices: what educational policies work, what social policies work, and what management policies work in the public and private sectors. Finally, this knowledge infrastructure must contain information on how to create new information. That is, the government must disseminate information on how to build policies that create knowledge about their own operation: policies designed for continuous improvement.

Continuous Improvement of These Proposals

Many of the ideas proposed in this volume are novel and are not yet tested. Many ideas that appear sensible will not work in practice. Others ideas, such as the need for service integration, are as familiar in the prescriptive literature as they are ignored in practice.

What both the novel and the familiar ideas have in common is a need for learning and disseminating what works. We must learn what policies work, and we must learn how to implement those policies in the face of obstacles to integration, change, and so forth.

Concluding Thoughts

Today, almost one in four children live in poverty. These rates are much higher for certain groups such as blacks and families headed by a single mother. With half of all marriages ending in divorce, no extended family is likely to be immune from these dislocations.

There is no ethical justification for children suffering on this scale in a land of plenty. Moreover, children are our future. Investing in them can pay off through higher living standards, lower crime rates, a lower burden on social services, and the higher taxes they will pay over their lives.

No single policy will reverse America's disappointing performance concerning poverty, teen pregnancy, and slow productivity and wage growth. Nevertheless, taken together, the policies described here can enhance the

chances of all Americans to live prosperous, middle-class lives. These policies will increase the likelihood that children will be born healthy, enter
school ready to learn, and stay there long enough to learn the skills they will
need in the workplace of the future. Policy innovations in the labor market
promise new entrants better prospects for finding a satisfying first job, and
all workers a greater likelihood of smoother transitions between jobs and of
continued learning on their jobs and throughout their careers. If successful,
these policies will promote higher productivity and rising living standards,
as well as make work more interesting for all.

BIBLIOGRAPHY

Adler, Paul S., Goldoftas, Barbara, and Levine, David I. 1997. "Ergonomics, Employee Involvement, and the Toyota Production System: A Case Study of NUMMI's 1993 Model Introduction." *Industrial and Labor Relations Review* 50, no. 3 (April): 416–437.

AFL-CIO Committee on the Evolution of Work. 1994. "The New American Workplace: A Labor Perspective." Report. February.

Akerlof, George. 1970. "The Market for 'Lemons': Quality Uncertainty and the Market Mechanism." *The Quarterly Journal of Economics* 84 (August): 488–500.

ALMIS Talent Bank Project Home Page 1996. [http://www.mesc.state.mi.us/netrex]

American National Standards Institute/Electronic Industry Association. 1992. "National Electronic Process Certification Standard: EIA 599." Washington, DC: ANSI/EIA.

Arthur, Jeffrey B. 1994. "Effects of Human Resource Systems on Manufacturing Performance and Turnover." *Academy of Management Journal* 37, no. 3 (June): 670–687.

Ashenfelter, Orley, and Rouse, Cecilia. 1997. *Income, Schooling, and Ability: Evidence from a Sample of Identical Twins.* Cambridge, MA: National Bureau of Economic Research.

Bane, Mary Jo, and Ellwood, David T. 1994. *Welfare Realities: From Rhetoric to Reform.* Cambridge, MA: Harvard University Press.

Barber, Benjamin. 1992. "The Politics of Education." *Afternoon Insights.* Interview, WYSO-FM, December 14. [Text at URL http://www.west.net/insight/london/barber.html]

Bartel, Ann P. 1994. "Productivity Gains from the Implementation of Employee Training Programs." *Industrial Relations* 33, no. 4 (October): 411–425.

Bartik, Timothy J. 1996. "Performance Standards and Welfare Reform." *Upjohn Institute Employment Research* (Spring): pp. 5–6.

Batavia, A.I., and Parker, S. 1995. "From Disability Rolls to Payrolls: A Proposal for Social Security Reform." *Journal of Disability Studies* 6, no. 1: 73–86.

Bates, Timothy. 1995. "A Bad Investment." *Inc.* (January): 27. [http://www.inc.com/incmagazine/archives/01950271.html]

Becker, Gary. 1975. *Human Capital.* 2nd ed. Chicago: University of Chicago Press.

Bendick, Marc, Jackson, Charles W., and Reinoso, Victor. 1993. *Measuring Employment Discrimination through Controlled Experiments.* Washington, DC: Fair Employment Council of Greater Washington, Inc. May.

Bennett, William, 1995. Testimony of William Bennett, *Contract with America—Welfare Reform: Hearing before the Subcommittee on Human Resources of the Committee on Ways and Means, House of Representatives.* 104th Congress, 1st ses. part 1 of 2. Serial 104-43. January 20, pp. 159–162.

Berg, Peter, Appelbaum, Eileen, Bailey, Thomas, and Kalleberg, Arne. 1996. "The Performance Effects of Modular Production in the Apparel Industry." *Industrial Relations* 34, no. 3 (Summer): 356–373.

Berkowitz, M. 1996. "Improving the Return to Work of Social Security Disability Beneficiaries." In *Disability, Work and Cash Benefits,* ed. Jerry Mashaw. Kalamazoo, MI: Upjohn.

Berkowitz, E., and Dean, D. 1996. "Lessons from the Vocational Rehabilitation/Social Security Administration Experience." In *Disability, Work and Cash Benefits,* ed. Jerry Mashaw, pp. 223–244. Kalamazoo, MI: Upjohn.

Birnbaum, Jeffrey. 1995."Politics & Policy: Like Dumbo's Feather, Prospect of Federal Grants Gives Cities the Confidence to Fly on Their Own." *Wall Street Journal,* August 24, p. A10.

Bishop, John H. 1992a. "Why United States Students Need Incentives to Learn." *Educational Leadership* 49, no. 6 (March): 15–18.

Bishop, John. 1992b. "High School Performance and Employee Recruitment." *Journal of Labor Research* 13, no. 1 (Winter): 41–44.

———. 1993. "Improving Job Matches in the U.S. Labor Market." *Brookings Papers on Economic Activity* 1: 335–400.

Bishop, John H., and Kang, S. 1991. "Applying for Entitlements—Employers and the Targeted Jobs Tax Credit." *Journal of Policy Analysis and Management* 10, no. 1 (Winter): 24–45.

Bishop, John H., and Montgomery, M. 1993. "Does the Targeted Jobs Tax Credit Create Jobs at Subsidized Firms?" *Industrial Relations* 32, no. 3 (Fall): 289–306.

Blake, Kathy. 1997. "Contract Feeders Open Up Jobs and Doors to Former Welfare Recipients." *Nation's Restaurant News* 31, no. 14 (April 7): 45.

Blank, Rebecca M., and Blinder, Alan S. 1986. "Macroeconomics, Income Distribution and Poverty." In *Fighting Poverty: What Works and What Doesn't,* ed. Sheldon H. Danziger and Daniel H. Weinberg. Cambridge, MA: Harvard University Press.

Blasi, Joseph, and Kruse, Douglas. 1991. *The New Owners.* New York: Harper Business.

Bok, Derek, and Dunlop, John. 1970. *Labor and the American Community.* New York: Simon and Schuster.

Bompey, Stuart H., and Stempel, Andrea H. 1995. "Four Years Later: A Look at Compulsory Arbitration of Employment Discrimination Claims after Gilmer v. Interstate/Johnson Lane Corp." *Employment Relations Law Journal* 21, no. 2 (September 2).

Borjas, George J., Bronards, Stephen G., and Trejo, Stephen J. 1992. "Self-Selection and Internal Migration in the United States." *Journal of Urban Economics* 32, no. 2 (September): 159–185.

Bound, John, and Freeman, Richard. 1992. "What Went Wrong? The Erosion of Relative Earnings and Employment Among Young Black Men in the 1980s." *Quarterly Journal of Economics* 107, no. 1 (February): 201–232.

Broeder, C. den. 1995. *The Match Between Education and Work: What Can We Learn from the German Apprenticeship System?* Onderzoeksmemorandum No. 118. Hague: Central Planning Bureau.

Brown, Charles. 1980. "Equalizing Differences in Labor Markets." *Quarterly Journal of Economics* 94, no. 1 (February): 113–134.

Calmfors, Lars. 1993. "Centralization of Wage Bargaining and Macroeconomic Performance: A Survey." Working papers 131. Economics Department, Organisation for Economic Co-operation and Development.

Campbell, John Y., and Mankiw, N. Gregory. 1990. "Permanent Income, Current Income, and Consumption." *Journal of Business & Economic Statistics* 8, no. 3 (July): 265-279.

Carbone, James. 1994. "Ford Comes Up with a Better Way to Design." *Electronic Business Buyer* 20, no. 4 (April): 120-123.

Card, David, and Krueger, Alan B. 1996. "Labor Market Effects of School Quality:

Theory and Evidence." Working Paper 5450. Cambridge, MA: National Bureau of Economic Research.

Carville, James. 1996. *We're Right and They're Wrong.* New York: Random House.

Citro, Constance F., and Michael, Robert T., eds. 1995. *Measuring Poverty: A New Approach.* Panel on Poverty and Family Assistance: Concepts, Information Needs, and Measurement Methods, Committee on National Statistics, Commission on Behavioral and Social Sciences and Education. National Research Council. Washington, DC: National Academy Press.

Clark, Kim. 1989. "Project Scope and Project Performance: The Effects of Parts Strategy and Supplier Involvement on Product Development." *Management Science* 35 (December): 1247–1263.

Clinton, William J. 1992. "Putting People First." *Journal for Quality and Participation* 15, no. 7 (October/November): 10–12.

———. 1995. "The New OSHA: Reinventing Worker Health." *National Performance Review* 10, no. 1:20–28.

Cook Philip J., and Ludwig, Jens. 1997. "Weighing the Burden of 'Acting White': Are There Race Differences in Attitudes Towards Education?" *Journal of Policy Analysis and Management* 16, no. 3 (Summer).

Corporation for Manufacturing Excellence. 1996. "Manufacturing Extension Partnership." [http://www.ncalmec.org/mep.htm] May.

Council for Basic Education. 1996. "Judging Standards in Education Reform, and State Standards: A Selective Comparison." Washington, DC. [http://www.summit 96.ibm.com/brief/papers/judging.html]

Crane, Jonathan. 1991. "Effect of Neighborhoods on Dropping Out of School and Teenage Childbearing." In *The Urban Underclass,* ed. Christopher Jencks and Paul E. Peterson. Washington, DC: Brookings Institution.

Currie, Janet, and Duncan, Thomas. 1995. "Race, Children's Cognitive Achievement and the Bell Curve." Working paper series (National Bureau of Economic Research); Working Paper No. 5240. Cambridge, MA.

Cusumano, Michael. 1985. *The Japanese Automobile Industry.* Cambridge: Harvard University Press.

Cutler, David M., and Katz, Lawrence F. 1991. "Macroeconomic Performance and the Disadvantaged." *Brookings Papers on Economic Activity* 2: 1–74.

———. 1992. "Rising Inequality? Changes in the Distribution of Income and Consumption in the 1980's." *American Economic Review* 82 (May): 546–551.

Danziger, Sheldon, and Gottschalk, Peter. 1995. *America Unequal.* New York: Russell Sage Foundation. Cambridge, MA: Harvard University Press.

DeLong, Brad, and Levine, David I. 1995a. "Welfare Reform That Makes Poor Kids Poorer Will Never Pay Off." *Los Angeles Times,* Sunday Forum, October 15, p. D2.

———. 1995b. "Not Such a Capital Idea." *San Francisco Chronicle,* December 5, p. A23.

———. 1996. "Dole Tax Cuts Ignore Deficits, Investment, Education, Future." *San Jose Mercury News.* August 26, p. 5E

Dickens, William, Kane, Thomas, and Schultze, Charles. 1997. *Does the Bell Curve Ring True?* Washington, DC: Brookings Institution.

Diebold, Francis X., Neumark, David, and Polsky, Daniel. 1997. "Comment on Swinnerton and Wial, 'Is Job Stability Declining in the U.S. Economy?' " *Industrial and Labor Relations Review* 49, no. 2 (January): 348–352.

DiIulio, John J. Jr. 1996. "Help Wanted: Economists, Crime, and Public Policy." *Journal of Economic Perspectives* 10, no. 1 (Winter): 3–24.

DiNardo, John E., and Pischke, Jorn-Steffen. 1996. "The Returns to Computer Use Revisited: Have Pencils Changed the Wage Structure Too?" NBER, Working Paper 5606. Cambridge, MA, June.

Dobb, Fred. 1996. *ISO 9000 Quality Registration Step by Step.* Woburn, MA: Butterworth-Heinemann.

Donahue, John J. III, and Siegelman, Peter. 1991. "The Changing Nature of Employment Discrimination Litigation." *Stanford Law Review* (May).

Downs, Anthony. 1992. "Regulatory Barriers to Affordable Housing." *Journal of American Planning Association* 58, no. 4 (Autumn): 419–421.

Drago, Robert. 1988. "Quality Circle Survival." *Industrial Relations* 27 (Fall): 336–351.

Duffy, Shannon P. 1995. "Casellas: EEOC Suffering Backlash." *Legal Intelligencer* (June 20): 1.

Dunlop, John T., and Weil, David. 1996. "Diffusion and Performance of Human Resource Innovations in the U.S. Apparel Industry." *Industrial Relations* 35, no. 4: 299–333.

Durkheim, Emile. 1951. *Suicide: A Study in Sociology.* New York: Free Press.

Eccles, Robert, and Mavrinac, Sarah. 1994. "Improving the Corporate Disclosure Process." Harvard Business School working paper.

Eisner, Robert. 1994. *The Misunderstood Economy: What Counts and How to Count It.* Boston: Harvard Business School Press.

Eissa, Nada. 1996. "Labor Supply Response to the Earned Income Tax." *Quarterly Journal of Economics* 11, no. 2 (May): 605–637.

Elias, Peter. 1994. "Occupational Change in a Working-Life Perspective: Internal and External Views." In *Skill and Occupational Change* , ed. Roger Penn, Michael Rose, and Jill Rubery. Social Change and Economic Life Initiative series. Oxford and New York: Oxford University Press.

Englander, Todd. 1989. "Ford: Quality Driven." *Incentive* 163, no. 1 (January): 23–24.

Enthoven, Alain C., and Singer, Sara J. 1996. "Managed Competition and California's Health Care Economy." *Health Affairs* 15, no. 1 (Spring): 39–57.

Farber, Henry S. 1992. "The Changing Face of Job Loss in the United States, 1981-1993." National Bureau of Economic Research, Working Paper No. 5596. Cambridge, MA.

Farley, Reynolds, and Frey, William H. 1996. "Changes in the Segregation of Whites from Blacks During the 1980s: Small Steps Towards a More Racially Integrated Society." Research Report 92-257, Population Studies Center, University of Michigan.

Federman, M., Garner, T.L., Short, K., Cutter, W.B., Boman, Kiely, J., Levine, D., McGough, D., and McMillen, M. 1996. "What Does It Mean to Be Poor in America." *Monthly Labor Review* 119, no. 5 (May): 3–17.

Finegold, David, and Levine, David I. 1997. "Institutional Incentives for Employer Training." *Journal of Education and Work* 10, no. 2 (June): 109–127.

Fischer, Claude S., Hout, Michael, Jankowski, Martin Sanchez, Lucas, Samuel R., Swidler, Ann, and Voss, Kim. 1996. *Inequality by Design.* Princeton: Princeton University Press.

Fisher, Roger, and Ury, William. 1991. *Getting to Yes: Negotiating Agreement Without Giving In.* 2nd ed. Boston: Houghton Mifflin.

Fix, Michael, and Struyk, Raymond J., eds. 1993. *Clear and Convincing Evidence: Measurement of Discrimination in America.* Washington, DC: Urban Institute Press.

Fortin, Nicole M., and Lemieux, Thomas. 1997. "Institutional Changes and Rising Wage Inequality: Is There a Linkage?" *Journal of Economic Perspectives* 11, no. 2 (Spring): 75–96.

Freeman, Richard B., and Rogers, Joel. 1993. "Who Speaks for Us? Employee Representation in a Nonunion Labor Market." In *Employee Representation:*

Alternatives and Future Directions, ed. Bruce E. Kaufman and Morris M. Kleiner. Madison, WI: IRRA.

―――. 1995. "Worker Representation and Participation Survey." Princeton: Princeton Survey Research Corporation.

Friedman, Milton. 1962. *Capitalism and Freedom,* ch. 6. Chicago: University of Chicago Press.

Gingrich, Newt. 1994. Remarks before the Washington Research Group Symposium in Washington, November 11. [Text at URL http://www.clark.net/pub/jeffd/ng0.html]

―――. 1995. "Address to the Nation" (marking 100 days as Speaker of the House), April 7. [http://www.agtnet.com/USNEWS/wash/gingri.htm]

Glaster, George, et al. 1994. *Sandwich Hiring Audit Pilot Program Report.* Washington, DC: Urban Institute.

Goldstein, Joseph. 1995. "Alternatives to High-Cost Litigation." *Cornell Hotel and Restaurant Administration Quarterly* 36, no. 1 (February): 28 ff.

Gore, Albert. 1993. *From Red Tape to Results: Creating a Goverment that Works Better and Costs Less: Report of the National Performance Review.* New York: Times Books.

―――. 1995. *Common Sense Government: Works Better and Costs Less.* Third report of the National Performance Review. Washington, DC: GPO.

Gottschalk, P., and Moffitt, R. 1994. "The Growth of Earnings Instability in the United States Labor Market; Comments and discussion." *Brookings Papers on Economic Activity* no. 2: 217–272.

Graedon, Joe, and Graedon, Teresa. 1996. "Verify All Your Prescriptions." *Cleveland Plain Dealer,* September 24, Final/All, p. 7E.

Grosskopf, Sheila, Hayes, Kathy, Taylor, Lori, and Weber, William. 1995. "On Competition and School Efficiency." Paper presented at the Western Economic Association, June.

Hall, Peter. 1986. *Governing the Economy.* Oxford: Polity Press.

Hanushek, Eric A. 1986. "The Economics of Schooling: Production and Efficiency in Public Schools." *Journal of Economic Literature* 24 (September).

―――. 1994. *Making Schools Work: Improving Performance and Controlling Costs.* Washington, DC: Brookings Institution.

Hayward, Becky, and Tallmadge, G. 1993. *Evaluation of Dropout Prevention and Reentry Projects in Vocational Education.* Draft final report, Research Triangle Institute. November.

Heckman, James, Smith, Jeffrey A., and Taber, Christopher. 1996. "What Do Bureaucrats Do? The Effects of Performance Standards and Bureaucratic Preferences on Acceptance into the JTPA Program." National Bureau of Economic Research Working Paper No. 5535, Cambridge, MA.

Heclo, Hugh. 1994. "Poverty Politics." In *Confronting Poverty,* ed. Sheldon Danzinger, Gary Sandefur, and Daniel Weinberg, 396–437. Cambridge: Harvard University Press.

Hedges, L.V. 1993. "Does Money Matter?" Unpublished working paper, University of Chicago.

Helper, Susan. 1990. "Comparative Supplier Relations in the U.S. and Japanese Auto Industries." *Business and Economic History,* Second Series 19, pp. 153–162.

―――. 1991a. "How Much Has Really Changed Between U.S. Automakers and Their Suppliers?" *Sloan Management Review* 32 (Summer): 15–28.

―――. 1991b. "Strategy and Irreversibility in Supplier Relations: The Case of the U.S. Automobile Industry." *Business History Review* 65, no. 4 (Winter): 781–824.

Helper, Susan, and Levine, David I. 1992. "Long-term Supplier Relations and Product

Market Structure." *Journal of Law, Economics, and Organization* (October): 561–581.

Henderson, Peter. 1995. "Why Vouchers Won't Work!" *Journal of Housing and Community Development* 52, no. 5 (September/October): 25–32.

Hendricks, K.B., and Singhal, V.R. 1996, 1997. "Quality Awards and the Market Value of the Firm. An Empirical Investigation." *Management Science* 42, no. 3 (March): 415–436.

———. 1997. "Does Implementing an Effective TQM Program Actually Improve Operating Performance? Empirical Evidence from Firms That Have Won Quality Awards." *Management Science* 43, no. 9 (September): 1258–1274.

Hennessey, John C. 1996. "Job Patterns of Disabled Beneficiaries." *Social Security Bulletin* 59, no. 4 (Winter): 3–11.

Herrnstein, Richard, and Murray, Charles. 1996. *The Bell Curve.* New York: Free Press.

Hirschman, Albert O. 1970. *Exit, Voice and Loyalty,* pp. 45–46. Cambridge: Harvard University Press.

Holusha, John. 1988. "Ford Profit Rises 8.9% To Record." *New York Times,* April 29, p. D1.

Howard, Philip K. 1994. *The Death of Common Sense.* New York: Random House.

Howenstine, E. Jay. 1986. "Foreign Housing Voucher Systems: Evolution and Strategies." *Monthly Labor Review* 109, no. 5 (May): 21–27.

Hoxby, Caroline Minter. 1994a. "Do Private Schools Provide Competition for Public Schools?" Working Paper Series, National Bureau of Economic Research, Working Paper No. 4978, Cambridge, MA.

———. 1994b. "Does Competition among Public Schools Benefit Students and Taxpayers?" Working Paper Series, National Bureau of Economic Research, Working Paper No. 4979, Cambridge, MA.

Hoxby, Caroline M. 1996. "All School Finance Equalizations Are Not Created Equal: (Marginal Tax Rates Matter)." Mimeo. Department of Economics, Harvard University.

Hoye, J.D., and Tegger, Steven. 1996. "School-to-Work Systems: Redesigning U.S. Education for the 21st Century." National Planning Association. *Looking Ahead* 18, no. 1 (June): 19–23, 20.

Hoynes, H., and Moffitt, R. 1995. "The Effectiveness of Financial Work Incentives in DI and SSI: Lessons from Other Transfer Programs." Institute for Research on Poverty. Discussion Paper 1073-95, University of Wisconsin, Madison.

Huselid, Mark, and Becker, Brian. 1996. "Methodological Issues in Cross-Sectional and Panel Estimates of the Human Resource–Firm Performance Link." *Industrial Relations* 35, no. 4 (Summer): 400–423.

Ichniowsky, Casey, Kochan, Thomas, Levine, David I., Olson, Craig, and Strauss, George. 1996. "What Works at Work: A Critical Review." *Industrial Relations* 35, no. 3 (Summer): 299–333.

Ichniowski, Casey, Shaw, Kathryn, and Prennushi, Giovanna. 1997. "The Effects of Human Resource Management Practices on Productivity." *American Economic Review* 87, no. 3 (June): 291–313.

Jaikumar, Ramchandvan. 1986. "Postindustrial Manufacturing." *Harvard Business Review* 64, no. 5 (November/December): 69–76.

Jargowsky, Paul A. 1994. "Ghetto Poverty among Blacks in the 1980s." *Journal of Policy Analysis and Management* 13, no. 2: 288–310.

Jarrell, Sherry, and Easton, George. "The Effects of Total Quality Management on Corporate Performance: An Empirical Investigation." *Journal of Business* (forthcoming).

Jencks, Christopher, and Peterson, Paul E., eds. 1991. *The Urban Underclass*. Washington, DC: Brookings Institution.

Jensen, Eric L. 1983. "Financial Aid and Educational Outcomes: A Review." *College and University* (Spring).

Kahn, Shulamit, and Lang, Kevin. 1992. "Constraints on the Choice of Hours of Work." *Journal of Human Resources* 27, no. 4 (Fall): 661–688.

Kamer, Gregory J., Abbot, Scott M., and Salevitz, Lisa G. 1994. "The New Legal Challenge to Participation," *Labor Law Journal* (January): 41–48.

Kane, Thomas. 1994. "College Entry by Blacks Since 1970: The Role of College Costs, Family Background, and Returns to Education." *Journal of Political Economy* 102, no. 5 (October): 878–911.

Kane, Thomas J., and Bane, Mary Jo. 1994. "The Context for Welfare Reform." In *Welfare Realities: From Rhetoric to Reform,* ed. Mary Jo Bane and David T. Ellwood, pp. 1–27. Cambridge: Harvard University Press.

Kelley, Maryellen R. 1996. "Participative Democracy and Productivity in the Machined Products Sector." *Industrial Relations* 35, no. 3 (July): 374–399.

Kendall, David B., and Pauly, Mark V. 1996. "Health Care Reform Starts with Tax Reform." *Wall Street Journal,* June 10, p. A10.

Kingsley, G. Thomas, and Turner, Margery Austin, eds. 1993. *Housing Markets and Residential Mobility*. Washington, DC: Urban Institute Press. Lanham, MD: Distributed by University Press of America.

Kirschenman, Joleen, and Neckerman, Kathryn M. 1991. "'We'd Love to Hire Them, But . . .': The Meaning of Race for Employers." In *The Urban Underclass,* ed. C. Jencks and P.E. Peterson, pp. 203–232. Washington, DC: Brookings Institution.

Kochan, Thomas A. 1995. "Using the Dunlop Report to Achieve Mutual Gains." *Industrial Relations* 34, no. 3 (July): 350–366.

Kochan, Thomas A., and Osterman, Paul. 1991. "Human Resource Development and Utilization: Is There Too Little in the U.S.?" Massachusetts Institute of Technology, Sloan School of Management, Cambridge, MA, February.

———. 1994. *The Mutual Gains Enterprise: Forging a Winning Partnership Among Labor, Management, and Government*. Boston: Harvard Business School Press.

Korneman, Sanders, and Winship, Christopher. 1996. "A Reanalysis of *The Bell Curve*," National Bureau of Economic Research, Working Paper No. 5230, Cambridge, MA.

Krafcik, John F. 1990. *Training and the Automobile Industry: International Comparisons*. Contractor Report. Washington, DC: Office of Technology Assessment, February.

Krueger, Alan. 1993. "How Computers Have Changed the Wage Structure: Evidence from Microdata, 1984–1989." *Quarterly Journal of Economics* 108, no. 1 (February): 33–60.

Krueger, Alan, and Kruse, Douglas. 1995. "Labor Market Effects of Spinal Cord Injuries in the Dawn of the Computer Age," National Bureau of Economic Research Warking Paper 5302, October.

Krueger, Alan, and Rouse, Cecilia. 1996. "The Effect of Workplace Education on Earnings, Turnover, and Job Performance." Mimeo. Princeton University. August.

Kruse, D., Krueger, A., and Drastal, S. 1996. "Computer Use, Computer Training, and Employment—Outcomes Among People with Spinal Cord Injuries." *Spine* 21, no. 7 (April): 891–896.

Kugler, Adriana D. 1996. "Job Referrals and Job Characteristics." Mimeo. UC Berkeley.

Law, Sally Ann, and Keltner, Brent. 1996. "Civic Networks: Social Benefits of On-line Communities." In *Universal Access to E-mail: Feasibility and Societal Implications,* ed. Robert H. Anderson, Tora K. Bikson, Sally Ann Law, and Bridger M. Mitchell, ch. 5, report MR-650–MF. Santa Monica CA: Rand. [http://www.rand.org/publications/ MR/MR650/mr650.ch5/ch5.html]

Lawler, Edward E. III, Mohrman, Susan, and Ledford, Gerald E. Jr. 1995. *Creating High Performance Organizations.* San Francisco: Jossey-Bass.

Leonard, Bill. 1996. "From School to Work." *HR Magazine* 41, no. 7 (July): 74–82.

Leonard, J. 1986. Labor Supply Incentives and Disincentives for the Disabled. In *Disability and the Labor Market,* ed. M. Berkowitz and M. Anne Hill, pp. 64–96. Ithaca, NY: ILR Press.

Leonard, Jonathan S. 1990. "The Impact of Affirmative Action Regulation and Equal Employment Law on Black Employment. " *Journal of Economic Perspectives* 4, no. 4 (Fall): 47–63.

Lerman, Robert I., and Pouncy, Hillard. 1990. "Why America Should Develop a Youth Apprenticeship System." Progressive Policy Institute, Policy Report No. 5, March. [http://www.dlcppi.org/texts/economic/appren.txt)

Leslie, Larry L., and Brinkman, Paul T. 1988. *The Economic Value of Higher Education.* London: Collier Macmillan.

Levin, Henry M. 1997. "Raising School Productivity: An X-Efficiency Approach," *Economics of Education Review* 16, no. 3 (June): 303–311.

Levin, Henry M. 1998. "Educational Vouchers: Effectiveness, Choice, and Costs." *Journal of Policy Analysis and Management* 17, no. 3 (forthcoming).

Levine, David I. 1991. "Just Cause Employment Policies in the Presence of Worker Adverse Selection." *Journal of Labor Economics* 9, no. 3.

———. 1995. *Reinventing the Workplace: How Business and Employees Can Both Win.* Washington, DC: Brookings Institution.

Levine, David I., and Helper, Susan. 1995. "A Quality Policy for America." *Contemporary Policy Issues* 13, no. 2 (April): 26–37.

Levine, David I., and Painter, Gary. "The NELS Curve: Replicating the Bell Curve with the National Educational Longitudinal Survey." *Industrial Relations* (forthcoming).

Libman, Gary. 1991. "Genesis of a Dream: As 6th-Graders, They Were Offered College Money If They Stayed in School. Where Are They Now?" *Los Angeles Times,* September 22, p. E1.

Lick, Larry. 1996. "Franklin's Monster Destroyed: An Overview and Analysis of the Demise of Public Housing." *Rental Housing News & Commentary.* [http://-doghouseonline.com/franklin.htm]

Locke, Edwin A., and Latham, Gary P. 1990. *A Theory of Goal Setting and Task Performance.* Englewood Cliffs, NJ: Prentice Hall.

"Look Out Landlords: Congress May Totally Revamp HUD Rent Subsidies and They Should Because It Is a Massive Failure." 1995. *Rental Housing News & Commentary* (November 18). [http:\\doghouseonline.com/hud2.htm#home]

Ludwig, Jens. 1996. "School Spending and Student Achievement." Mimeo. Georgetown University, Washington, DC.

Lynch, Lisa. 1994. "Payoffs to Alternative Training Strategies at Work." In *Working Under Different Rules,* ed. Richard B. Freeman. New York: Sage, pp. 63–96.

Lynch, Lisa M., and Black, Sandra E. 1995. "Beyond the Incidence of Training: Evidence from a National Employer Survey." NBER Working Paper No. 5231. Cambridge, MA.

MacDuffie, John Paul. 1995. "Human Resource Bundles and Manufacturing Performance: Organizational Logic and Flexible Production Systems in the World Auto Industry." *Industrial and Labor Relations Review* 48, no. 2 (January): 197-221.

MacDuffie, John Paul, and Helper, Susan. 1997. "Creating Lean Suppliers: Diffusing Lean Production Throughout the Supply Chain," *California Management Review* 39, no. 4 (Summer): 118–151.

MacDuffie, John Paul, and Kochan, Thomas A. 1995. "Do U.S. Firms Invest Less in Human Resources-Training in the World Auto Industry?" *Industrial Relations* 34, no. 2 (April): 147–168.

McNeil, Patricia. 1996. "Redesigning Our High Schools." In *CenterWork* 7, no. 3 (Summer): p. 4.

McPherson, Michael, and Shapiro, Morton. 1991. *Keeping College Affordable: Government and Educational Opportunity.* Washington, DC: Brookings Institution.

Malcomson, James M. 1997. "Contracts, Hold-Up, and Labor Markets." *Journal of Economic Literature* 35, no. 4 (December): 1916–1957.

Manski, Charles, and Wise, David. 1983. *College Choice in America.* Cambridge: Harvard University Press.

Marcotte, Dave E. 1996. "Has Job Stability Declined? Evidence from the Panel Study of Income Dynamics." Mimeo. DeKalb, IL, Northern Illinois University.

Marks, Denton. 1984. "Incomplete Experience Rating in State Unemployment Insurance." *Monthly Labor Review* 107, no. 11 (November): 45–49.

Mashaw, Jerry L., and Reno, Virginia, eds. 1996. "Balancing Security and Opportunity: The Challenge of Disability Income Policy. Final Report of the Disability Policy Panel." Washington, DC: National Academy of Social Insurance.

Matthes, Karen. 1991. "From Welfare to the Workplace: America Works." *Personnel* 68, no. 8 (August): 23.

Mayer, Susan, and Jencks, Christopher. 1993. "Recent Trends in Economic Inequality in the United States: Income versus Expenditure versus Material Well-being." In *Poverty and Prosperity in the USA in the Late Twentieth Century,* ed. Dimitri B. Papadimitriou and Edward N. Wolff. New York: St. Martin's Press.

———. 1995. "Has Poverty Really Increased Among Children Since 1970?" Center for Urban Affairs and Policy Research Working Paper 94-14, Northwestern University.

Microcredit Summit. 1997. Declaration and Plan of Action, February 2–4. [http://www.microcreditsummit.org/declaration.htm]

Miller, Jane E., and Korenman, Sanders. 1994. "Poverty and Children's Nutritional Status in the United States." *American Journal of Epidemiology* 140, no. 3.

Mills, Richard P. 1995. "A Nickel on the Dollar." In *National Issues in Education: Elementary and Secondary Education Act,* ed. John. F. Jennings, pp. 19–34. Bloomington, IN: Phi Delta Kappa.

Mishel, Lawrence, Bernstein, Jared, and Schmitt, John. 1997. *The State of Working America, 1996–97.* Armonk, NY: M.E. Sharpe, for Economic Policy Institute.

Moffitt, Robert. 1992. "Incentive Effects of the U.S. Welfare System: A Review." *Journal of Economic Literature* 30: 1–61.

Morris, Charles J. 1996."Will There Be a New Direction for American Industrial

Relations?—A Hard Look at the TEAM Bill, the Sawyer Substitute Bill, and the Employee Involvement Bill." *Labor Law Journal* (February): 89–107.

Moss, Philip, and Tilly, Chris. 1995. *"Soft" Skills and Race: An Investigation of Black Men's Employment Problems.* New York: Russell Sage Foundation. [http://epn.org/sage/rstill.html].

Munnell, Alicia H., et al. 1996. "Mortgage Lending in Boston: Interpreting HMDA Data." *American Economic Review* 86, no. 1 (March): 25–53.

Murray, Charles. 1993. "Welfare and the Family: The U.S. Experience." *Journal of Labor Economics* (January).

———. 1994. "Does Welfare Bring More Babies?" *Public Interest* (Spring): 17–30.

National Federation of Independent Businesses (NFIB). 1992. *Small Business Problems and Priorities.* Washington, DC: NFIB.

Neumark, David, Bank, Roy J., and Van Nort, Kyle D. 1995. "Sex Discrimination in Restaurant Hiring: An Audit Study." National Bureau of Economic Research, Cambridge, MA.

Newman, Sandra, and Schnare, Ann. 1992. "Beyond Bricks and Mortar." Urban Institute Report No. 92-3, Washington, DC.

Nickel, Stephen. 1997. "Unemployment and Labor Market Rigidities: Europe vs. North America." *The Journal of Economic Perspectives* 11, no. 3 (Summer): 55–74.

Nishiguchi, Toshihiro. 1990. "Strategic Dualism: An Alternative in Industrial Society." Ph.D. dissertation, Oxford University.

Nulty, Peter. 1992. "I Have a Dream." *Fortune* 126, no. 11 (November 16): 142–144.

OECD. 1993. "Enterprise Tenure, Labor Turnover and Skill Training." *Employment Outlook* (July): ch. 4.

———. 1994a. *The OECD Jobs Study: Evidence and Explanations, Part II: The Adjustment Potential of the Labour Market.* Paris: OECD.

———. 1994b. *Vocational Training in Germany: Modernisation and Responsiveness.* Paris: OECD.

Okun, Arthur. 1975. *Equality and Efficiency: The Big Tradeoff.* Washington, DC: Brookings.

Olson, Mancur. 1982. *The Rise and Decline of Nations: Economic Growth, Stagflation, and Social Rigidities.* New Haven: Yale University Press.

O'Regan, K.M., and Quigley, J.M. 1996. "Teenage Employment and the Spatial Isolation of Minority and Poverty Households." *Journal of Human Resources* 31, no. 3 (Summer): 692–702.

"Oregon Safety Committees Touted." 1993. *Occupational Safety and Health* 62, no. 9 (September): 26–27.

Osborne, David, and Gaebler, Ted. 1992. *Reinventing Government.* Reading, MA: Addison-Wesley.

Osterman, Paul. 1994. "How Common Is Workplace Transformation and Who Adopts It?" *Industrial and Labor Relations Review* 47, no. 2 (January): 173–188.

Parsons, D.O. 1991. "Measuring and Deciding Disability." In *Disability and Work: Incentives, Rights and Opportunities,* ed. Carolyn L. Weaver. Washington, DC: AEI Press.

Parsons, Donald O., and Bound, John. 1991. "The Health and Earnings of Rejected Disability Insurance Applicants: Comment; Reply." *American Economic Review* 81, no. 5 (December): 1419–1434.

Pauly, Mark V., Danzon, Patricia, Feldstein, Paul, and Hoff, John. 1992. "A Plan for Responsible National Health Insurance." *Health Affairs* 10, no. 1 (Spring): 5–25.

Pauly, Mark V., and Goodman, John C. 1995. "Tax Credits for Health Insurance and Medical Savings Accounts." *Health Affairs* 14, no. 1 (Spring): 126–139.

Peterson, P.E., Greene J.P., and C. Noyes. 1996. "School Choice in Milwaukee." *Public Interest* 125 (Fall): 38–56.

Piven, Frances Fox, and Ellwood, David. 1996. "Controversy." *American Prospect* 27 (July–August): 14–15. [http://epn.org/prospect/27/27-cnt.html]

Port, Bob, and Solomon, John. 1995. "OSHA never saw 75% of Fatal Sites." *San Jose Mercury News,* September 5: 1E, 5E.

Porter, Michael. 1992. *Capital Choices.* Washington, DC: Council on Competitiveness Report and Harvard Business School.

Poterba, James M., and Summers, Lawrence H. 1991. "Time Horizons of American Firms: New Evidence from a Survey of CEOs." Washington, DC: Council on Competitiveness. October.

Potter, Edward E., and Youngman, Judith A. 1995. *Keeping America Competitive: Employment Policy for the Twenty-first Century.* Lakewood, CO: Glenbridge.

Public/Private Ventures. 1996. "Community Change for Youth Development: Building Neighborhood Supports for Young People." (Philadelphia [http:\\epn.org/ppv/ ppccyd.html]).

Putnam, Robert D. 1993. *Making Democracy Work: Civic Traditions in Modern Italy.* Princeton: Princeton University Press.

Rector, Robert. 1992. "How the Poor Really Live: Lessons for Welfare Reform." *Heritage Foundation Backgrounder* 875 (January). 31.

Reich, Robert B. 1989. "The Origins of Red Tape." In *The Resurgent Liberal,* pp. 34–50. New York: Times Books.

Riley, Richard. 1996. Secretary of Education, cover letter to state education officials. Application for State Grants under the Technology Literacy Challenge Fund. November. [http://www.ed.gov/Technology/TLCF/ltr.html.]

Roditi, Hannah Finan. 1992. "High Schools for Docile Workers." *The Nation,* March 16, pp. 341–343.

Rose, Steven. 1994. *On Shaky Ground: Rising Fears about Incomes and Earnings.* Washington, DC: NCEP.

Rosenbaum, James E. 1995. "Changing the Geography of Opportunity by Expanding Residential Choice: Lessons from the Gatreaux Program." *Housing Policy Debate* 6, no. 1, 231–269.

Rothstein, Richard. 1993. "The Myth of Public School Failure." *American Prospect* 13 (Spring). [http://epn.org/prospect/13/13roth.html]

Rowe, Mary P. 1990. "People Who Feel Harassed Need a Complaint System with Both Formal and Informal Options." *Negotiations Journal* (January): 1–12.

Rubin, Victor, and Kaplan, Seth. 1995. "Coordination of Youth Employment and Training Programs in Oakland." Mimeo, University-Oakland Metropolitan Forum, Berkeley: University of California.

Sander, William. 1996. "Catholic Grade Schools and Academic Achievement." *Journal of Human Resources* 31, no. 3 (Summer): 540–548.

Schellhardt, Timothy D. 1996. "Company Memo to Stressed-Out Employees: 'Deal With It.' " *Wall Street Journal,* October 2, p. B1.

Schmidt, Stefanie R. 1996. "Does Head Start Improve the Life Prospects of Poor Children?" *Jobs & Capital* 5 (Spring): 26–31.

Shapiro, Carl, and Stiglitz, Joseph E. 1984. "Equilibrium Unemployment as a Worker Discipline Device." *American Economic Review* 74, no. 3 (June): 433–444.

Shea, Martina. 1995. "The Dynamics of Economic Well-Being." Census, No. P70-42. Washington, DC: Bureau of the Census.

Shell, Ellen Ruppel. 1996. "Where the Guys Are." *Washington Post*, April 7, Sunday, final edition.

Shook, Robert. 1990. *Turnaround: The New Ford Motor Company*. Englewood Cliffs, NJ: Prentice Hall.

Siebert, Horst. 1997. "Labor Market Rigidities: At the Root of Unemployment in Europe." *The Journal of Economic Perspectives* 11, no. 3 (Summer): 37–54.

Smitka, Michael. 1989. *Competitive Ties: Subcontracting in the Japanese Automobile Industry*. P.h.D. dissertation, Columbia University.

Sockell, Donna. 1984. "The Legality of Employee-Participation Programs in Unionized Firms." *Industrial and Labor Relations Review* 37 (July): 541–556.

Stamps, David. 1996. "Will School-to-Work Work?" *Training* 33, no. 6 (June): 72–81.

Starr, Paul. 1988. *The Limits of Privatization*. Report of the Economic Policy Institute, Washington, DC.

Statistical Abtstract of the United States. 1995. Washington, DC: GPO.

Stecklow, Steve. 1997. "Arizona Takes the Lead in Charter Schools—For Better or Worse." *Wall Street Journal,* January 2, p. A1.

Steiber, Jack. 1984. "Employment-at-Will: An Issue for the 1980's." *1983 IRRA Proceedings.*

Stern, David, Dayton, C., Paik, I., and Weisberg, A. 1989. "Benefits and Costs of Dropout Prevention in a Program Combining Academic and Vocational Education: Third-Year Results from Replications of the California Peninsula Academies." *Educational Evaluation and Policy Analysis* 11, no. 4: 405–415.

———. 1995. *School to Work: Research on Programs in the United States*. London: Falmer Press.

Tan, Hong W., and Batra, Geeta. 1995. "Enterprise Training in Developing Countries." Private Sector Development Department, World Bank.

Tanner, Michael. 1994. "Ending Welfare as We Know It." *Policy Analysis,* Cato Institute, No. 212 (July 7) [http://www.cato.org/pa-212.html]

Topel, Robert H. 1984. Experience Rating of Unemployment Insurance and the Incidence of Unemployment." *Journal of Law & Economics* 27, no. 1 (April): 61–90.

Treadway, Joan. 1996. "Study Is Based on Race, Family." *New Orleans Times-Picayune,* February 1.

U.S. Bureau of Labor Statistics. 1994. *Workplace Injuries and Illnesses in 1993,* USDL-94-600. Washington, DC: GPO.

U.S. Commission on the Future of Worker-Management Relations, 1994. *Fact-Finding Report.* Washington, DC: Departments of Labor and Commerce.

———. 1995. *Final Report.* Washington, DC: Departments of Labor and Commerce.

U.S. Council of Economic Advisers. 1995. *Economic Report of the President, 1995,* Washington, DC: GPO.

———. 1996a. *Economic Report of the President 1996.* Washington, DC: GPO.

U.S. Council of Economic Advisers (with the U.S. Department of Labor, Office of the Chief Economist). 1996b. *Job Creation and Employment Opportunities: The United States Labor Market, 1993-1996.* Washington, DC: GPO, April 23. [http://www2.whitehouse.gov/WH/EOP/CEA/html/labor.html]

U.S. Department of Education. 1996a. *Revenues and Expenditures for Public Elementary and Secondary Education: School Year 1993–94.* NCES. [http://www.ed.gov./pubs/96303.html.]

———. 1996b. NCES. *Digest of Education Statistics.* Washington, DC: GPO.

————. 1996c. NCES. *1995 Survey of Advanced Telecommunications in U.S. Public Schools, K–12.* Washington, DC: GPO.

U.S. Department of Labor. 1989. *Investing in People. Report of the Commission on Labor Force Quality and Labor Market Efficiency.* Washington, DC: GPO.

————. 1991. *Secretary's Commission on Achieving Necessary Skills.* (SCANS). *What Work Requires of Schools: A SCANS Report for America 2000.* Washington, DC: GPO.

————. OSHA (Occupational Safety and Health Administration). 1995a. "Review and Analysis of State-Mandated and other Worker Protections Programs." Mimeo. (June).

————. 1995b. *The New OSHA.* Washington, DC. [http://www.osha-slc.gov/Reinventing]

————. (Office of the Chief Economist). 1995c. *What's Working (and What's Not): A Summary of Research on the Economic Impacts of Employment and Training Programs.* Washington, DC: GPO. January.

————. 1995d. *Working Together for Public Service. The final report of the Task Force on Excellence in State and Local Government Through Labor-Management Cooperation.* Washington, DC: GPO. [http://www.ilr.cornell.edu/lib/ bookshelf/e_archive/ LaborExcellence/]

————. America's Job Bank. 1996a. [http://www.abj.dni.us/]

————. 1996b. *America's Labor Market Information System.* Washington, DC: ALMIS.

U.S. Equal Employment Opportunity Commission (EEOC). 1995. *Policy Statement on Alternative Dispute Resolution.* Reprinted in the *Daily Labor Reporter,* July 18, n. 137 BNA.

U.S. Executive Summary. 1996. Public/Private Ventures. "Executive Summary: Making a Difference: An Impact Study of Big Brothers/Big Sisters." [http:// epn.org/ppv/ppbbbs.html].

U.S. Federal Quality Institute. 1991. *Introduction to Total Quality Management in the Federal Government.* Washington, DC: GPO.

U.S. General Accounting Office (GAO). 1992a. *Quality Management: Survey of Federal Organizations.* GAO/GGD-93-9BR.s. Washington, DC: GPO.

————. 1992b. *Workplace Safety and Health Programs Show Promise.* Testimony before the House Committee on Education and Labor. GAO/T-HRD-92-15. Washington, DC: GPO.

————. 1994. *Report on Workplace Regulation.* Washington, DC: GPO. June.

————. 1996. *SSA Disability: Program Redesign Necessary to Encourage Return to Work.* GAO/HEHS-96-62, Washington, DC: GPO.

U.S. National Academy of Social Insurance. 1996. *Balancing Security and Opportunity: The Challenge for Disability Income Policy,* Washington, DC: GPO. The Executive Summary is reprinted in the *Journal of Disability Policy Studies* 7, no. 2: 67–78.

U.S. Office of Federal Procurement Policy (OFPP). May 1995. *Guide to Best Practices for Past Performance, Interim Edition.* Washington, DC: GPO. [http://www. far.npr.gov/bestp/bestpract.html.]

U.S. Office of the Vice-President. September 1993. *Regulatory Systems.* Accompanying Report of the *National Performance Review.* Washington, DC: GPO.

U.S. Social Security Administration. 1995. *Red Book on Work Incentives 1993.* No. 64-030. Washington, DC: SSA, August.

Waring, Marilyn. 1988. *If Women Counted.* San Francisco: Harper & Row.

Weber, Max. 1946. *From Max Weber: Essays in Sociology.* Trans., ed., and with an intro. by H.H. Gerth and C. Wright Mills. New York: Oxford University Press.

Weil. David. 1991a. "Comment, on James Porteba's 'House Price Dynamics: The Role of Tax Policy and Demographics.' " *Brookings Papers on Economic Activity,* no. 2: 184–188.

———. 1991b. "Enforcing OSHA: The Role of Labor Unions." *Industrial Relations* 30, no. 1 (Winter): 20–36.

Weiler, Paul. 1990. *Governing the Workplace: The Future of Labor and Employment Law.* Cambridge: Harvard University Press, 1990.

Weisbrod, Burton A. 1991. "The Health Care Quadrilemma—An Essay on Technological Change, Insurance, Quality of Care, and Cost Containment." *Journal of Economic Literature* 29, no. 2 (June): 523–552.

West, Edwin G. 1997. "Education Vouchers in Principle and Practice: A Survey." *World Bank Research Observer* 12, no. 1 (February): 83–103.

Wever, Kirsten S. 1995. *Negotiating Competitiveness: Employment Relations and Organizational Innovation in Germany and the United States.* Boston: Harvard Business School Press.

Wilder, Margaret G., and Rubin, Barry M. 1996. "Rhetoric Versus Reality." *Journal of the American Planning Association* 62, no. 4 (Autumn): 473–491.

Wilensky, Harold. 1983. "Political Legitimacy and Consensus." In *Evaluating the Welfare State: Social and Political Perspectives,* ed. S.E. Spiro and E. Yuchtman-Yaar, pp. 51–74. New York: Academic Press.

Wilson, Pete. "Competitive Government: A Plan for Less Bureaucracy, More Results, State of California." Report. n.d.

Witte, John F., Sterr, Troy D., and Thorn, Christopher A. 1995. *The Fifth-Year Report: The Milwaukee Parental Choice Program.* Department of Political Science and The Robert M. La Follette Institute of Public Affairs, University of Wisconsin–Madison. December. [http://144.92.45.20/faculty/witte/report95.htm]

Witte, John F., and Thorne, Christopher A. 1996. "Who Chooses? Voucher and Interdistrict Choice Programs in Milwauke." *American Journal of Education* 104, no. 3 (May): 187–217.

Wolff, Edward N. 1996. "Trends in Household Wealth During 1989–1992." Paper submitted to the Department of Labor. New York, NY: New York University.

Womack, James, et al. 1990. *The Machine That Changed the World.* New York: Rawson Associates.

World Institute on Disability. 1996. *National Return to Work Forum.* Report on conference proceedings, January 26–28, Oakland CA.

Yinger, John. 1996. *Closed Doors, Opportunities Lost: The Continuing Cost of Housing Discrimination.* New York: Russell Sage Foundation.

Zemsky, Robert. 1994. *On Measuring a Mirage: Why U.S. Training Numbers Don't Add Up.* Philadelphia: The National Center on the Educational Quality of the Workforce.

INDEX

Rubin, Victor, 39
Rural labor market, 202–203

S

Safety
  preventive measures, 219–220
  regulations, 43, 154–158, 169
Sander, William, 95
SAT exam, 111
Schellhardt, Timothy D., 15
Schmidt, Stefanie R., 89
Schmitt, John, 6, 33
Schnare, Ann, 176
School(s). *See* Education
School choice programs, 91–95, 247,
  252, 254–255
School-to-Work Opportunities Act of
  1994, 96
School-to-work programs, 96–99,
  255
Schultze, Charles, 78
Segregation, residential, 179–180
Service providers, incentives for, 53,
  60–61
Sexual harassment, 149, 158–162
Shapiro, Carl, 29
Shapiro, Morton, 106
Shea, Martina, 17
Shell, 42
Shook, Robert, 36, 37, 47, 49
Siebert, Horst, 28
Siegelman, Peter, 159, 160
Singer, Sara J., 119
Singhai, V.R., 51
Single-parent households, 5, 18, 20,
  21
Skill standards
  in education, 64, 90–91, 111, 248,
  250
  job, 110–111, 136–138, 248
Small Business Administration, 168
Smitka, Michael, 47
Social science research, 225–227, 241

Social Security Administration, 204,
  206, 207–208, 209, 211, 212,
  216, 219, 220
Social Security Disability Insurance
  (SSDI), 204, 205–207, 208, 213,
  220
Social services. *See* Welfare system
Sockell, Donna, 163
Solomon, John, 154
Spending. *See* Consumption
Stamps, David, 98
States
  and decentralization, 52–53, 55–59
  disincentives of
    command-and-control rules, 42
  and school funding, 85
  and school reform, 87–88, 90–91
  statistical data collection by, 128
Statistical system, federal, 123–133,
  226
Stecklow, Steve, 95
Steiber, Jack, 159
Stempel, Andrea H., 161
Stern, David, 27, 98, 99
Stiglitz, Joseph E., 29
Stock market
  diversified/indexed investments,
  121–122
  employee ownership plans, 165–166
Stovepipe focus
  in automobile industry, 35
  of government programs, 38–39
Stove-pipe focus, in public sector,
  38–39
Struyk, Raymond J., 24, 159
Student Loan Reform Act, 107
Students. *See* College education;
  Education
Supplemental Security Income (SSI),
  204, 206, 207, 212, 220
  work incentives of, 209, 213
Suppliers
  under command-and-control rules,
  36, 42
  and flexible workplace, 47–48, 52–53

ABOUT THE AUTHOR

David I. Levine is an associate professor at the Haas School of Business, University of California, Berkeley. Levine is also editor of the journal *Industrial Relations,* associate director of the Institute of Industrial Relations, and director of research at U.C. Berkeley's Center for Organization and Human Resource Effectiveness. His research examines what management policies such as training and quality programs contribute to high-skill/high-performance workplaces. He also focuses on the role and design of public policies to promote such high-performance workplaces. His research on workplaces is summarized in his recent book, *Reinventing the Workplace* (Brookings, 1995), and in a volume he coedited, *The New American Workplace* (Cambridge University Press, 1998).

Levine was an undergraduate at Berkeley and has taught at the Haas School since receiving his Ph.D. in economics from Harvard University in 1987. He recently returned from spending a year and a half in Washington serving as a senior economist at the Department of Labor and at the Council of Economic Advisers.